CARIBBEAN WITH KIDS

BE A TRAVELER - NOT A TOURIST!

CRITICAL ACCLAIM FOR
OPEN ROAD TRAVEL GUIDES!

*Whether you're going abroad or planning a trip in the United States, take Open Road along on your journey. Our books have been praised by **Travel & Leisure, The Los Angeles Times, Newsday, Booklist, US News & World Report, Endless Vacation, American Bookseller, Coast to Coast**, and many other magazines and newspapers!*

Don't just see the world – experience it with Open Road!

ABOUT THE AUTHORS

Paris Permenter and John Bigley, a husband-wife travel writing team, are the authors of *Caribbean For Lovers, The Southwest's Best Bed & Breakfasts, Day Trips from San Antonio and Austin, Texas Barbecue* (named Best Regional Book by the Mid-America Publishers Association) and other travel guides. They have contributed many articles to leading travel magazines and newspapers, and are frequent television and radio talk show guests. They reside in the Texas Hill Country near Austin.

HIT THE OPEN ROAD -
WITH OPEN ROAD PUBLISHING!

Open Road Publishing now has guide books to exciting, fun destinations on four continents. As veteran travelers, our goal is to bring you the best travel guides available anywhere!

No small task, but here's what we offer:

• All Open Road travel guides are written by authors with a distinct, opinionated point of view – not some sterile committee or team of writers. Our authors are experts in the areas covered and are polished writers.

• Our guides are geared to people who want great vacations, great value, and great tips for both standard tourist sights *and* fun, unique alternatives.

• We're strong on the basics, but we also provide terrific choices for those looking to get off the beaten path and *experience* the country or city – not just *see* it or pass through it.

• We give you the best, but we also tell you about the worst and what to avoid. Nobody should waste their time and money on their hard-earned vacation because of bad or inadequate travel advice.

• Our guides assume nothing. We tell you everything you need to know to have the trip of a lifetime – presented in a fun, literate, no-nonsense style.

• And, above all, we welcome your input, ideas, and suggestions to help us put out the best travel guides possible.

CARIBBEAN WITH KIDS

BE A TRAVELER - NOT A TOURIST!

Paris Permenter & John Bigley

OPEN ROAD PUBLISHING

1st Edition

TABLE OF CONTENTS

Contents

Contents

Contents

Contents

Contents

1. INTRODUCTION

A new family-friendly attitude is blowing across the Caribbean like a fresh tradewind. Parents who have vacationed here before are discovering the fun of introducing their children to favorite island attractions. Families are playing together and staying together in some of the Caribbean's premier destinations, creating warm holiday memories that will last for generations.

Throughout the Caribbean, you'll find resorts with kids' programs to keep youngsters busy and happy as well as beaches where the whole family can play in the waves, snorkel in shallow waters, or just build sand castles until the sun sets over another perfect day. And if you're ready to take a break from constantly watching the budget as well as the kids, you'll also find many all-inclusive resorts that leave the worries of "how much is left in the vacation budget?" at the door.

Regardless of what you're looking for in an island vacation for the family, there's a place for you in the Caribbean. After you've looked throught this book, selecting your next Caribbean family getaway will be "no problem, mon!"

2. OVERVIEW

Ready to cast off those jackets, feel the sun on your face and the sand between your toes? Watch your children romp in the sand, be introduced to new cultures, and share a few days with you that you'll all remember the rest of your lives?

Then it's time to head to the Caribbean. While you may be shoveling snow, the islands are still blessed with weather that's just right for a day of snorkeling, scuba diving, or just sunning.

While they may all share the powdery sand, the aquamarine waters, and the near-perfect weather, Caribbean destinations can be as different as the seashells found along their beaches. Some islands are large and span hundreds of miles; others can be covered in an afternoon bicycle excursion. Culturally, these islands vary from French to Dutch to English; language and currency differ as well. Political structures range from crown colonies to independent nations.

Before we start examining the individual differences, let's look at the region as a whole. The Caribbean spans an area that stretches over 2,000 miles east to west and 1,000 miles north to south, starting just off the coast of Florida and arching down to the coast of South America.

This part of the world is blessed with year-around sunshine, with water warmed by Caribbean currents and shores cooled by gentle trade winds. Winter and summer temperatures differ by only about five degrees.

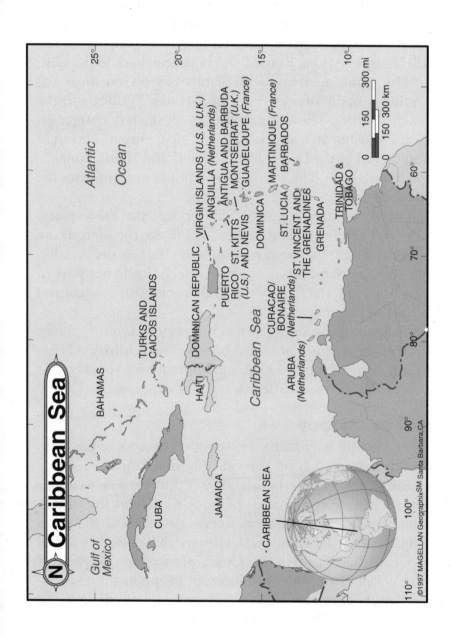

Caribbean Sea

Gulf of Mexico

Atlantic Ocean

BAHAMAS

TURKS AND CAICOS ISLANDS

CUBA

JAMAICA

HAITI

DOMINICAN REPUBLIC

PUERTO RICO (U.S.)

VIRGIN ISLANDS (U.S. & U.K.)

ANGUILLA (Netherlands)

ST. KITTS AND NEVIS

ANTIGUA AND BARBUDA

MONTSERRAT (U.K.)

GUADELOUPE (France)

DOMINICA

MARTINIQUE (France)

ST. LUCIA

BARBADOS

ST. VINCENT AND THE GRENADINES

GRENADA

CURACAO/ BONAIRE (Netherlands)

ARUBA (Netherlands)

TRINIDAD & TOBAGO

Caribbean Sea

CARIBBEAN SEA

0   150   300 mi
0 150 300 km

©1997 MAGELLAN GeographixSM Santa Barbara,CA

If you look at a map of the Caribbean, you'll see that the islands arch out like a cracking whip, with the largest islands to the west and the small islands to the east, curving on down to South America and ending in a "snap" with the ABC islands: Aruba, Bonaire, and Curaçao back to the west.

The whole formation of islands is referred to as the Antilles, usually divided into the Greater Antilles and the Lesser Antilles. The Greater Antilles, as the name suggests, are the Caribbean's largest islands: Cuba, Hispaniola (an island shared by the Dominican Republic and Haiti), Jamaica, and Puerto Rico. The term Lesser Antilles encompasses the other islands.

Often, the area is just divided up into the Eastern and Western Caribbean. The Eastern islands are the same as the Lesser Antilles; the Western islands are the Greater Antilles and the Cayman Islands. Although technically not part of the Caribbean, the Bahamas also shares its azure waters and perpetual summer.

The multiple names given to this region is your first hint at the diversity the Caribbean boasts. The Caribbean holds an endless fascination for us, and hopefully for you, because it *does* offer so many different types of experiences.

RICH IN HISTORY

The islands have such varied cultures because of the many nations that fought over this valuable area. During this time of unrest, protecting the islands was a major job. Magnificent forts were constructed of stone to defend the islands from marauding buccaneers. Today you can tour El Morro in San Juan, stroll along the lemon sherbet-colored walls of Fort Christiansvaern in St. Croix, photograph the city of Puerto Plata from the Fortaleza San Felipe in the Dominican Republic, or visit imposing Brimstone Hill in St. Kitts, known as the "The Gibraltar of the Caribbean."

Once the islands were settled, many prospered with sugar cane plantations. Today you can tour the islands' heritage of huge plantation houses. In Jamaica, tours provide a peek at the lavish lifestyle once enjoyed by plantation owners at Great Houses such as Rose Hall near Montego Bay, and the newly opened Barnett Estate Plantation also near Montego Bay, with a jitney tour of the sugar, banana, and mango plantation and fine dining in a restored sugar mill.

WINTER GETAWAYS

At one time, wintering in the Caribbean meant wealth. Today you'll still find the rich and famous crowd heading to the islands for a little sun, but getaways are affordable for almost everyone.

There's nothing quite like stepping off an airplane, still in layers of clothing, into the Caribbean sunshine. This is the peak season in the islands, a time when travelers from around the globe come to enjoy a respite from the cold.

DIFFERENT CULTURES

Although every island boasts a rollicking Caribbean spirit, their cultures also borrow heavily from their founding fathers. Aromas of fine French food fills the air of Martinique, St. Martin, St. Barthelemy, and Guadeloupe. Dutch architecture creates picturesque waterfront communities in Aruba, Bonaire, Curaçao, Saba, Sint Maarten, and Sint Eustatius. A rich Spanish atmosphere pervades the islands of the Dominican Republic and Puerto Rico. Anguilla, the British Virgin Islands, Montserrat, the Cayman Islands and the Turks and Caicos still operate as British dependencies. In the former British colonies of the Bahamas, Antigua and Barbuda, Barbados, Dominica, Grenada, St. Kitts and Nevis, St. Lucia, Trinidad and Tobago, and Jamaica, the British influence is still strongly felt, with driving on the left side of the road and the Royal family smiling back from postage stamps.

CHECK OUT THE WATER

The true island treasures that every Caribbean nation shares are miles of beaches lapped by clear, warm water. The activities in the water are endless: sailing, windsurfing, water-skiing, the list goes on and on. If you'd like to stay above the water, head to the boating capital of the Caribbean, the British Virgin Islands. Several resorts offer combination packages with a week's stay split between a hotel and a yacht.

If you want to venture beneath the waves, you'll find the top dive destinations to be the Cayman Islands, Turks and Caicos, and Bonaire. Divers can hand feed sharks on guided dives in the Bahamas or pet sting rays at Grand Cayman. Or if you're just looking to snorkel, coral reefs are scattered just yards from shore throughout this region.

3. PLANNING YOUR TRIP

WHEN TO GO

Weather is usually a minor factor in planning a Caribbean vacation. It's almost a boring topic, with day after day of spring-like conditions, sometimes punctuated by brief afternoon showers.

One weather topic that concerns most potential Caribbean travelers is hurricane season. These deadly storms are a threat officially from June through November, although the greatest danger is during the later months, basically August through October. (September is the worst.)

But don't forget that the Caribbean is a huge region. Just as a blizzard in Connecticut wouldn't influence travelers to Miami or Denver, a tropical storm doesn't necessarily mean a risk to the whole region. We've been in the Western Caribbean when storms were picking up force in the eastern reaches and never felt a gust of wind or saw a wave over ankle high.

To minimize the chances of a hurricane ruining or postponing your trip, plan a vacation outside the hurricane season or outside the hurricane zone. In the far southern reaches, the islands of Aruba, Bonaire, and Curaçao (also known as the ABC islands) and Trinidad and Tobago are below the hurricane zone and should be safer bets during the summer and fall months.

Overall, the weather in the Caribbean is predictably wonderful. In the summer, days peak at about 95, with lows in the 70s. In the winter, temperatures run about 5 to 10 degrees cooler. The sea remains warm enough for comfortable swimming year around. (Don't forget: The Bahamas are technically not part of the Caribbean, and the temperatures there are slightly cooler.)

However, when to visit the Caribbean may be based more on budget than weather. Prices can vary as much as 40 percent between high and low season.

High season generally extends from December 15 through April 15. During this time, prices are at peak and rooms can even be difficult to reserve (especially during the holiday season). Prices soar during Christmas week. After the holidays, package prices (although sometimes not room rates) drop during January. They rise again by February and remain high until mid-April.

Low season covers the summer and early fall months, for two reasons. First, these are the warmest months in the Northeast, the area of the country that often flees to the sunny Caribbean during the chilly winter months so demand is down. Second, this is hurricane season.

WHAT TO PACK

When it comes to packing, there's no doubt that less is more. This axiom is especially true for a Caribbean vacation, where the order of the day is casual and cool. Most guests are comfortable in shorts and T-shirts in the day, switching to something "elegantly casual" in the evening hours: smart shorts sets or simple sundresses for women, khakis and polos for men, and "school clothes" for kids.

We keep a permanent packing list for our Caribbean trips. For a four-night trip, we bring:

His

1 pair casual slacks
2 T-shirts
1 pair jeans or very casual pants if you'll be horseback riding
2 polo or short sleeve shirts
2 pair of shorts
2 swimsuits
1 pair walking shoes
1 pair walking sandals
1 pair swim shoes

Hers

1 pair casual slacks (for the plane)
1 pair nice slacks or khakis
1 casual skirt
1 pair jeans or casual pants if you'll be horseback riding
1 dress
1 T-shirt
2 short sleeve/sleeveless blouses
2 pair of shorts
2 swimsuits
1 pair sandals or tennis shoes
1 pair evening sandals
1 swimsuit cover-up
1 pair swim shoes

Kids

3 pair shorts
1 pair jeans or casual pants if you'll be horseback riding
3 T-shirts
1 old T-shirt to wear while swimming
2 dinner outfits, similar to school clothes
2 swimsuits (one to wear and one to dry)

1 pair beach shoes
1 pair sandals
1 pair sneakers
1 pair swim shoes
    We also carry all the necessary accessories (which, on some islands, can be expensive or difficult to buy):
film and camera, extra camera battery
sunscreen (usually two bottles of different strengths)
snorkel gear (and certified divers must bring a "C" card)
aqua shoes
insect repellent
all prescriptions (in prescription bottles)
2 pairs of sunglasses each
paperback book or two
antiseptic for bug bites
aloe vera lotion for sunburn
first aid kit with aspirin, stomach medicine, bandages, children's aspirin, etc.
passports
airline tickets
mini-address book for postcard writing

    Parents with infants will find baby needs readily available on most islands. In a few cases, disposable diapers are difficult to locate (on small islands like Little Cayman). If you have favorite brands, bring them from home. Prices are likely to be steeper on the islands, and the selection can be limited.

BOSCOBEL BEACH IN JAMAICA

Perhaps no other resort in the Caribbean sees as many children travelers as Boscobel Beach in Jamaica (see "Best Places to Stay with Children" for more on that special resort). Concierge Coral Purvil gives these packing tips for family travelers headed to Boscobel Beach or to any Caribbean resort:

Parents, it is advisable to bring along the following:

1) Any special medication your children may be taking.

2) Pack sneakers since some activities, e.g. tennis, are more comfortable to do in sneakers rather than sandals.

3) Bring along rubber soled shoes for the entire family. This will come in especially handy if your family decides to book the tour to climb the world famous Dunn's River Falls.

4) Bring along your children's favorite toys or baby's comfort sheets, blankets, pillows or any other item that children are attached to.

5) Remember to bring swimsuits and sunblock for the entire family.

6) It would help if you bring floaters (arm or otherwise) for younger children. This is safer in the water.

7) One of the activities for the eight to 12 age group includes an off-property picnic trip. In this case it would help if children have their own backpacks to pack their swimsuits, sunblock, etc. to take along with them.

8) For babies, bring along wipes, diapers, formula, or baby food, bottles and cups and utensils.

9) You are advised to bring along your favorite CDs. While the rooms are equipped with CD players, CDs are not provided.

10) Bring along at least one pair of long pants and a collared shirt. This will come in handy if you want to dine in our award-winning, adults-only Italian restaurant—The Allegro—which has a dress code.

11) For divers who are certified, it is advisable to bring along your certificate.

PASSPORTS

Specifics vary from country to country (and are covered in each island's chapter later in this book) but plan to bring along either a current passport or a certified birth certificate and a photo ID. Passports are the easiest form of entry (plus you'll get the neat immigration stamps as a free souvenir). In Trinidad and Tobago, a passport is mandatory; a certified birth certificate and ID will NOT be accepted as proof of citizenship.

Obtaining a Passport

To obtain a passport, you may apply in person at the nearest passport office (see chart) or at one of the several thousand federal or state courts or U.S. post offices authorized to accept passport applications. Not every post office will accept passport applications; it's usually one of the largest offices in the city. For your first passport application, you must apply in person.

We can't stress enough the importance of applying for a passport early. The heaviest demand period is January through August (because of summer travel), with September through December being the speediest period. Even during the latter, however, you should allow at least eight weeks for your passport application to be processed.

To obtain a passport, first get an unsigned passport application (DSP-11) from your local passport office or post office which handles passport applications. Do NOT sign the application.

Provide proof of US citizenship. This can be an expired passport, a certified birth certificate (that means one with a raised, impressed, embossed, or multicolored seal). If you do not have a certified copy of your birth certificate, call the Bureau of Vital Statistics in the city where you were born. You also must provide identification, which could be an expired passport, a valid driver's license, a government ID card or certificate of naturalization or citizenship. (Here's what won't work: Social Security card, learner's permit, temporary driver's license, credit card, expired ID card.)

Next, provide two identical photographs of yourself no larger than 2x2 inches (the image of your head from the bottom of your chin to the top of your head must not be less than one inch or more than 1-3/8 inch). Passport photos can be either color or black and white but they may not be Polaroid's or vending machine photos. The easiest way to get passport photos is to go to one of the quick copy stores and ask for passport shots.

Passports for adults 18 and over are $65 and are valid for 10 years. You may pay in person by check, bank draft, or money order. At passport agencies you may also pay in cash; some (but not all) post offices and clerks of court accept payment in cash.

When you receive your passport, sign it. The next step is to fill in page four in pencil with your address and a contact in case of emergency.

Need to talk with someone? The only public phone number for passport information is to the National Passport Information Center (NPIC). You can call here for information on passport emergencies, applying for a US passport, or to obtain the status of a passport application. Automated information is available 24 hours a day and live operators can be reached on workdays from 8am to 8pm, Eastern Standard Time. (Services are available in English, Spanish, and by TDD.) This is a toll call; the charge is 35 cents per minute for the automated system or $1.05 per minute for live operators. *Call Tel. 900/225-5674 for either automated or live service; Tel. 900/225-7778 for TDD service. Calling from a number blocked from 900 service? Call Tel. 888/362-8668 (TDD Tel. 888/498-3648); you will be required to pay by credit card at a flat rate of $4.95 per call.*

US PASSPORT OFFICES
Boston Passport Agency
Thomas P. O'Neill Federal Building
10 Causeway Street
Suite 247
Boston, MA 02222-1094
Region: Maine, Massachusetts, New Hampshire, Rhode Island, upstate New York, and Vermont

Chicago Passport Agency
Kluczynski Federal Building
230 S. Dearborn Street
Suite 380
Chicago, IL 60604-1564
Region: Illinois, Indiana, Michigan, and Wisconsin

Honolulu Passport Agency
First Hawaiian Tower
1132 Bishop Street
Suite 500
Honolulu, HI 96813-2809
Tel. 808/522-8283
Region: American Samoa, Federated States of Micronesia, Guam, Hawaii, & Northern Mariana Islands

Houston Passport Agency
Mickey Leland Federal Building
1919 Smith Street
Suite 1100
Houston, TX 77002-8049
Region: Kansas, Oklahoma, New Mexico, and Texas

Los Angeles Passport Agency
Federal Building
11000 Wilshire Boulevard
Suite 1000
Los Angeles, CA 90024-3615
Region: California (all counties south of an including San Luis Obispo, Kern and San Bernardino), and Nevada (Clark County only)

Miami Passport Agency
Claude Pepper Federal Office Building
51 SW First Avenue
3rd Floor
Miami, FL 33120-1680
Region: Florida, Georgia, Puerto Rico, South Carolina, and U.S. Virgin Islands

National Passport Center
31 Rochester Avenue
Portsmouth, NH 03801-2900
Applications Handled: Applications for Passport by Mail (Form DSP-82) and workload transfers from regional passport agencies

New Orleans Passport Agency
Postal Services Building
701 Loyola Avenue
Suite T-12005
New Orleans, LA 70113-1931
Region: Alabama, Arkansas, Iowa, Kentucky, Louisiana, Mississippi, Missouri, North Carolina, Ohio, Tennessee, and Virginia (except DC suburbs)

New York Passport Agency
376 Hudson Street
New York, NY 10014
Tel. 212/206-3500
Region: New York City and Long Island
Note: New York Passport Agency only accepts emergency
applications from those leaving within two weeks.

Philadelphia Passport Agency
US Custom House
200 Chestnut Street
Room 103
Philadelphia, PA 19106-2970
Region: Delaware, New Jersey, Pennsylvania, & West Virginia

San Francisco Passport Agency
95 Hawthorne Street
5th Floor
San Francisco, CA 94105-3901
Region: Arizona, California (all counties North of and including Monterey, Kings, Oulare, and Inyo), Nevada (except
Clark Co.), and Utah

Seattle Passport Agency
Henry Jackson Federal Building
915 Second Avenue
Suite 992
Seattle, WA 98174-1091
Region: Alaska, Colorado, Idaho, Minnesota, Montana,
Nebraska, North Dakota, Oregon, South Dakota, Washing-
ton, and Wyoming

Stamford Passport Agency
One Landmark Square
Broad and Atlantic Streets
Stamford, CT 06901-2667
Region: Connecticut and Westchester County (New York)

Washington Passport Agency
1111 19th Street, N.W.
Room 300
Washington, D.C. 20524
Region: Maryland, Northern Virginia (including Alexandria, Arlington County, and Fairfax County), and the District of Columbia

Special Issuance Agency
1111 19th Street, N.W. Room 300
Washington, D.C. 20524

Passports for Kids

For islands requiring passports, all travelers must have their own passport. If your child is between the ages of 13 and 18, he or she will need to appear in person, accompanied by a parent or guardian. Parents or guardians may obtain a passport for children under age 13.

If your child is too young to sign his name, the mother or father must print the child's name and sign their own name. Then, in parenthesis by the parent's name, write the word (mother) or (father) to identify who signed for the child.

The fee for a passport for any child under 18 is $40. The children's passport is valid for five years.

CHILDREN TRAVELING WITHOUT BOTH BIRTH PARENTS

Children traveling without both birth parents should also travel with a notarized letter from the non-present parent stating permission for the child to travel with the other parent. Why all the fuss? The number of parental kidnappings has skyrocketed and foreign countries are trying their best to stop parental abductions from entering their borders. In Mexico, law requires that a child traveling along or with only one parent carries a written, notarized consent letter from the absent parent. (This includes children traveling with grandparents.) Generally, this is not a problem in the Caribbean but better safe than sorry.

US CONSULATES AND EMBASSIES

Emergency Situations

When we think of the State Department assisting Americans abroad, we usually picture political tensions in the Middle East or Americans who have run into trouble with the law.

However, the State Department's Bureau of Consular Affairs will also assist travelers during an emergency situations, such as a hurricane.

The State Department sets up a task force to disseminate information on the crisis, including responding to relatives and friends who are inquiring about the safety of those abroad.

If you are involved in an emergency situation, go to the nearest US embassy or consular office and register. Bring along your passport and a location where you can be reached. The Embassy can also assist you with these situations:

Lost Passport: If you lose your passport or have it stolen, first report the loss to the local police. Get a police declaration then report to the consul for a replacement passport. If you have extra passport photos, bring these along. It also helps to travel with a copy of the identification page of your passport tucked somewhere in your belongings. In case of a lost passport, this will speed along the reissuance.

Medical Assistance: Contact the consular office for a list of local doctors, dentists, and medical specialists. If you are injured or become seriously ill, a consul will help you find medical assistance and, at your request, inform your family or friends. The State Department cannot assist you in funding an emergency trip back to the States—that's what travel insurance is all about.

Financial Assistance: Lose your money? The consular office can help you contact your family, bank, or employer to arrange for them to send you funds.

U.S. EMBASSIES AND CONSULATES ABROAD
BAHAMAS
American Embassy
Queen Street
Nassau, Bahamas
Tel. 242/322-1181 or 328-2206

BARBADOS
American Embassy
Canadian Imperial Bank of Commerce Bldg.
Broadstreet
Bridgetown, Barbados
Tel. 246/436-4950

American Consulate
ALICO Building
Cheapside
Bridgetown, Barbados
Tel. 246/431-0225

CUBA
Swiss Embassy (USINT)
Calzada between L and M
Vedado
Havana, Cuba
Tel. 537/33-4401

DOMINICAN REPUBLIC
American Embassy
Calle Cesar Nicolas Penson and Calle Leopoldo Navarro
Santo Domingo, Dominican Republic
Tel. 809/221-2171

JAMAICA
American Embassy
Jamaica Mutual Life Center
2 Oxford Road
Kingston, Jamaica
Tel. 876/929-4850 to 4859

NETHERLANDS ANTILLES
American Consulate General
J.B. Gorsiraweg No. 1
Willemstad, Curaçao
Tel. 599-9/461-3066

TRINIDAD AND TOBAGO
American Embassy
15 Queen's Park West
Port of Spain, Trinidad
Tel. 868/622-6371

Several islands also have available resident consular agents:

CAYMAN ISLANDS
American Consular Agent
George Town, Grand Cayman
Tel. 246/949-7955

ANTIGUA AND BARBUDA
American Consular Agent
Hospital Hill, Nelson's Dockyard P.O.
English Harbour, Antigua
Tel. 268/460-1569
Assists Americans in Antigua & Barbuda, St. Kitts & Nevis, and the British West Indies.

DOMINICAN REPUBLIC
American Consular Agent
Calle Beller 51, Second Floor, Office 6
Puerto Plata, Dominican Republic
Tel. 809/586-4204

JAMAICA
American Consular Agent
St. James Place, 2nd Floor, Gloucester Avenue
Montego Bay, Jamaica
Tel. 876/949-7955
Assists Americans in Jamaica.

Foreign Embassies in the United States
For diplomatic relations with the US and to assist their citizens while in the US, other nations have embassies located within the US. These offices can help with specific questions on the country's entry requirements, political situations, etc.

Embassy of Antigua and Barbuda
3216 New Mexico Avenue, N.W.
Washington, DC 20016
Tel. 202/362-5122 or 5166

Embassy of the Bahamas
2220 Massachusetts Avenue, N.W.
Washington, DC 20008
Tel. 202/319-2660

Embassy of Barbados
2144 Wyoming Avenue, NW
Washington, DC 20008
Tel. 202/939-9200

Embassy of Switzerland
Cuban Interests Section
2639 16th Street, NW
Washington, DC 20009
Tel. 202/362-5122 or 5166

Consulate of the Commonwealth of Dominica
820 2nd Avenue, Suite 900
New York, NY 10017
Tel. 212/599-8478

Embassy of the Dominican Republic
1715 22nd Street., NW
Washington, DC 20008
Tel. 202/332-6280

Embassy of France
4101 Reservoir Road, NW
Washington, DC 20007-2172
Tel. 202/944-6200 or 6187

Embassy of Jamaica
1520 New Hampshire Avenue, NW
Washington, DC 20036
Tel. 202/452-0660

Embassy of the Netherlands
4200 Linnean Avenue, NW
Washington, DC 20008
Tel. 202/244-5300

Embassy of St. Kitts and Nevis
3216 New Mexico Avenue, NW
Washington, DC 20016
Tel. 202/686-2636

Embassy of St. Lucia
3216 New Mexico Avenue, NW
Washington, DC 20016
Tel. 202/364-6792

Embassy of Trinidad and Tobago
1708 Massachusetts Avenue, NW
Washington, DC 20036
Tel. 202/467-6490

British Embassy
3100 Massachusetts Avenue, NW
Washington, DC 20008
Tel. 202/462-1340

CUSTOMS AND ENTRANCE REQUIREMENTS
US Customs

Arriving home means a trip first through immigration
and then through US Customs. (A few islands have Customs

Pre-Clearance so you can go through the declaration before returning home, usually a faster process.)

You'll complete a customs declaration form, one per household, identifying the total amount of your expenditures while out of the country. Each person has an exemption of either $400, $600 or $1200 (depending on the island you visited). Families can pool their exemptions so a family of four can bring back $1600, $2400, or $4800 worth of merchandise without paying duty.

Canadian Customs: After a 48 hour absence or more, Canadians may return home with goods valuing $100; a written declaration may be required. After a seven day's absence or more (one per calendar year), Canadians may return home with goods valuing $300. A written declaration is required. Travelers age 16 and over may include up to 200 cigarettes and 50 cigars and 1 kilogram of tobacco. Travelers who meet the age requirements set by their province or territory may return with up to 1.4 liters of wine or liquor. Original works of art valued at $20 or more are duty free.

Some items cannot be brought back to the US. These include:

- books or cassettes made without authorized copyright ("pirated" copies)
- any type of drug paraphernalia
- firearms
- fruits and vegetables
- meats and their by-products (such as paté)
- plants, cuttings
- tortoise shell jewelry or other turtle products (which you will see sold in the Cayman Islands, among others)

Here are some tips to make your passage through Customs a little easier:

- keep your sales slips
- pack so your purchases can be reached easily

• get a copy of the "Know Before You Go" brochure (Publication 512) from the US Customs Service at your airport or by writing the US Customs Service, PO Box 7407, Washington, DC 20044.

Immunizations

Immunizations are not required for any islands in the Caribbean. Travelers should have their immunizations current however and anyone traveling should make sure their tetanus inoculation was within the past five years.

Check with your pediatrician several months before departure to make sure your children's shots are up-to-date.

USING TRAVEL SPECIALISTS/AGENTS

Travel agents offer a (usually) free service, making hotel and air reservations and issuing airline tickets. They can shop around for the lowest rate for you and often know about sales that aren't known to the general public.

Stop by a travel agency and talk to an agent during an off-peak time, usually early morning or mid-day. Tell him or her your likes and dislikes and your budget range. The agent can help you start to narrow your choices to a few islands and perhaps a few resorts. Pick up some brochures, head home, and talk over the choices with your family.

Now the fun part: doing some research. Rent some travel videos. Look at some guidebooks and travel magazines. Get on the Internet and check out some travel forums for other people's views. Talk about your options.

When you have your minds made up—or at least narrowed down—return to the travel agent for some help. If it's a large office, ask for the agent who specializes in the Caribbean.

Now the agent can assist you with the nitty-gritty of the travel task: making your reservations. Often you'll need to put down a deposit on reservations or packages. This deposit may be non-refundable so make sure that you have made your final selection both in terms of resort and travel dates.

GETTING TO THE CARIBBEAN BY AIR

Getting to the Caribbean is an easier job that it once was. Daily flights serve most islands. Most connections from major mainland US cities are made through Miami or San Juan's Luis Muñoz Marin Airport, the American Airlines hub for Caribbean flights from Chicago, Dallas, New York, and Miami. From San Juan, American Eagle serves many neighboring islands.

Those air arrivals are met with expanded and improved airports on many islands. Terminals in Aruba, Jamaica (Montego Bay), Bermuda, St. Kitts, San Juan, Puerto Rico and the Cayman Islands offer new and improved facilities.

The following carriers offer flights to at least one Caribbean destination. You'll find that the flight schedule varies by season (the most flights, and for some airlines the *only* flights, are offered during peak season from mid-December to mid-April).

• Air Aruba	*Tel.*	*800/88-Aruba*
• Air Canada	*Tel.*	*800/776-3000*
• Air Jamaica	*Tel.*	*800/523-5585*
• ALM	*Tel.*	*800/327-7230*
• American Airlines	*Tel.*	*800/433-7300*
• Bahamasair	*Tel.*	*800/222-4262*
• BWIA	*Tel.*	*800/538-2942*
• Carnival	*Tel.*	*800/824-7386*
• Cayman Airways	*Tel.*	*800/422-9626*
• Continental	*Tel.*	*800/231-0856*
• Delta	*Tel.*	*800/221-1212*
• Kiwi	*Tel.*	*800/538-5494*
• Northwest	*Tel.*	*800/447-4747*
• Prestige Airways	*Tel.*	*800/299-8784*
• TWA	*Tel.*	*800/892-4141*

• United   *Tel.   800/538-2929*
• USAirways   *Tel. 800/428-4322*

HELPING YOUR KIDS ENJOY FLYING

• Talk to you kids about flying, from the sounds they'll hear to the layout of the plane and the behavior that will be expected of them.

• Book seat assignments early so the family sits together. (If you're flying on a charter carrier that doesn't pre-assign seats, get to the airport extra early to ensure that your group will stay together.)

• Order special kid's meals from the airline reservation number at least a day in advance. Special meals, available at no extra charge, contain kid favorites and also help make children feel part of the trip.

• Minimize your luggage. You'll travel lighter (remember the "lug" in luggage!) and check-in will be faster.

• Arrive at the airport early. Check-in for international flights is two hours before departure at most airports.

• Consider preboarding if you want to get seated before the mad dash onto the plane begins. However, if your child is restless, this will only add to total time on the ground before takeoff.

• Bring bottles and pacifiers for young children to ease the pressure on the inner ear during take off and landings. For older children, bring chewing gum.

• Pack some special activities in a secret "goody bag" to keep your child's hands busy until the trip is underway.

• Bring extra batteries for older children's electronic games and headsets.

Several airlines offer package deals that provide a complete vacation: room, transfers, air, and, for all-inclusives, meals, drinks, and tips. Is this cheaper than putting a package together on your own? Usually. Check it out for yourself by calling the hotel reservation numbers, asking for their room rate and adding it to the cost of an airline ticket. You'll usually see a substantial savings, since, after all, the airlines are buying rooms in bulk and therefore have much more purchasing power than an ordinary consumer.

Packages are also offered by charter airlines, carriers that offer service at lower cost, usually with few frills. (Often only one class of service is available, seat assignments are given only at check-in, and carry on allowances may be only one bag per passenger due to an increased number of seats onboard.) Some companies offering Caribbean service include Adventure Tours, FunJet, Apple Vacations, GoGo, and others. See your travel agent for information on charters available from your area.

If you're concerned about the credibility of a charter company or a tour package, check it out before signing on that dotted line. Call the **American Society of Travel Agents**, *Tel. 703/739-2782*, or write 1101 King Street, Alexandria, VA 22314 to see if complaints have been lodged against the company. Another good source of information is your local Better Business Bureau.

If you don't want the package vacation, some of these charters also sell "air-only," just the airline tickets themselves.

Child Restraint Devices

Parents flying with infants or small children may also want to pack another important piece of equipment: a child restraint device or CRD. The Federal Aviation Administration strongly recommends that children under 40 pounds be secured in a CRD.

A CRD should have hard sides and back. It attaches to the seat through channels; you just thread the seatbelt through the channels to secure the device. Many carriers will say they are approved for motor vehicles and on aircraft; another tip is to look for the "FMVSS.213" insignia. Some car carriers recently issued work both in planes and automobiles but don't assume that every carrier will perform both functions. Carriers shouldn't be wider than 16 inches or they won't fit the airline seat properly. Also, make sure the carrier correctly fits your child; the shoulder straps should come out of the seat back just above the child's shoulders.

Children under 20 pounds should face the rear of the seat; kids 20-40 pounds face out.

Once you're on the flight, the CRD can be used in seats that face forward and are not in an exit row. The window seat is best.

If you have questions and would like more information on air safety for children, call the **FAA consumer information hotline**, *Tel. 800/322-7873*.

GETTING AROUND THE CARIBBEAN
By Air
Want to island-hop? It's fun and, if you're visiting small islands, a necessary part of a Caribbean vacation.

Two carriers offer special passes designed for island hopping. **LIAT**, Tel. *869/462-0700*, and **BWIA**, *Tel. 800/327-7401*, each offers a special pass that permits you to hop from island to island—with certain restrictions. The catch is that you must make all your travel in one direction, except for the return flight back to the island from which you started. These passes must be purchased and ticketed (a very important detail) outside the Caribbean. They cannot be purchased in the islands.

By Ferry

Ferry travel is available between some islands: Trinidad and Tobago, St. Martin and both St. Barts and Anguilla, St. Kitts and Nevis, the British Virgin Islands and St. John and St. Thomas, and others.

Ferry travel between islands can be a fun way to extend your knowledge of the region and to travel like a local. Prices are generally very economical but expect timetables to be taken less seriously than you might expect. Arrive plenty early and bring along your passport for voyages between countries such as Anguilla and St. Martin.

By Bus

Public transportation can be a fun and inexpensive way to travel around the island and feel like a local. However, you'll find that it's not the fast way. Be prepared for plenty of stops and starts (on many islands buses stop anywhere they're flagged). Smaller islands such as Anguilla do not have bus service. To flag down a bus or taxi in the islands, hold out your hand and pat down, like you're bouncing a ball.

By Car

Modes of transportation vary from island to island, but for the most part taxis are the best means of travel. Even the smallest islands like tiny Salt Cay in the Turks and Caicos have taxi service, and you'll find that they're generally operated by professionals who are happy to talk about their island. We've had some of our most interesting conversations about island life with taxi drivers, who are well informed about history and tourist attractions. Often drivers will present their business card at the end of the journey in case you have further need for transportation.

Car rentals can be expensive in the islands but on some islands, such as Anguilla, present a more economical option than taxis. If you'll be doing some exploring, a rental car is often the easiest and most economical way to get around.

Prices vary by island, type of vehicle, and even time of year. Most car rentals begin at about US $30-40 per day; expect to pay about $10 more per day for a 4X4 vehicle. Prices are higher on some islands such as St. Barts where rental cars average about $60 a day in the winter months, falling to about $35 a day during the summer. In this sellers' market, major credit cards are accepted but most request a two- or three-day minimum rental.

On many islands, a temporary driver's license is required; you can usually obtain this from the rental agency by presenting a valid driver's license. Prices vary from about $5-10. You must also show a major credit card.

Remember that driving is on the LEFT side of the road on Caribbean islands with a British heritage including Anguilla, Cayman Islands, Jamaica, St. Kitts and Nevis, the US and British Virgin Islands, and others. Even though driving is on the left side, many vehicles are right hand drive; however, most 4X4s have a left-hand stick shift.

Even if you won't be driving during your stay, remember that driving is on the left and stress this to your family members. Crossing a road becomes a challenge under these circumstances: remind everyone to look RIGHT then left. Take special care when getting out of tour vans, taxis, and buses.

Throughout most islands, speed limits are far lower than those in the US and Canada. Speed limits are maximum 30 mph on many islands (20 mph in some areas). Look for tall traffic bumps called "sleeping policemen" to slow down speeders.

FAMILY ACCOMMODATIONS

Whatever you're looking for in the way of accommodations— high-rise hotel, seaside bungalow, contemporary condominium, small traditional hotel, or private villa — you'll find it in the Caribbean.

Just as varied as the type of accommodations is the range of prices of these properties. Everything from budget motels with Spartan furnishings to private islands that attract royalty and Hollywood types is available.

This guidebook covers things in between, places where the everyday vacationing family can enjoy safety and comfort in surroundings where fun can flourish. The resorts, hotels, and villas featured on these pages cover all levels of activity. Some offer around-the-clock fun and evening theme parties for their guests; others point the way for families to find their own entertainment. Some are located on the beach; others up in the mountains with grandiose views. Some are full-service properties with everything from beauty salons to jewelry shops; others are simple accommodations where the guests enjoy dinner in former greathouses built over 200 years ago.

Choosing a Caribbean accommodation is even more important than selecting a hotel at other destinations. You'll find that a Caribbean hotel, unlike a property in a downtown US city, for example, becomes your home away from home. This is not just where you spend your nights, but also a good portion of your days, languishing on the beach, lying beneath towering palms, and luxuriating in a warm sea.

What form will your paradise take? White sandy beaches? Rugged limestone cliffs that fall into baby blue water? Mountainside vistas? A resort with daily activities and a complete children's program? Or a quiet getaway where the only footprints are your own?

The choice is yours.

Resorts. What is a resort? A resort is a hotel, but a hotel is not necessarily a resort. Confused?

Actually the distinction is fairly simple. A resort is a place where you could, if you chose, stay your entire vacation. You'll find restaurants, watersports, shops, you name it, all within the hotel grounds. It's a place that caters to the leisure traveler, although you may also see a mix of business travelers at some properties.

Resorts offer many different packages. These include:

EP, European Plan. This is a room-only plan. You've paid for a place to sleep but all meals, drinks, and recreation are extra.

MAP, Modified American Plan. Breakfast and dinner are included. This is a good option for those who plan to be out exploring the island during the day.

AP, American Plan. All meals are included. This is not an all-inclusive plan however, since drinks may or not be included and usually watersports, tips, and any other kind of recreation are not part of the package.

All-inclusive Resorts. As the name suggests, all-inclusive means that all activities, meals, drinks, transfers, and tips are included in the price.

This all-inclusive policy means that you're free to try anything you like without getting out the credit cards. You've already paid for it in the package price.

Some folks don't like all-inclusive because of the concern (not unfounded) that once you've paid for the whole package you'll be unlikely to leave the property to sample local restaurants and explore the island.

If your family wants to try it all: scuba diving, sailing, windsurfing, golf, or tennis, an all-inclusive is just the ticket for you as well. The one-price-pays-all policy will be a better deal than paying for individual lessons.

Our family loves all-inclusive resorts, but we are careful to balance a stay there with island tours or visits to off-property restaurants. Even with these extra expenditures, we've found most of these resorts to be economical choices. Our family has enjoyed several all-inclusive stays which have relieved strain (both on parent-child relations and on the budget) as the kids to be able to order whatever they want without an eye on the pocketbook. It makes it even easier to get picky eaters just to "try" a bite of a new dish like fungi or callaloo when you know that you've already paid for it.

The all-inclusive concept was born in Jamaica over a decade and a half ago with SuperClubs. "Here all our guests are equally rich because you can't spend money while you're here," says founder John Issa. With an all-inclusive vacation, you're enjoying a stay without tips, bar tabs, transfers, or bills of any kind.

Today Jamaica is still the king of the all-inclusive market, and properties offer fun for travelers of all ages. Some popular all-inclusive chains in the Caribbean especially popular with families are Beaches (part of the Sandals family), SuperClubs, Club Med and Jack Tar (although the location in Jamaica recently became an adults-only property).

Condominiums. Like your own island apartment, condominiums give you the freedom of housekeeping, whether that means doing a quick load of laundry or making bowls of cereal in the morning. Condominiums are not found on every island but are an especially popular option on Grand Cayman.

MONEY SAVING TIPS

• Consider bringing some food with you or making a stop at a supermarket.

• Pick up coupon booklets. These can offer 10%-off coupons and other bargains at eateries. This type of booklet is often distributed at the visitors' booth at the airport arrival area.

• Look for two-for-one specials (popular on Sunday nights).

• Buy rum on island and make your own cocktails. Buy soft drinks and juices for the kids.

• Double check the gratuity. Some restaurants add a 15% gratuity to the bill, so make sure you don't inadvertently tip twice.

• Check for laundry facilities if you rent a condominium.

• Look for early bird specials at some restaurants. Dining before 6pm can save money and it's smart with children.

• Make sure you understand whether the menu prices you are reading are marked in US or local currency.

• Look for free attractions. Remember, a stop doesn't necessarily have to be labeled "tourist attraction" to be fun and educational. We always make a stop at the local grocery store to compare brands and have a look at local specialties. Outdoor food markets are also terrific fun. Buy a banana or pineapple from a local vendor for an impromptu picnic.

Small hotels. If you're looking for peace and quiet, small inns offer good getaways and a chance to immerse yourself in more of the local atmosphere. Often the owners of the inn reside right on property, so you'll receive personal attention.

Our favorite inns make us feel like we're guests of the family returning for another stay. We enjoy chatting with other guests, usually experienced travelers, and with the owners, who give us an insight into island life. Over the years, we've shared dinner conversations with hoteliers about hurricanes, gardening, local specialties, local sports, and island life in general. It has given us a perspective on these destinations that we would never have received at a larger property.

How do small properties feel about kids? This book includes only small properties that welcome families but for other properties you'll have to ask. Some do not allow children, period. That includes anyone under age 18. Others welcome children during non-peak months. And still others welcome kids with open arms any time of year.

Villas. For some families, the idea of a real getaway is a private villa, without other guests. Your family gets the treat of feeling like you're living on the island in your own home, except for the occasional visit by a cook or maid who is there to meet your special requests, to introduce you to island cuisine, and to make you feel pampered in what really is your home away from home. There's no better solution for families who want to enjoy a vacation together with plenty of room, facilities to satisfy even picky eaters, and a genuine island atmosphere.

The top islands for villa getaways are St. John and St. Thomas in the US Virgin Islands, Jamaica, and Barbados.

Like resorts, villas come in different budget categories, but generally are more pricey than a hotel or resort stay. Also, you should not assume that every villa comes with the range of facilities you might expect from a resort.

Before you select a villa, check on some details. Is maid service offered? Many villas offer maid service before your arrival and after your departure; additional cleaning can be arranged for a surcharge. At other properties, you may have daily maid service. Check with your villa management company.

Can you send a deposit for groceries and have a cook stock up before your arrival? Finding a refrigerator and cabinets ready with your favorites can be a big boost after a long flight. Is cook service available? Many villas can arrange for cook service as you choose: three meals a day, dinner only, or just one special meal. In Jamaica, villas typically include cook service. Check your options. Is the villa air-conditioned? Don't assume your villa is air conditioned; ever-present trade winds make this an optional feature. If it's more of a necessity than an option to you, inquire.

Do you need to rent a car? Many villas are located away from the resort areas. See if you should rent a car to avoid pricey taxi rides for long hauls. Is there a minimum stay? Unlike hotel minimums of three nights, villas often require a minimum seven night rental.

4. BASIC INFORMATION

The Caribbean is the land of "no problem" and, for the most part, it's just that. Here's a look at some basic details to make your family's visit carefree.

Business Hours

Business hours vary from island to island but plan for most shops to be open 8am to noon, often closing from noon to 2pm. When cruise ships are in port, however, look for shops to keep their doors open throughout the day.

Cost of Travel

This item really varies by island. Some islands are pricey and proud of it. Destinations like Anguilla and St. Barts are aimed at travelers who won't flinch at high price tags. Other destinations, such as Puerto Rico, Jamaica, the US Virgin Islands, and St. Martin, offer plenty of elegant properties but also a mix of modest accommodations.

Crime

In today's world, there's no escape from crime, period. However, in general, crime is an infrequent problem in this region and often the result of travelers taking a vacation from their everyday precautions. On vacation, use the same common sense you would exhibit at home, especially at night. Don't bring expensive jewelry. Use safes and safety deposit boxes provided by hotels. Also, don't leave valuables on the beach while you are in the water—one of the most common scenarios for theft.

Also, make sure your children know some basic information in case you are separated. Children should know the name of the hotel where you are staying. Also, make sure that very young children know your name, first and last, rather than just Mommy or Daddy.

Depending on the island you visit (Jamaica is the most notable example), you may be offered illegal drugs from a smooth-talking local salesman. These ingenious entrepreneurs offer their goods both on and off land. We've had more than one swim interrupted by salesmen in canoes, boats, and, once, even on horseback in the shallow water. A polite "no, thank you" usually ends the transaction without further problems.

Marijuana, or *ganja* as it's known locally, is illegal throughout the Caribbean. Drug penalties are becoming stiffer, and drug prevention measures more stringent in many countries. Customs carefully screens bags (using dogs in most cases) both when leaving the island and when returning to the mainland.

Have a good talk with teenagers before a trip to the islands. They're prime targets for ganja salesmen, especially in Jamaica. Explain to teenagers that they may be approached and offered drugs for sale, and also explain to them how to politely refuse and move on without further discussion.

We also caution vacationers not to carry any packages that they have not personally packed. We have been approached by locals asking us to mail packages for them once we arrived in the US. The requests may have been legitimate, but the risk is too great.

Etiquette

The citizens of the West Indies are modest, conservative people who generally frown upon displays of skin. Although nudity or topless bathing is permitted on some beaches, it is typically not practiced by locals. Most islanders follow a more conservative style of dress than seen in US beach communities, perhaps echoing back to the European influences felt on many isles.

Bathing suits are appropriate only for swimming; when off the beach grab a cover up. Bare chests are also frowned upon outside the beach. However, leisure wear — T-shirts, shorts, sundresses and sandals—will be readily accepted in any Caribbean community.

Throughout the West Indies, it is customary to greet folks before blurting out a question or request. A polite "good morning" or "good afternoon" will help you fit in and get your interaction off to a good start.

Electricity

Fortunately you don't need to worry about bringing many electrical appliances on a family Caribbean vacation. For those who insist on carrying a hair dryer (which many resorts will supply), electric shaver, or curling iron, however, know that the electric current may not be the same as that you have at home. And on those islands where it is, you may find yourself faced with electric outlets that don't at all resemble those you use every day.

Most Caribbean islands do offer 110 power, 60 cycles with American plugs (after all, American travelers make up the biggest portion of their business). However, on the French islands, St. Kitts and Nevis, and many others, you'll find 220 volts. The French islands use 220 AC, 60 cycles, and all appliances made in the US and Canada will require French plug converters and transformers. Most hotels offer both voltages and different plug configurations but bring converters to be safe.

Festivals

The Caribbean is undoubtedly one place that knows how to party. Besides a whole slew of national holidays (more than found in the US and Canada), you'll also find that the islands celebrate with many special festivals. The biggest blowout on every island is Carnival, scheduled at different times on different islands. Like Mardi Gras, this party lasts for many days (and nights) and may or may not be the best time for your family's visit.

Many smaller festivals are also planned throughout the year on every island. Some can be a wonderful glimpse into another culture, from music that echoes back to the island's early days to flavorful foods that give a taste of the island's bounty.

Be forewarned, however: islands just about shut down during any festival or holiday. Don't expect shops and stand-alone restaurants outside the hotels and resorts to be open for business.

Here's a sampling of some of the festivals planned annually in this region:

January
Bahamas: Junkanoo parades
Jamaica: Maroon Festival
St. Kitts and Nevis: Carnival parade
USVI: Crucian Christmas Children's Parade

February
Curaçao: Carnival
Jamaica: Bob Marley Birthday Bash
Trinidad and Tobago: Carnival

March
Anguilla: Moonsplash
Bahamas: Winter Sailing Championships
St. Maarten: Heineken Regatta
Trinidad and Tobago: Leatherback turtle nesting period

April
Barbados: Congaline Festival
Cayman Islands: Schooner race

Jamaica: Carnival
St. Maarten: Carnival
Tobago: Goat and Crab Race
USVI: Rolex Cup Regatta, St. Thomas Carnival

May

BVI: Spring Caribbean Arts Festival
Cayman Islands: Annual National Children's Festival of
  the Arts
Curaçao: KLM Jazz Festival
Trinidad: Steelpan Competition
Turks and Caicos: Annual Regatta

June

Cayman Islands: Annual Million Dollar Month
  International Fishing Tournament
Puerto Rico: Casals Festival
St. John, USVI: Carnival

July

Cayman Islands: Summer Bash Weekend
Puerto Rico: Barranquitas Artisans Fair
Tobago: Tobago Heritage Festival
Turks and Caicos: Rake and Scrape Festival

August

Jamaica: Jamaica Independence Day Parade
Turks and Caicos: Cactusfest

September

BVI: Foxy's Wooden Boat Regatta
Puerto Rico: Inter-American Festival of the Arts
Turks and Caicos: National Youth Day

October
    Cayman Islands: Pirates Week
    USVI: St. Croix Jazz and Caribbean Music and Art
    Festival

December
    Anguilla: Christmas Fair
    Nassau, Bahamas: Night of Christmas Music
    Jamaica: Devon House's Christmas Fair
    Puerto Rico: Criollisimo Show, Dec.; Lighting of the
    Giant Christmas Tree; Nutcracker Suite Ballet
    St. Lucia: Christmas Folk Festival
    Turks and Caicos: Christmas Tree Lighting Ceremony
    St. Croix, USVI: Christmas Spoken Here

Health Concerns
    Stomach problems from food and water are at a mini-
mum in the Caribbean. Most stomach distress is caused by,
not the food itself, but by larger-than-usual amounts of food
(a problem visitors to the all-inclusive resorts will easily understand due to massive buffets).
    Nothing will ruin a vacation any faster than a sunburn,
your biggest danger in the Caribbean. You'll be surprised,
even if you don't burn easily or if you already have a good
base tan, how easily the sun will sneak up on you. At this
southern latitude, good sunscreen, applied liberally and often, is a must.
    Bring along children's sunblock for tender young skin.
Reapply often and make sure that it goes everywhere, even
into thin hair. Many parents bring along a T-shirt for children to wear in the water. Young snorkelers can fry like fish
in these waters and while snorkeling it's especially easy to
forget that your back is exposed.
    Also bring along mosquito and bug repellent. The worst
insect in the Caribbean are sand fleas. Popularly known as
no-see-'ums, these pesky critters raise itchy welts where they
bite, usually along the ankles. Use an insect repellent if you'll

be on the beach near sunset, the worst time of the day for these unwelcome beach bums.

Here are a few other dangers to share with your family:

• Fire coral: There are many varieties but all edged in white and will burn you if you brush against it. The safest thing is to teach children not to touch any kind of coral because coral will die if touched.

• Jellyfish: These cause painful stings with their tentacles.

• Manchineel trees: These present an unusual danger. These plants have highly acidic leaves and fruit. During a rain, water dropping off the leaves can leave painful burns on your skin and the tree's tiny apples will also burn when stepped on. In most resorts, manchineel trees have been removed or are clearly marked, often with signs and with trunks painted red. Don't let kids touch the trees or play beneath them.

• No-See-Ums: Tucked into that oh-so-wonderful sand lie tiny sand fleas, waiting to bite when the sand cools. You won't feel their bites, but just wait a day or two: welts like jumbo mosquito bites will make themselves apparent and they'll itch for days. To avoid the no-see-ums, stay off the sand at sunset. The fleas are most active when the sand cools.

• Scorpionfish: This mottled pinkish fish hangs out on coral and is so ugly it actually looks dangerous.

• Sea urchins: These are painful if you step on their brittle spines. We recommend bringing old sneakers or swim shoes for every member of the family.

• Stingrays: These are dangerous only if stepped on and can be avoided by dragging your feet when wading.

Language

English is the primary language of most Caribbean islands, but you'll quickly find that you may not understand everything, especially if locals are talking to one another.

English is spoken with a distinct Caribbean lilt, a delightful sing-song rhythm. Each island has its own patois as well; local words are often a mixture of African languages dating back to the island's slave days. Jamaica's patois is perhaps the most distinctive and also most difficult to understand.

Money and Banking

You'll find that US currency is accepted on many Caribbean islands, although you'll often receive change back in the local currency.

We recommend using a credit card for everything but tips and street purchases. Besides avoiding the hassle of currency conversion (and back again when you leave), you'll usually receive the best possible exchange rate on a credit card. The credit card company shops for the best exchange rate for you—saving you some extra pennies and time along the way.

Currency exchange rates shift as suddenly as sand on a beach, but here are some conversion rates at press time:

Aruba florin (AWG)
$1US=1.79AWG
$1CAD=1.25AWG

Barbados dollars (BBS)
$1US=2.01BBS
$1CAD=1.40BBS

Dominican pesos (DOP)
$1US=14.72DOP
$1CAD=10.25DOP

Cayman dollars (KYD)
$1US=83 cents KYD
$1CAD=58 cents KYD

Trinidad dollars (TTD)
$1US=6.20TTD
$1CAD=4.32TTD

Nudity

Depending on the island you visit (the French islands
are the most notable example, although it is practiced on
other islands as well), your family may very well encounter
topless bathers. A routine part of sunbathing for European
women, topless vacationers are often seen on many beaches.
We've explained to our children that topless sunbathing, like
different foods and different languages, is just another example of the cultural differences that make travel interesting and necessary.

Post Office

Don't forget to bring along your friends' addresses for
those obligatory postcards. Most resorts sell postcard stamps
and generally the front desk will handle mailing. It's also
fun to make a stop in the local post office to buy a selection
of local stamps, which might begin a lifelong philatelic interest for your youngster. Stamps are also a good way to learn
more about island life, from the national bird to the past
leaders.

Telephones

Telephone service from the Caribbean is generally very
good, although it is expensive. Generally the highest rates
are found on islands that are not part of the US dialing system such as the French and the Dutch isles. A brief phone
call from these islands can be as much as US $40.

However, even on islands near the US and part of the
US dialing system such as the Turks and Caicos, rates are
pricey, often as much as US $2.50 per minute. Make the call
directly from your hotel room and you'll also be slapped

with hotel telephone surcharges, sometimes as much as 100-200% of the call itself.

The answer? Make a quick call and ask the receiver to call you back. Calls from the mainland to the islands are much less pricey.

Fax service is available at just about all the resorts and is another good way to keep in touch. Many charge nothing to receive a fax and only a few dollars to transmit.

Television

Most Caribbean resorts offer far more television than you'll probably want. Satellite transmissions mean that you're only steps away from all the network channels.

Some resorts recognize that not all guests want a television and do not offer sets in the rooms.

Time

The Caribbean straddles two time zones. The western islands—Jamaica and Cayman—fall in the Eastern time zone, the same as the east coast of the US.

The eastern islands fall in the Atlantic time zone, one hour ahead of Eastern time.

Also, most islands do not observe Daylight Savings Time. During the summer months, the western islands are the same as the Central time zone; the eastern islands the same as the Eastern time zone. A few islands, such as the Turks and Caicos, do observe Daylight Savings Time, however.

Tipping

Between 10 and 15% is traditional for tips for waitstaff and taxi drivers. Some islands typically add tips to restaurant bills so check before paying.

5. GETTING THE KIDS READY:
LEARNING ABOUT OTHER CULTURES THROUGH BOOKS

One of the best ways to build excitement about an upcoming trip is to start the vacation before you ever leave home. Look for Caribbean restaurants in your area or select a Caribbean recipe for your family to make together and try. Read about the region. Rent movies that feature island locales. Surf the Internet and look for island news, notices, and even photos of your destination and resort.

We've compiled here a list of books for different ages, from preschool through teens. Introducing your children to the islands through books can be a way to enrich your experience and to minimize culture shock, helping young travelers learn to appreciate and enjoy the differences between countries.

BOOKS
Picture Books

Bloom, Valerie and David Axtell (Illustrator). Fruits : A Caribbean Counting Poem. Henry Holt, 1997.

This preschool book follows a young Jamaican girl and her sister as they count tropical fruits, including guava, sweetsop, and guinep. The book is written in Jamaican patois.

Lessac, Frane. My Little Island. Harpercrest, 1985.
Aimed at babies to preschoolers, this colorful book follows a young boy and his friend back to the island of his birth.

Elementary Readers
Agard, John, Grace Nichols, Cynthia Jabar (Illustrator). No Hickory No Dickory No Dock : Caribbean Nursery Rhymes. Candlewick Press, 1995.
Ages 4-8 will enjoy these lilting nursery rhymes.

Burgie, Irving, and Frane Lessac (Illustrator). Caribbean Carnival : Songs of the West Indies. William Morrow, 1992.
For ages 4-8, this collection includes easy piano and guitar arrangements for many calypso and folk songs. Irving Burgie is the composer of "Day-O," "Jamaica Farewell," and other calypso classics, and includes those tunes as well as "Michael Row the Boat Ashore" and "Yellow Bird."

Caribbean Canvas. Boyds Mills Press, 1994.
This collection of poems and proverbs of West Indian writers is accompanied by folk paintings with all the beauty and color of the region.

Conolly, Yvonne, Gloria Cameron, and Sonia Singham. Mango Spice : 44 Caribbean Songs. A&C Black, 1994.
Ages 9-12 will enjoy this book of spirited songs.

Elder, J.D., Bess Lomax Hawes, and Alan Lomax (Compiler). Brown Girl in the Ring : An Anthology of Song Games from the Eastern Caribbean. Pantheon Books, 1997.

This collection of 68 children's songs includes not only the music and the lyrics but also the stories behind them.

Gunning, Monica and Frane Lessac (Illustrator). Not a Copper Penny in Me House : Poems for the Caribbean. Mills Press, 1993.
For all age levels, this collection of poems talks about growing up in the Caribbean.

Hallworth, Grace (Editor) and Caroline Binch (Illustrator). Down by the River : Afro-Caribbean Rhymes, Games, and Songs for Children. Cartwheel Books, 1996.
For ages 4-8, this collection includes rhymes, chants, and games of Afro-Caribbean origins. Girls will love the jump rope rhymes and hand-clapping games.

Joseph, Lynn and Sandra Speidel (Illustrator). Coconut Kind of Day : Island Poems. William Morrow, 1990
For ages 4-8, this book of poems follows a Trinidad girl through her day.

Rau, Dana Meachen and Katie Lee (Illustrator). Undersea City : A Story of a Caribbean Coral Reef. Soundprints Corp. Audio, 1997.
This story follows a land hermit crab in the Dominican Republic in his search for a new shell.

Sherlock, Philip and Petrina Wright (illustrator). The Illustrated Anansi : Four Caribbean Folk Tales. MacMillan Publishers Ltd., 1995.
Ages 4-8 enjoy the tales of the Caribbean's most popular folk character: spider named Anansi.

Staub, Frank. Children of Cuba. Carolrhoda, 1996.
For ages 4-8, this book portrays the daily life of Cuban children against the backdrop of their history and customs.

Young Adult Books

Abodaher, David J. Puerto Rico : America's 51st State (An Impact Book). Franklin Watts, 1993.

This book looks at the history of the Caribbean's fourth largest island and includes discussion on the debate for statehood.

Black, Clinton V. Pirates of the West Indies. Cambridge University Press, 1989.

Teens can learn more about the real pirates of the Caribbean with this volume.

Broberg, Merle. Barbados (Let's Visit Places and Peoples of the World). Chelsea House Publishers, 1989.

This guide covers all of Barbados in a language for young readers: history, people, culture, and topography.

Dolan, Sean. Juan Ponce De Leon (Hispanics of Achievement). Chelsea House Publishers, 1995.

Ferris, Jean. Song of the Sea (American Dreams). Flare, 1996.

This novel follows Rose as she escapes from a British sea captain and meets up with Jean LaFitte.

Taylor, Theodore. Timothy of the Cay. Flare, 1994.

This sequel to the immensely popular The Cay follows Philip and Timothy after their rescue.

HELP YOUR CHILD BRING HOME VACATION MEMORIES

Every vacationer wants to return home with memories of the experience that will help him relive the trip time after time. Adults rely on cameras to capture these memories, but children all too often fall prey to overpriced souvenirs as a poor substitute.

There is a way to help your child bring back vacation memories — without breaking your trip budget. No matter where you travel, free (or low cost) souvenirs are yours for the asking. Your children can collect everything ranging from postcards to matchbooks and placemats. They are available in restaurants, campgrounds, motels, tourist attractions, and service stations, potentially every place your family might stop. By showing your child the fun of searching for (not just buying) souvenirs, you can involve him in the excitement of seeking out free souvenirs and keep him away from the trinket stands which plague so many tourist attractions.

Your first step begins before the vacation at your neighborhood five-and-dime. Buy each child an inexpensive photo album ($1-2) with adhesive pages. These pages allow small fingers to stick memorabilia in the book, and they will survive several rearrangements before you have to resort to glue.

Keep an eye out for these souvenirs:

Restaurants: You'll find special children's placemats in many family restaurants, often with pictures or a map of local attractions. Free children's menus, containing a game or a puzzle, are available in many restaurants. And don't overlook tiny sugar packets with the restaurant's name or picture on it. These can act as miniature postcards, ready to assume a place in your child's scrapbook.

Postcards: For about a quarter each, you can carry home a professional photo of almost any attraction in the world. These are a great bargain, and a much better buy than the slides sold at many places, which have often faded under fluorescent lights. And if you've heard your child complain "I never get any mail," encourage them to send a postcard to themselves! They'll act as miniature vacation diaries when they return home, and give returning vacationers a little something to look forward to as well.

Matchbooks: Many restaurants and hotels give away free matchbooks. Minus the matches, of course, these make good additions to the scrapbook. Also, your young travelers may want to start a matchbook collection in a jar once they return home.

Foreign Money: A sample of foreign currency can be a good souvenir and a great way to learn about a country. Foreign coins can be fun to collect and could even interest your child in an entirely new hobby.

Stamps: Foreign stamps are also an excellent and inexpensive way to bring home souvenirs. Your child will learn about the government, national heroes, and often the national bird and flower through stamps.

6. SPORTS & RECREATION

The Caribbean presents a variety of sporting opportunities, whether it's for the toddler or teen, the non-swimmer or the certified scuba diver. Here's an overview of some of the top activities in the Caribbean.

Some of these sporting activities such as scuba diving require previous knowledge and skills; others can be learned with a quick lesson on site. Whatever activities you and your family select, know your limitations and the limitations of your children before signing up for any of these sports. For watersports, make sure that life vests are available. The scruples of the sports operator should not mandate your safety level and don't forsake safety for fun. Know what you can and cannot do.

UNDERWATER ACTIVITIES
Scuba Diving

The Caribbean is universally recognized as one of the world's top dive destinations. Thousands of sites lure divers of all abilities, from beginners looking for shore excursions and shallow reef dives to advanced divers seeking wreck and cave explorations.

You'll find professional assistance from dive operators on every island, including resort courses where you'll have the opportunity to sample diving after a one-day course. Full certification courses will award you a "c" card, and advanced courses to teach you the use of scuba computers, the skills of drift diving, and even underwater photography.

Resort courses can be a good way to introduce your teens to the world of scuba diving without sacrificing much of your vacation. Only children age 12 and over are allowed to participate. The day begins with a lesson on scuba diving, followed by practice in the resort pool. When comfortable with the gear, new divers and the divemaster head offshore for a shallow water dive. It's a thrilling introduction to a new sport and is available at most larger resorts (complimentary at many all-inclusives).

Other novice divers decide to go for full certification and take courses at home before the big vacation. You can opt to do everything but your certification dive at home and then finish up in the Caribbean if you'd like.

Incredible visibility, measured at 100 to 150 feet, helps make these islands such spectacular dive destinations. With year-around water temperatures of 77 to 83 degrees, visitors can dive comfortably and enjoy an underwater playground that's filled with marine life.

Although good scuba spots are found off most islands, top scuba destinations are Grand Cayman, the Bahamas, Turks and Caicos, Anguilla (wreck diving for advanced only).

Tethered Scuba

For those curious about the undersea world but not ready to take the plunge for a full certification course, several outfits in the islands offer a tethered scuba experience to depths of 20 feet. In Grand Cayman and St. John, tethered scuba operators give you the option of shallow scuba diving. You'll start with a simple class on use of the gear then wade out for a shallow water dive. At all times, you are connected to the air tank floating on the surface by a 20 foot tube. With this tube, you'll breathe just like any other scuba diver.

Submarines

For more underwater fun, several islands are home to submarines that give you the chance to see beneath the waves without ever getting wet. Atlantis submarines, found on Grand Cayman, St. Thomas, Barbados, and Aruba, plunge to a depth of 100 feet below the surface.

On other islands, semi-submersible subs are another option. On these vessels, the boat never submerges but visitors walk down into a glass hull for a look at the undersea world. These are a good choice for the budget conscious and for those whose children might not do well in the enclosed environment of a true sub.

Underwater Photography

A great way to get your children interested in the world beneath the sea is with an inexpensive underwater camera. Disposable models are available for about $15 and are good to a depth of 10-15 feet. They're perfect for capturing the memories of a snorkel trip or even for wading out in the clear waters and taking a picture of the beautiful corals.

Snorkeling

Snorkeling is an excellent introduction to the underwater beauty and rich marine life found in the Caribbean waters. Many scenic reefs can be enjoyed with equipment as limited as a mask and a snorkel.

Just yards from shore, you can enjoy a look at colorful corals, graceful fans, and fish like friendly sergeant majors, butterfly fish, and shy damselfish.

Most resorts offer snorkel equipment for little or no charge. To prevent your mask from fogging, rub saliva on the inside of your lenses. Dishwashing liquid and special alcohol-based non-fogging formulas may also be used.

Even non-swimmers can enjoy a look below the waves with snorkel gear. Don a mask, stand in the shallows, and just stick your head in the warm water for a look at another world just inches away.

UNDERWATER ADVENTURE COSTS

These costs represent average prices for underwater activities (in US dollars):

Snorkel Equipment Rental:	free-$8
Half Day Snorkel Trip:	$20-$35
Full Day Snorkel Trip:	$38-$45
One Tank Scuba Dive:	$35-$45
Two Tank Scuba Dive:	$55-$65
Night Scuba Dive:	$25-$50
Resort scuba course:	$75-$90
Scuba Certification Course:	$250-$400

ABOVE WATER FUN

Sailing excursions are another popular way to enjoy the islands. Charters, sunset cruises, booze cruises, rollicking "pirate" cruises, and more are offered to entertain vacationers. Do it yourselfers will find plenty of smaller watercrafts: ocean kayaks, Sunfish, Hobie cats, waverunners, and more.

Rental prices vary by location, but expect to pay anywhere from $25 to $100 an hour, depending on type of vessel. Catamaran rentals run about $35-$40 per hour.

Yachting is another favorite sport. While it may sound like the stuff of a vacation for only the rich and famous, many families enjoy yacht excursions in the Caribbean. Yacht companies in the US Virgin Islands, British Virgin Islands, Sint Maarten, and others offer both bareboat (where you captain the vessel) and crewed yachts. A crewed yacht is similar to a floating hotel. Your meals will be cooked for you and you can help set the course for the day. The size of the vessels vary, so you can choose to have a yacht just for your family or share with others.

Water Toys

You'll find plenty of less serious water fun in the islands as well, especially at the major resort centers. Waverunners, aqua trikes, viewboards, Sunsearcher floats, banana boat rides, paddle cats, paddleboats, and toys for kids of all ages are available for rent. Look along the busier beaches throughout the region: Orient Beach on St. Martin, Seven Mile Beach in Negril, Jamaica, and Seven Mile Beach on Grand Cayman. Top resorts also offer a good array of water toys, often available for guests to use free of charge.

It's also fun to take along some of your child's water toys. Small pails, shovels, and even spoons can keep youngsters busy for hours.

Parasailing

If you or your older children are ready to enjoy a bird's eye view, sign up for a parasail ride. Cost averages about $45 for the ride, which lasts about than 10 minutes.

WATERSPORTS COSTS

The following represent average prices for watersports activities (in US dollars):

Windsurfing rentals per hour:	$20-$30
Wave Runner rentals per half hour:	$35-$60
Sailboat rentals per hour:	$20-$30
Ocean kayak rentals per hour:	$15-$22
Catamaran rentals per hour:	$35
Glass bottom boat ride per trip:	$22-$33
Dinner cruises:	$45-$68
Day sail cruise:	$35-$100

Fishing

Fishing is a popular activity on many Caribbean islands. Several different types of fishing are available throughout the region:

Shore Fishing: From the beach and the shallow waters just beyond, anglers find plenty of challenge. One advantage of shore fishing is that you can enjoy it with just a minimum of scheduling and cost. Bonefish, tarpon, permit, common pompano, and barracuda are some species commonly caught from the shore.

Reef Fishing: The many miles of reefs in the Caribbean provide a playground for fishermen looking for light tackle action. After chumming to attract the fish, a variety of species can be sought, usually with live bait such as squid and conch. At the reef, group, jack crevalle, mutton snapper, yellowtail snapper, and others are common catches.

Deep Sea Fishing: Charters seek gamefish including blue marlin, yellowfin tuna, wahoo, dolphin (dorado) and barracuda, all caught year-around. Strikes can occur as close as a quarter mile from land at the point where the turquoise shallows drop into inky darkness. Chartering a boat is not an inexpensive proposition, but for many visitors it's the highlight of their trip. A half day charter begins at about US $400 and may range as high as $1000 for a full day trip aboard a large charter with state-of-the art equipment and tackle. Blue marlin, dolphin (not the mammal but a popular gamefish), yellowfin tuna, blackfin tuna, skipjack tuna, and wahoo are favorites with deep sea anglers.

FISHING COSTS

Prices for fishing excursions vary by operator, by island, and by time of year, but here's a cost estimate in US dollars (tipping, which is traditional, is extra):

Deep sea charters, full-day	$450-$1,000
Offshore charters, half-day	$325-$650
Bone, tarpon and reef fishing, full day	$300-$600
(up to four anglers, $50 for each additional fisherman)	
Bone, tarpon, and reef fishing, half day	$200-$400
(up to four anglers, $50 for each additional fisherman)	
Bonefishing guide, half day	$250
(maximum two anglers)	

Hiking and Walking

Hikers will find marked trails on many islands. Some are self-guided walks and can be enjoyed by any family member, others are recommended only for serious hikers.

Note that mid-day heat can be intense, especially once you enter the interior of the island away from the cooling breezes on the beach. Always carry water with you and be aware of signs of heat exhaustion and sunstroke.

Horseback Riding

Horseback riding is an excellent opportunity to tour some of the island's quieter sections and to romp along the beach. Some operators also offer pony rides for children.

Use your best judgment with horseback operators. Ask your hotel concierge for recommendations and check out the operation. Does the equipment look well tended? Do the horses look healthy? While there are several top-notch riding facilities in the Caribbean, a few have very old equipment. If your children have not had experience with horses, make sure you select a reputable operator.

7. FOOD & DRINK

For most travelers, dining is an important part of their trip. After all, not everyone will snorkel, scuba dive, or fish, but everyone eats three times a day. It's also a chance to further delve into a national culture, to learn more about the bounty of the land and the sea.

A richly diverse region, the Caribbean presents a full menu of offerings that reflect the many cultures that settled this area. From East Indian rotis served throughout Trinidad and Tobago to Dutch keshi yena served on Aruba, Curaçao, and St. Maarten, the islands are a cornucopia of cultures and cuisines.

One thing island cuisines have in common is attention to flavor. Dishes are rich with flavor and are often spicy. Some dishes trace their origin back to the earliest days of the island when the Arawak Indians first barbecued meats. Later, distinctive seasonings were developed by Africans who came to the islands as slaves. A century later, Chinese and East Indian influences made their way to the islands, when indentured laborers who replaced slaves after emancipation also brought their own culinary talents. Today curried dishes grace nearly every menu, using local meats such as goat, chicken, and seafood.

You will find, however, that at most resorts local dishes are "toned down" to more American tastes. Also, many resort restaurants also offer plenty of American dishes for even the pickiest eater in the family. Beyond the resorts, you'll find fast food outlets on many islands. Don't laugh, even a trip to a fast food eatery can be a cultural experience. In Aruba, we enjoyed an inexpensive lunch under the golden arches, surrounded by locals speaking in Papiamento.

Here's a sampling of island dishes found on many Caribbean menus:

Breakfast
- ackee and saltfish, the national dish of Jamaica. Ackee is a small fruit that is harvested only when it bursts and reveals its black seeds; before that time the fruit is poisonous. Ackee is cooked and resembles (and tastes) much like scrambled eggs.
- johnny cakes and boiled fish for breakfast in the Bahamas

Soups
- pepperpot, a spicy stew
- *asopao*, a chicken and rice soup in Puerto Rico.
- *stoba di cabrito* (goat stew) in Curaçao

Entrees
- fried fish
- stewed lamb with *pan bati* (pancake) on Dutch islands
- *keshi yena* (a hollowed wheel of Edam cheese filled with meat and baked to combine flavors) on Dutch islands
- conch (pronounced konk), a shellfish served chopped, battered and fried in conch fritters
- Grouper, a large fish caught in the waters just offshore, also appears on every menu
- flying fish
- fried plantains
- pattie, a turnover filled with spicy meat that's a favorite lunch snack with locals in Jamaica
- jerk, pork, chicken, or fish is marinated with a fiery mixture of spices including fiery Scotch bonnet peppers, pimento or allspice, nutmeg, escallion, and thyme. This is a favorite dish in Jamaica.

• *empanadillas*, little meat turnovers in Puerto Rico.

• roti, a burrito-like fast food that traces its roots to India; served in Trinidad and Tobago. Look for "buss up shot" at most diners; this is a roti that's torn up like a "busted up shirt" and is eaten with a fork rather than by hand.

Side dishes

• peas (usually red beans or pigeon peas) and rice: the number one side dish in the Caribbean

• cou-cou (a cornmeal and okra dish) in Barbados

• jug-jug (a dish made of Guinea corn and green peas) in Barbados

• christophine, a type of squash

• dasheen (a root vegetable similar to a potato)

• *mofongo*, fried plantains mixed with fried pork rinds and seasoned with garlic, in Puerto Rico

• afungi, a pudding of cornmeal and okra

• fungi (pronounced foon-gee), a tasty accompaniment that's somewhat like cornbread dressing; in the Virgin Islands.

Dessert

• ducana, a pudding made from grated sweet potato and coconut, sugar, and spices, and boiled in a banana leaf

• *flan*, a wonderful custard

• *tembleque*, a custard made with coconut milk and sprinkled with cinnamon in Puerto Rico.

RESTLESS RESTAURANT DINING

OK, this is a warning: service in Caribbean restaurants is not speedy. Whether you are going to a resort restaurant for a nice night out or a side of the road jerk stand, recognize that these are not American fast food joints. Service will not be speedy. You will wait. Your kids will wait.

And they may not wait gracefully. Evening meals can stretch out for several hours at some Caribbean restaurants, and even the most patient diners can become restless. Here are a few tips for dealing with young (and not so young) restless diners:

• consider buffets. Many resorts offer buffet lunches, and buffet serving is often offered at least once a week (most do a "beach night" and serve barbecue).

• move around. Consider placing the order, then taking the kids out for a walk.

• bring activities. The wait for food is a perfect time to catch up on postcard writing, travel diaries, and other "desk" activities for schoolage children.

• use the time to discuss your day and plan the next day's activities. Go around the table and ask everyone what their favorite activity that day was. What has been their favorite food? Their favorite song on the island?

8. BEST PLACES TO STAY WITH KIDS

BOSCOBEL BEACH, *Oracabessa, Tel. 876/975-7330. Toll-free US reservations number Tel. 800/GO SUPER. Winter rates $409-$663 for three nights, per person; Summer rates from $319-$503 for three nights, per person. Credit cards accepted.*

Boscobel Beach is a dream come true both for children and for parents. Called "The Country Club by the Sea," this all-inclusive property puts the emphasis on family fun, starting with a top-notch children's center and program.

Four children's centers are designed to provide age-appropriate activities for young vacationers from 9am to 10pm daily. Kids Coordinators make the day fun with exercise classes, tennis lessons, island excursions, bicycle tours, nature walks, picnics, fashion shows, reggae dance classes, and more.

Children are divided in groups by age. "Tiny Town", for children three years and under, is themed on "Goldilocks and the Three Bears" and includes a life-sized dollhouse, an audiovisual center, and a slumber annex; the center is open until 5pm daily. Four to seven year olds head to "The Bears' Bungalow" for super Nintendo games, an audio-visual area, artistic indoor play area, and an arts and crafts center. Kids eight to 12 years find more advanced fun with CD interactive games and even a girls' make-up room. An teens have their own getaway, "Teens Jump-Up Club" for ages 13 to 17 with a computer learning area, CD juke box, pool table, and ping pong. Need personalized child care? In a typical Jamaican way, that request is no problem. SuperNannies are available for a small fee 24 hours daily.

Kids' needs are met throughout the resort, from a 24-hour nurses station (with a doctor on call around the clock) to a gift shop that carries baby food and diapers. All rooms include mini-refrigerators for special kids' needs as well as color TV with cable.

Adults also find plenty of activity in the 207-room resort. One restaurant is adults-only for a quiet evening out. Four lighted tennis courts, golf at Breezes Runaway Bay Golf and Beach Resort, volleyball, a fitness room, windsurfing, waterskiing, scuba diving, and much more are available.

Up to two children under age 14 (one per parent) stay, play, and eat free. Each additional child is charged $50 per day.

TYPICAL TEENS' PROGRAM

9am	Jump-Up Club Opens
9:30am	Teens' orientation
10am	Watersports on beach
10:30	Tie Die, arts and crafts center
11am	Scavenger Hunt
1pm	Pool tournament
2pm	Reggae Dance Class
2:30pm	Beach Volleyball
3:30pm	Fashion show rehearsal
8pm	Welcome party
10:30pm	Jump-Up Club Closes

BEACHES NEGRIL, *Negril, Jamaica, Toll-free US phone number 800/BEACHES. Winter rates from $600 per person for two nights in a deluxe room, all-inclusive. Credit cards accepted.*

This $25 million property is the answer to all those couples who enjoyed a vacation at Sandals but then wanted to take the kids back the next time. Part of the Sandals family, Beaches brings the all-inclusive fun those couples-only resorts are known for to families, singles, and couples.

Beaches is perched on Negril's famous Seven Mile Beach and offers something for everyone. Three swimming pools, a sports complex with tennis, volleyball and basketball courts, watersports, you name it, it's here. Kids have a full Kids Camp with age appropriate activities. Youngsters especially enjoy the Sega Center, where the latest videos (some being test marketed here!) are available—with no token or coins!

Dining is arranged so families can enjoy time together and apart. Two gourmet restaurants are for adults only while children especially enjoy a pasta bar with brick oven pizza and a Beach Grill, exclusively for kids between 5pm and 9pm.

RENAISSANCE GRAND BEACH RESORT, *St. Thomas, US Virgin Islands, Tel. 340/775-1510, Fax 340/775-2185. Toll-free US phone number 800/HOTELS-1. Winter from $335, summer from $155. Credit cards accepted.*

The Renaissance has proven that you can't keep a good resort down. Struck by 1995's Hurricane Marilyn, the resort rose like an eternal phoenix to reopen even grander than before. From the moment you step in the open-air lobby and look through to powdery beach and Caribbean sea beyond, you'll enjoy a resort that features an airy tropical decor. Rooms here, constructed up one of St. Thomas' steep hillsides, look out on the palm-shaded beach and the turquoise sea as well.

Family activity here centers on the sea as well. Step out on the beach, pull up a chaise lounger, and enjoy a lazy day in the sun or look for fun on the water in the form of snorkeling, sailing, kayaking, or windsurfing.

Dining opportunities include two specialty restaurants as well as poolside lunches (kids love the resident iguana begging for french fries)!

The Kid's Club features daily, year-around fun for kids ages 4-12. Activities vary.

A special family rate is available with a 50% discount on the price of a second room for children traveling with parents. Children under 18 stay free when sharing a room with parents using existing bedding. A children's menu is available in all restaurants and through room service as well.

SAMPLE SCHEDULE OF KIDS' CLUB ACTIVITIES

Supervised fun at the Renaissance Grand Beach Resort varies from week to week, but here's a sample of kids' fun:

Sunday: 9:30am- 1pm: Beach Brunch. This beach party with beach Olympics, sandcastle building, kite flying, brunch and ice cream social provide a half day of fun; there is a $12 charge per child.

Monday: 12:30-5pm Mystery Monday. Magic tricks and show, mystery games, and a pirate hunt keep little ones guessing; there is a $10 per child charge which includes snack.

Tuesday: 1pm - 1:30 Mommy and Me Learn to Swim. Bring children age 2-5 for a swimming lesson; free.

Wednesday: 9am. - 1pm Kid's Caribbean Carnival. Limbo lessons, carnival games and prizes, T-shirt designs and more bring a St. Thomas spirit to the day; $12 per child charge includes lunch.

Noon-4pm Kid's Deep Sea Discover. Pool games, fish craft, and a trip to Coral World; $13 per child charge includes admission and lunch.

Thursday: 1pm - 1:30pm Swimming instruction for ages 2 and up offered free of charge.

6:30pm - 9:30pm Kid's Club Pizza Party with movies, games, and pizza available for $12 per child.

Friday: 12:30pm - 5pm Friday Fantasy. Nature hikes, iguana hunt, poolside bingo, shell craft, and other events keep young nature lovers happy; $10 per child charge includes snack.

Saturday: 6:30pm - 9:30pm Kid's Cartoon Club with cartoons, games and dinner lets parents enjoy a quiet dinner out; $12 per child charge.

WYNDHAM SUGAR BAY BEACH CLUB & RESORT, *6500 Estate Smith Bay, St. Thomas, US Virgin Islands. Tel. 340/777-7100, Fax 340/777-7200. Toll-free US reservations number 800/WYNDHAM. Winter from $396, summer from $288. Credit cards accepted.*

This 300-room resort is a real rarity in the US Virgin Islands: an all-inclusive property. Here, families can stay, play, and eat for one easy price. "We believe that parents deserve a holiday from high vacation costs," said Bob Marshall, general manager. "Our all-inclusive offerings allow the entire family to enjoy a full breakfast, lunch, and dinner daily, including spectacular theme dinners and all day snacks." Perched high atop by seaside hill, the resort offers spectacular views of St. John and the British Virgin Islands.

The all-inclusive package includes all meals and drinks, an ice cream bar, day and night tennis, all non-motorized watersports, use of snorkel equipment, use of fitness center and Jacuzzi, daily activity programs, nightly entertainment, and beach volleyball.

The KidsKlub keeps young vacationers age three to 12 busy and happy. From 9:30am to 5pm daily, children stay occupied with activities such as kite flying, sea shell hunting, crab races, arts and crafts, and more.

The whole family finds plenty of fun as well. Much of the activity centers around the spectacular pool area. Here three interconnecting pools are alive with the sounds of children's laughter as well as the roar of a man-made waterfall. Visitors reach the pool area across a suspended bridge (look in the hibiscus for a resident iguana on the way down!) and a casual dining area lies just steps away. Beyond the pool area, the beach offers plenty of watersports and has some good snorkeling just yards from the shore, a site where we spotted about 40 small squid one afternoon.

The Wyndham Sugar Bay also boasts the island's only indoor resort amphitheater. Movies are shown here when guests are ready to take a break from the sun and the KidsKlub also uses the site for a weekly movie showing.

Check with the resort for special summer offerings where kids under 12 can stay free with parents and older children can stay in an adjoining room for half price.

FRANKLYN D. RESORT (FDR), *St. Ann, Jamaica, Tel. 876/973-3067-70, Fax 876/973-3071. Toll-free reservations Tel. 800/654-1FDR or 888/FDR-KIDS. $1,700-$2,205 per person for 7 days. Credit cards accepted.*

FDR has one of the most unique programs in the Caribbean for vacationing families. Each guest is assigned a Girl Friday on arrival. She works with the family throughout their entire stay, supervising the kids, washing out bathing suits, or even making sandwiches for hungry young travelers.

All guests stay in one-, two-, or three-bedroom suites. Breakfast, lunch, dinner (and a special kiddies dinner) are included along with all beer, soft drinks, bar drinks, and wine. Guests have use of all sports facilities including sailing, windsurfing, snorkeling, glass bottom boat, kayaking, bicycles, tennis court, and gym.

The children's mini-club includes computer training, satellite TV room, disco, Super Nintendo games, donkey rides, picnics, arts and crafts, kiddies slides and paddling pools, and kiddies disco.

FDR offers a unique service: the chance for couples to get married and honeymoon with their new family. With an increase in second marriages involving children, FDR now offers a special $400 wedding package that includes everything a couple needs to get married. The new family can have time together—and apart, thanks to the Girl Friday.

ALMOND BEACH VILLAGE, *Speightstown, Barbados, Tel. 407/872-2220, Fax 407/872-7770. Toll-free reservations Tel. 800/425-6663. Winter rates from $460, summer from $375. Credit cards accepted.*

The Village caters to both couples and families. A children's program keeps the little ones happy while the two of you play a round of nine-hole golf, enjoy watersports right on property, or just lounge around the long expanse of sand.

The Kid's Club is set in the Village's Family Entertainment Center on the southern edge of the property. Here 64 guest rooms are specially reserved for family travelers and swimming pools, a playground, an ice cream shop, a pizza parlor, a restaurant with a special kids' menu and more make even the youngest traveler feel welcomed. Registration in the Kid's Club is complimentary as part of the all-inclusive program, whether families are staying within the Family Entertainment Center or elsewhere on the property.

The Kid's Club Nursery is for children up to the age of four, with a child to caregiver ratio of three to one. The nursery is open from 9am to 5pm daily, closed for the lunch hour. Kids five and up enjoy various activities appropriate to their age. With a child to caregiver ratio of 12 to one, school-age children are grouped from 5 to 7 and 8 to 12. Child fun includes board games, a mini-pool table, VCR, Jukebox, and Foozeball. Outside the center, supervised fun includes watersports, arts and crafts, beach games, on-site nature walks, storytime, treasure hunts, and more. Parents can enroll children in the program for all or part of a day or just for a single activity. Children can also be escorted to lunch or dinner by Kid's Club staff while parents enjoy a meal out.

Almond Beach takes special care with child safety. Children are supervised by staff at all times. Playrooms are kept locked and children in the Kid's Club are returned only to an adult known by the children or one previously identified as a family member or friend.

The Family Plan for both single and two parent families permits the first child under 16 to stay free when traveling with one or two paying adults (except for standard rooms). All other children are charged US $50 per night (except for standard and deluxe rooms).

SONESTA BEACH RESORT AND CASINO CURAÇAO, *Piscadera Bay, Curaçao, Tel. 011/599-9-736-8800, Fax 011/599-9-462-7502. Toll-free reservations Tel. 800/766-3782. Winter rates $230-$335, Summer rates $160-$220. Credit cards accepted.*

This elegant hotel holds the position as the island's best, stretched along a wide swath of beach just a short ride from either the airport or the city. Built in 1992, the 248-room property is designed in the style of the Netherlands Antilles architecture. Cool lemon walls contrast with chili pepper-colored roofs, all framed by stately palms. The property is a veritable oasis on this dry island.

We especially liked the low-rise, open-air quality of this resort, starting with the lobby, where you'll arrive to a view over a cascading fountain across the palm-shaded pool and out to the sea. Every room includes either a balcony or patio (ask for a ground floor room for direct beach access) and at least a partial view of the ocean.

Children age five to 12 can join the Just Us Kids program, offered Wednesday through Sunday from 10am to noon and 1:30pm to 4:30pm. On Saturday evenings, a dinner program is also available. For younger siblings, the Just Us Little Kids program is available for toddlers age 2 to 4 from 10am to noon on Wednesdays and Fridays.

Children's menus are available at all resort restaurants and through room service with child favorites such as hot dogs, burgers, and pizza.

Sample Schedule for Just Us Kids

Wednesday

10am	Register at Guest Services Desk
10:30am	Color, paint, and watch movies
Noon	Lunch with parents
1:30pm	Registration
2pm	Sand sculpturing contest and swimming on Sonesta Beach
3:30pm	Playtime and prizes in Kids Center
4:30pm	Parent pickup

Thursday

10am	Registration
10:30am	Jewelry crafts in the Kids Center
Noon	Lunch with parents
1:30	Registration
2pm	Treasure hunt on the Sonesta Beach
3pm	Board games in the Kids Center
4:30pm	Parent pick-up

Friday

10am	Registration
10:30am	Sports (tennis, volleyball, aerobics)
Noon	Lunch with parents
1:30	Registration
2pm	Games on Sonesta Beach including balloon toss, bucket races
4pm	Arts and Crafts
4:30pm	Parent pick-up

Saturday

10am	Registration
10:30am	Walk then games at Kids Center
Noon	Lunch with parents
1:30pm	Registration
2pm	Just Us Kids bingo with prizes
4:30pm	Parent pick-up

Saturday evening

6:30pm	Pizza and movie in Kids Center ($5 charge per child)
9pm	Parent pick-up

Sunday

10am	Registration
10:30	Swimming in pool
Noon	Lunch with parents
1:30pm	Arts and crafts—making masks
4:30pm	Parent pick-up

HYATT CERROMAR, *Dorado, Puerto Rico, Tel. 787/796-1234, Fax 787/796-4647. Toll-free reservations Tel. 800/233-1234. Winter from $405, summer from $205. Credit cards accepted.*

Hyatt Cerromar and its sister resort, Hyatt Dorado, share 1,000 acres west of San Juan, and guests enjoy reciprocal privileges at the two resorts. Connected by a free shuttle system, guest cards are honored at both resorts. The Hyatt Cerromar is a favorite with families because of its water activities, and special children's programs.

Cerromar is home to Camp Hyatt Cerromar Beach, open to guests at both resorts. This year-around program provides activities for children ages 3 to 12, including new activities focusing on the environment, culture, and geography of Puerto Rico.

The 504 rooms of the seven-story hotel are located in a single complex. Rooms include a TV, hair dryer, bathrobes, mini bar and coffee maker, in-room safe, and balcony or patio.

Activities at Cerromar center around the River Pool, billed as the world's longest freshwater swimming pool. Guests can ride colorful floats down the pool's 1,776-foot length or plummet into the waters from a high-rise water slide. Built at a cost of over $3 million, the pool features bridges, a swim-up bar, waterfalls and several islands. A wheelchair lift ensures that all guests have access to the pool. Nearby, a beach bohio serves lunch and snacks.

For the more adventurous, watersports are available on Cerromar's strip of beach. At the Windsurfing School and Watersports Center (Puerto Rico's only certified windsurfing school), lessons are offered by Lisa Penfield, two-time women's windsurfing champion and former member of the U.S. Olympic team. Guests learn in the reef-protected calmer waters of nearby Hyatt Dorado. These placid waters are also enjoyed by Cerromar snorkelers and ocean swimmers who arrive at the neighboring property via the free shuttle.

Fourteen tennis courts, jogging paths, bicycling and in-line skating are also available for guests.

Popular with families, the open-air Swan Cafe looks out on a lagoon filled with black swans and colorful koi and serves breakfast, lunch, and dinner. For more formal dining, Medici's Northern Italian restaurant and the JASS (Japanese, American, Steak and Sushi) offer elegant fare. Popular lunch spots include the golf pro shop, golf bohio, and beach bohio.

ATLANTIS RESORT, *Paradise Island, New Providence Island, Bahamas, Tel. 242/363-3000, Fax 242/363-2593. Toll-free reservations Tel. 800/321-3000. Winter from $195, summer from $130. Credit cards accepted.*

The vacationers looked up through the sea water, the sun filtering down in liquid shafts and illuminating the hundreds of fish around them. Suddenly, the light was blocked by an sinister silhouette —a shark.

Directly overhead, the six-foot predator swam with deliberate slowness, making schools of yellow grunts scurry closer to sheltering rocks.

But, unlike the school of fish and the large spiny lobster on the sandy floor below, the tourists were not worried. The visitors in the 100-foot long clear tunnel — the parents with the little boy in a stroller, the teenagers wearing a three-day sunburn, and the couple on their first trip to the Caribbean — just delighted in the view. Surrounded by thousands of tropical fish, sharks, manta rays, and sea turtles in the world's largest open-air aquarium, they had the experience of scuba diving without ever getting wet.

The tunnel and the 14-acre water gardens surrounding it are found at the Atlantis on Nassau's Paradise Island. The hotel is one of the most lavish properties in the entire Caribbean. For all its niceties, the hotel is just a backdrop to the 3.2 million-gallon saltwater habitat, the largest outdoor, open-air aquarium in the world. A 14-acre waterscape, where over 40 waterfalls splash and churn sea water into fish-filled lagoons that weave among walkways and bridges. Over three million gallons of sea water fill the observation tanks, each carefully constructed of man-made stone and coral formations to simulate a marine environment.

Guests flock to the Predator Lagoon for a close-up look at the half dozen reef sharks that swim a constant pattern alongside barracudas and rays. Above the water's surface, guests watch for the shark's tell-tale fin to break the lagoon's surface; underwater, encased in the clear tunnel, they stand within inches of the sharks. The Predator Lagoon is popular with all ages of visitors, from small children who delight at the diving turtles and crawling spiny lobsters to the older visitors and non-swimmers looking for the sensation of scuba diving without getting wet.

Water activities continue above the surface as well. Near Predator Lagoon, a rope suspension bridge swings and sways over the water. Nearby water tricycles churn across Paradise Lagoon, a salt water lagoon that opens to the sea. Here in the calm, protected waters the resort hopes to introduce tropical fish to be enjoyed by beginning snorkelers and children who are not ready to tackle the mild waves on the beach. The most popular spot with children is the Lazy River Ride, which meanders through the Waterscape for a quarter mile. Kids hop on an inner tube and set off on a journey pushed by a gentle current. Nearby, Goombay Baths and Slides are a series of saltwater pools where kids can tumble from one to another. Kids also enjoy a children's pool with a sand play area, an Adventure Water Walk with computer-controlled geysers and fountains, and the calm waters of Paradise Lagoon, a good place to receive an introduction to snorkeling or swimming.

Camp Paradise offers supervised activities from 9am to 5pm. Children 5-12 will find a full schedule of activities including searching for buried treasure, Bahamian crafts and storytelling, nature walks, sand castle building, computer games, and talent shows.

During peak season and holidays, Camp Paradise "Night Life" stretches from 3pm to 11pm. Kids are entertained with an evening program while adults play in the casino, watch a show, or enjoy a romantic dinner.

WYNDHAM PALMAS DEL MAR RESORT AND VILLAS, *Humacao, Puerto Rico, Tel. 787/852-6000, Fax 787/852-2230. Toll-free reservations Tel. 800/WYNDHAM. Winter rates from $249 for double occupancy, summer from $179. Credit cards accepted.*

For vacationers looking to getaway from the glitz of San Juan, Wyndham Palmas del Mar is an excellent choice. Located 45 minutes from the capital city, the resort lies tucked on the Caribbean side of the island near the town of Humacao. Actually a compendium of resorts that range from standard hotel rooms to a bed and breakfast inn to luxury condominiums, Palmas is a city in itself, with a staff of over 500 employees.

Although three and a half miles of groomed beach (plus another six miles of nearly deserted beach) tempt vacationers to soak up sun and sometimes rolling surf, the sports facilities offer plenty of opportunities to stay busy. The Golf Club features a championship course designed by Gary Player with holes offering views of El Yunque rain forest, the sea, and the nearby island of Vieques. The largest tennis center in the Caribbean has classes for players of every level.

Children 3-13 find plenty of fun at the Palmas Adventure Club. From 8:30 to 4:30, the daily program offers a full slate of activities: Olympic beach games, swimming, kayaking, miniature golf, water sports, hikes, talent shows, arts and crafts, pony rides, fishing, tennis, and a play ground. The program is available on a half or full day basis. Drop your child off in the morning or afternoon for $22 for the half day ($90 for a five half days) or $28 for the full day program ($112 for five full days). A kids' night out program allows parents to enjoy an evening of adult fun while the kids have evening activities and a snack from 6pm to midnight ($20 per child).

CLUB MED PUNTA CANA, *Provincia La Altagracia, Dominican Republic, Tel. 809/686-5500, Fax 809/687-2896. Toll-free US phone number 800/CLUB-MED. Winter from $120 per person. Credit cards accepted.*

One of the top Club Meds with families, this family village is located five minutes from Punta Cana airport. Guests can select from 334 rooms, each with air conditioning. each have a king or two twin beds and a private bath with shower.

Families have a full menu of activity options from which to choose: water-skiing, sailing, snorkeling, tennis, golf, soccer, windsurfing, horseback riding, basketball, volleyball, aerobics, scuba diving, whatever you choose. Seven tennis courts keep players busy. Facilities also include swimming pool, theater, TV room, and two specialty restaurants as well as a main dining room. At the village, a doctor and two nurses staff an infirmary.

Club Med runs special Kids Free weeks throughout the year, with one kid free per paying parent or legal guardian. (Only the land portion is free, not air packages.)

Children age two and up have plenty of activity at three children's clubs: Petit, Mini, and Kids Club for age-appropriate activities. The fun starts at 8:30am and continues until 9pm and includes a range of free activities, from puppet shows to arts and crafts. One of the top activities is the Circus Workshop, while other sporting events include windsurfing, kayaking, archery, tennis, soccer, basketball, snorkeling, and even a scuba experience in the pool for kids starting at the age of four! Kids can join in for the entire day or just stop by to participate in one activity. Lunches and dinners are supervised and taken early so parents can enjoy dinner later.

A one-time initiation fee of $30 per family with the same last name and annual membership of $50 for kids 12 and over, $20 for kids under 12 is charged.

PART TWO

ANGUILLA

Well known among the well-to-do, Anguilla is a favorite getaway for those really looking to get away. Don't expect mega-resorts on this isle; it is definitely for families looking to discover their own fun.

And that's an easy order to fill. This tiny island is the king of the Caribbean beach world, a mecca for beach buffs in search of that perfect stretch of sand. Although only 16 miles from end to end and little more than 35 square miles in all, the island packs in over 30 beaches and numerous nearby cays to tempt sunlovers, snorkelers, sailors, scuba divers, and those just looking for a good beach walk or hike. A few beaches bustle with activity but most are quiet and interruption-free, just pristine boundaries between land and sea.

Fun is also easy to find thanks to the friendliness of the Anguilla people. Anguillians pride themselves on their hospitality. Local residents greet cars with a wave and exchange "good morning" greetings with those they meet. Crime is as rare as you can find anywhere and, if you get lost, just pull over and ask for help. There's a welcoming spirit here that's shared with visitors and instantly makes your family feel right at home.

Anguilla also boasts a high safety factor. Rent a car, buzz around the island, pull over and dine at side of the road joints; you'll feel safe.

All this safety and seclusion does come at a price, however. The island aims for the upper market traveler, who is not shocked by three figure dinner tabs and per night accommodation rates equal to those found in three or four-night budget packages on some other islands. There are some medium-range properties that we have included in this chapter, but by and large Anguilla is for those who don't have to keep an eye on the pocketbook.

ARE WE THERE YET?

By Air

Air travelers arrive at Wallblake airport either by American Eagle from American's hub in San Juan, Puerto Rico or by connection from nearby Sint Maarten (either plane or ferry). The flight from Sint Maarten to Anguilla takes approximately seven minutes and costs about US $70 round-trip (daylight fare); air charter between the two airports runs about $300 per person. Service from Sint Maarten is available on WINAIR, *Tel. 264/497-2238 or 264/497-2748, Fax 264/497-3351.*

Additional service to Anguilla is available from LIAT, *Tel. 800/468-0482, 264/497-5000,* with daily flights from Antigua, St. Kitts, and St. Thomas. Tyden Air, *Tel. 800/842-0261, 264/842-0261, or 264/497-2719, Fax 264/497-3079,* has charter service anywhere in the Caribbean and day tours to St. Barts, Nevis, and Virgin Gorda as well as daily flights to Sint Maarten. Tyden also offers flights to St. Thomas and St. Kitts. Air Anguilla, *Tel. 264/497-2643,* offers flights to Sint Maarten. Flying time from San Juan is one hour.

By Ferry

Visitors also arrive by ferry from St. Martin. The 20-30 minute ride from Marigot on the French side of St. Martin to Blowing Point, Anguilla costs US$10 each way (plus a US $2 departure fee each way). The trip takes 20 to 25 minutes.

To take the ferry to Anguilla, stop by the open air ferry station on the north end of the market in Marigot. Go up to the window, pay your $2 departure tax, and sign up on the manifest sheet, listing your name, passport number, and nationality. The ferry fee will be collected on board.

Entry Requirements

Upon arrival in Anguilla by either ferry or plane, visitors show proof of citizenship. Passports are the easiest way to show citizenship; official photo ID along with a birth certificate with a raised seal can also be shown. A return or onward ticket is also necessary.

Getting Around the Island

If you'll be traveling around the island very much, by far the most economical transport is a rental car. Taxis are readily available but are not cheap, so a rental car is preferable for most guests. You can ask for a taxi to be dispatched at the airport or the ferry port in Blowing Rock.

Public transportation is not available on Anguilla. Taxi service, both in cars and 12-passenger vans, is available throughout the island. All taxis are on a call basis. We used Austin's Taxi Service, *Tel. 264-497-6660, beeper 2111-239*, and can recommend this service for its thorough knowledge of the island.

Rental car prices vary with operator and model, but a typical mid-size or a jeep runs about $35 per day. A three-month Anguillan permit is required of all drivers. The fee is US $6; this license can be obtained from the rental car companies.

WHICH ONE IS MY ROOM?

SONESTA BEACH RESORT, *Rendezvous Bay West , Tel. 264/497-6999, Fax 264/497-6899. Toll-free reservations Tel. 800/SONESTA. Winter rates start at $290 for a garden view and $410 for a junior suite; off season prices fall to $180 and $260 respectively. Credit cards accepted.*

One of Anguilla's most family-friendly resorts, Sonesta Anguilla is one of the most memorable resorts in the Caribbean. Styled like something right out of 1001 Arabian Nights, this lavish resort dazzles with mirrored tiles, elaborate mosaics, and a unique Moroccan architecture perched right on the edge of a three-mile-long beach.

One hundred guest rooms include private balconies, marble baths, TVs, mini bars, hair dryers, safes, cool tile floors, and a decor that continues the Moroccan theme in pastel Caribbean shades. Oceanfront rooms have spectacular views of the long beach and beyond to the hills of St. Martin. Guest facilities include complimentary use of snorkel gear, sea kayaks, windsurfers, and Sunfish as well as two tennis courts (for day and night play), fitness center, gift shops, children's playground, and freshwater pool. Rental bikes are available.

By Anguilla standards, the Sonesta is one of the best deals on the island. Children 12 and under share a room with parents at no additional charge.

MALLIOUHANA, *Meads Bay, Tel. 264/497-6111, Fax 264/497-6011. Toll-free reservations Tel. 800/835-0796. $320-$415 in high season; low season rates $240-$290.*

This intimate, 56-room hotel is perched on cliffs overlooking a tranquil sea and yet another example of a perfect Anguillian beach. Guest rooms here are private, spread among 25 manicured acres.

Complimentary facilities include use of snorkeling and fishing gear, waterskiing, cruises to nearby cays, windsurfing, Sunfish, Prindle catamarans, four tennis courts (three lit for night play), two pools, Jacuzzis, fitness facilities, and children's playground.

CAP JULUCA, *Maundays Bay, Tel. 264/497-6779, Fax 264/497-6617. Toll-free reservations Tel. 888/8JULUCA. From $620 in high season; low season rates start at $290. Credit cards accepted.*

Cap Juluca, named for the native Arawak Indian Rainbow God, is an exclusive getaway for those looking for privacy and pampering. The 58 guest rooms and junior suites, seven suites, six pool villas all offer complimentary mini bar, marble baths, and hair dryer. Some units include kitchen with refrigerator and dining room. Guest facilities include three tennis courts, croquet, beach, pool, Sunfish, kayaks, windsurfing, fitness center, snorkel trips and sunset cruises.

Cap Juluca offers a children's program called "Cap Juluca Kids" during the peak family season: Easter holidays and the months of July and August. The program is complimentary for guests and includes a full day of activities and theme field trips several times a week as well as lunch and a Cap Juluca kids' T-shirt. The program runs Monday through Friday from 9am to 5pm.

"At Cap Juluca we're providing a holiday for the entire family," says Kerman Beriker, general manager. "With Cap Juluca's Kids, parents have time to enjoy each other while knowing their children are in excellent hands themselves, as well as learning."

Children have the opportunity to learn through themed activities such as "Anguilla Today," a day of fun that highlights the island's residents, animals, ponds, and the sea; "Amerindians and Arawaks," with a visit to an island cave to hunt for fossils and crystals; "Fishing and Salt Production," to explore a fishing village; "Boat Racing," with a visit to the island's traditional boat builders. The most popular trip explores Gavanah Cave where the island's first archaeological find, a giant rodent fossil, was discovered in 1868. The rodent weighed 345 pounds but, to the relief of everyone, hasn't resided on the island in over 100,000 years!

After the two-hour field trips, children enjoy activities at the resort including puppet shows, journal writing, music, photography, nature hikes, games, and arts and crafts. The program is available for children age four to 12.

Babysitting is available for children under four. Children's rooms are half-price from June through October.

COVE CASTLES, *Shoal Bay West, Tel. 310/440-4225, 264/ 497-6801, Fax 264/497-6051. Toll-free reservations Tel. 800/ 223-1108. $795 for one-bedroom villa, $595 for one-bedroom beach house in high season.*

This villa resort caters to the guest looking for privacy, peace, and quiet. These stark white two- and three-bedroom getaways have a contemporary exterior and a tropical decor inside. Complimentary amenities include snorkeling, Sunfish sailboats, sea kayaks, bicycles, tennis, video players and library, concierge service, cable TV, and a personal housekeeper. Also available at additional charge are deep sea fishing, sailing excursions, tennis instruction, massage, and more.

WHAT ARE WE DOING NEXT?

If this is your first visit to the island, invest in an island tour led by one of the tour companies or a taxi driver. **Guided island tours** are available from most taxi drivers for $40 for one or two people, $5 for each additional person and will help give you a good overview of the island. From there, you can rent a car and motor around to the beaches and natural attractions scattered around the island (remember, though, driving is on the LEFT).

Anguilla is home to several small museums. The National Trust is currently at work on a museum in The Valley, but several privately owned collections welcome visitors. The **Heritage Collection**, *Pond Ground, Tel. 264/497-4440*, is the work of Colville Petty, an authority on Anguilla's rich history. Housed in part of Petty's home, the museum spans the entire range of the island's history, from its Amerindian days to the 1967 Revolution. Kids enjoy the collection of Arawak artifacts, including an Arawak shell necklace, a hollowed conch shell that served as an early drinking vessel, and spindle whorls, used to spin cotton to make hammocks and religious symbols for the Arawaks are also on display. This fascinating museum is open Monday through Saturday, 10 to 5pm and Sunday by appointment. Talking to Colville Petty about the island's history is well worth the price of admission. Admission is US $5, children under 12 are $2.

Anguilla enjoys a rich West Indian culture. Have a look at the traditional song and dance with a visit to the **Mayoumba Folkloric Theatre**, *La Sirena Hotel, Tel. 264/497-6827*, a group that plays every Thursday night at La Sirena hotel in Meads Bay. Call for reservations.

Kids five to 10 years old also have a unique opportunity to interact with Anguillians. Children are invited to a weekly Saturday morning **storytime** at the new Anguilla National Library, *The Valley, Tel. 264/497-2441*, a Caribbean-style building designed by a local architect. The National Library is seeking assistance with the purchase of books, computers, software, and audiovisual materials. Contact the Anguilla Library Service, The Valley, Anguilla, BWI, *Tel. 264/497-2441*.

Sports

Young swimmers will find many opportunities for **snorkeling**. A marked snorkel trail is found off Shoal Bay East. Maintained by the National Trust, the site has been mapped and can be easily followed by most snorkelers. Stop by the National Trust office at the National Museum in The Valley or ask your hotel's concierge for a map of this snorkel trail. Laminated for use underwater, the maps are available from the National Trust for a $5 deposit, $4 is returned when the map comes back to the office. To check on the snorkel trail or to obtain a map, call the National Trust, *Tel. 264/497-5297.*

Certified **scuba divers** in your family can enjoy a look at one of seven wrecks that lie in the waters off Anguilla. Four were sunk in 1990 as part of an ecological program and all the wrecks are intact and upright on the ocean floor. Anguilla has two dive operations, located in Sandy Ground and Island Harbour. Rates average about $45 US for a single tank dive, $80 for a two-tank dive, and $55 for a night dive.

Regardless of your children's ages and swimming abilities, you'll discover that one of Anguilla's best assets is its **beaches**. Miles of shining sand pave the perimeter of this island, which is often cited as one of the top beach destinations in the Caribbean (with good reason). The atmosphere at the various beaches varies from playful to placid. Regardless of which beach you select, the mood is friendly and low-pressure.

A few beach vendors are found on the island's busiest stretch of sand, **Shoal Bay**, but even here the sales are very low-key and you'll be able to enjoy undisturbed sunbathing all afternoon. Shoal Bay is a true classic, one of the best in the Caribbean. Nearly chalk white sand stretches for two miles. Shoal Bay has the most typical "beach" atmosphere in Anguilla, with casual eateries sprinkled along the sand. Beach chairs and umbrellas are rented by the day for a few dollars. This beach is a terrific choice for a family day of fun in the sun. Young swimmers generally find the water calm, and snorkeling is excellent on the northeast end of the beach.

Other good beach choices include **Sandy Ground**, stretching alongside the community of Sandy Ground (a favorite with boaters, windsurfers and water-skiers, so not the best choice for those with young swimmers), **Rendez-vous Bay**, at the Sonesta Anguilla (great for beachwalking), **Maundays Bay**, at Cap Juluca (good for beachwalking). A good adventure is to take a boat out to one of the many cays and islets surrounding Anguilla. Check with boat operators for a day trip to **Prickly Pear Cays** or **Sandy Island**, both known for their snorkeling, or for a unique experience load up everyone for a day trip to one of the uninhabited islands: **Anguillita Island, Sombrero Island**, or **Dog Island**. A boat can drop you for a full day's excursion, most departing from Sandy Ground. Bring along a picnic lunch and feel like Swiss Family Robinson.

Horseback riding is available through El Rancho Del Blues, *Blowing Point, Tel. 264/497-6164*. One hour rides on the beach and in the countryside are offered at 9, 11, 2:30, and 4:30; riding lessons are also available.

If you've got any football (soccer to Americans) fans in the family, drop by the Ronald Webster park, located north of the Post Office in The Valley. You'll find a game most weekend afternoons.

WHAT CAN I BUY?

Shopping is not one of Anguilla's strong points, especially for kids looking for small souvenirs. Artist's galleries are sprinkled throughout the island, but these are pricey reminders of an island vacation.

The Sonesta Anguilla resort has several good gift shops; both the clothing store and general store have reasonably priced items. Cap Juluca has a nice gift store but take out a loan first.

A good option is an afternoon of shopping in St. Martin. Take a ferry ride to Marigot, St. Martin for a day at the market. Kids of all ages find trinkets, clothes, jewelry, shells, carvings, and other goodies in all price ranges. The market is colorful, fun, and friendly.

PRACTICAL INFORMATION

Currency. The Eastern Caribbean (EC) currency is legal tender. Value is set at $1US=2.68EC. US dollars are also accepted.

Driving. Driving is English style, on the LEFT.

Electricity. The island has 110 volt electrical currents.

Information. For more information on Anguilla, contact the Anguilla Tourist Board, *Tel. 800/553-4939* , or write Anguilla Tourist Information Office, *P.O. Box 1388, Old Factory Plaza, The Valley, Anguilla.* Staff members are available from 8 to 5 Atlantic Standard Time (one hour ahead of Eastern Standard Time).

Information on Island. While on the island, stop by the Tourist Board office in The Valley at Factory Plaza, *Tel. 264/ 497-2759.*

Web site. Internet users can find some good up-to-date Anguilla information on the Web site: *http:// www.candw.com.ai/~atbtour.*

ISLAND REPORT CARD	
Transportation to island	B
Transportation around island	B+
Family Resorts	B
Family Restaurants	B-
Friendly atmosphere	A+
Activities for kids	B+
Weather	A
New cultures for kids to experience	A
Safety	A+

ANTIGUA

What Antigua boasts are beaches: 365 of them, the tourism folks claim. There's a beach for every activity level: stretches of white sand border turquoise waters teeming with marine life, beaches where your family can walk and hardly see another soul, beaches where you can shop for local crafts and buy a burger at beachside grill, and beaches where you can just curl up under a tall coconut palm and sit until the sun sinks into the sea and marks the end of another Caribbean day.

Pre-Colonial Antigua was originally inhabited by the Siboney Indians. In 1493 Christopher Columbus named the island in honor of Santa Maria de La Antigua of Seville, a saint at whose namesake church Columbus had prayed before his journey to the Americas.

Antigua has had close ties to England, ever since an English patrol from St. Kitts landed on the island in 1632 and claimed it for the mother country. Since 1981, however, the twin island nation of Antigua and Barbuda has held the status of an independent country.

This 108-square mile limestone and coral island is somewhat scrubby with rolling hills, especially on the southern reaches. The capital city is St. John's, home of most of the tourist shopping and the cruise port.

The south shore of the island is favored by yachties, who call into Nelson's Dockyard at English Harbour.

ARE WE THERE YET?
By Air

Air travelers will arrive at V.C. Bird International Airport, located near the capital city of St. John's. Served by American Airlines, Continental, and BWIA from the US as well as Air Canada and BWIA from Canada, the airport is also a bustling hub for airlines such as LIAT for many inter-island flights.

Antigua is also a popular destination for many cruise ships. The terminal is located in downtown St. John's and is within walking distance of the main shopping areas.

Entry Requirements

US and Canadian visitors must show a passport or a birth certificate and photo ID as well as an onward or return ticket.

Getting Around the Island

Taxi travel is the most common means of transportation, especially for families not comfortable with driving on the left side of the road. Taxi fares from the St. John's area to Nelson's Dockyard on the far side of the island run about $50 US round trip.

Rental cars are available; a temporary Antiguan driver's license is required. The license can be obtained at the V.C. Bird International Airport or at any Antiguan police station. We found that some roads are a little bumpy, and that a full tank of gas (as well as a spare tire) was recommended for visitors who would be traveling out on the island away from the major destinations.

WHICH ONE IS MY ROOM?

CURTAIN BLUFF HOTEL, *Tel. 268/462-8400, Fax 268/462-8409. Toll-free US phone number 800/672-5833. Winter rates from $655 double occupancy. Credit cards accepted.*

This exclusive hotel is located on a private peninsula with two beaches. The all-inclusive property includes all meals, drinks, afternoon tea, watersports, tennis, golf, and even mail service so you can send those postcards home.

Kids age two to five stay in the parents' room for $65 per night. Children over five years pay the extra person charge of $150 per night.

Note: Children are not permitted from mid-January through mid-March, peak season. At other times, kids are welcomed but are restricted from the bar and from the restaurant after 7pm.

Baby-sitting is available.

HAWKSBILL RESORT, *St. John's, Tel. 268/462-0301, Fax 268/462-1515. Toll-free reservations Tel. 800/223-6510. Winter rates from $375, summer from $276. Credit cards accepted.*

Located just a few minutes from St. John's, this quiet resort is our favorite kind: quiet, restful, and located on, not one, but four superb beaches. With a primarily British contingency, the resort is somewhat reserved but just a few minutes from the action of St. John's. Kids' supper is served from 6pm to 7pm.

CLUB ANTIGUA AT JOLLY BEACH, *Jolly Beach, Tel. 268/462-0061, Fax 268/462-1827. Toll-free US and Canada reservations Tel. 800/777-1250. Winter rates from $216 for double occupancy, $300 for family room; summer rates from $189 for double occupancy, $280 for family room. Credit cards accepted.*

This all-inclusive resort is a favorite with family travelers. Set on a half-mile of private beach, the resort offers travelers 470 guest rooms, ranging from standard accommodations to junior suites. The all-inclusive package includes three meals daily, snacks, beverages, tennis, watersports (including windsurfing, snorkeling, waterskiing and sunfish sailing), daily sports such as bicycling, volleyball, step aerobics, Calypso dance lessons, and more, and a children's program.

The children's program operates for young visitors from age four to 12 years. The supervised program includes board games, crafts, painting classes, excursions, shopping trips, and nature hikes.

JOLLY HARBOUR MARINA CLUB, *Jolly Harbour, Tel. 268/462-7771, Fax 268/462-7772. Toll-free US and Canada reservations Tel. 800/777-1250. Winter rates from $100 for double occupancy, from $85 during summer months. Credit cards accepted.*

Popular with families, these waterfront condominiums are located a short walk from the beach. The villas include an upstairs bedroom with a queen sized bed and balcony. The second bedroom has two twin beds. The ground floor includes a fully equipped kitchen, and patio that looks out on the harbour.

Guests can take a shuttle to the commercial center at the marina which includes over 40 businesses. Guests can enjoy a game of tennis or squash (for a fee) or use the swimming pool (free). Baby-sitting services are available. Villa residents can also buy passes to neighboring Club Antigua. Day memberships at the Jolly Harbour Golf Club are available. Daily memberships are $50 per day and include all meals, beverages, and use of resort facilities.

Visitors to the Marina Club can take an MAP plan with breakfast and dinner at select marina restaurants for about $30 per person per day.

WHAT ARE WE DOING NEXT?

Antigua's most family activity is a trip to its splendid **beaches**. Some of the most popular spots are Dickenson Bay, where you'll find beach bars and watersports action, Hawksbill beaches on Five Island peninsula, home of a clothing-optional beach, and Runaway Beach, also lively with watersports activities.

If it's beach seclusion you're after, then consider a day to Antigua's sister island, **Barbuda**. Day trips to this uncommercialized island, which is also popular with bird watchers because of its population of frigate birds, are available from several operators. Barbuda lies about 30 miles north of Antigua.

Nature lovers will also find plenty of activity on Antigua. **Scuba diving and snorkeling** is a popular activity. Certified divers can enjoy a variety of dives, from walls to wrecks.

Antigua is also rich in historic attractions as well. The most visited is **Nelson's Dockyard National Park**. Built in 1784, this dockyard was the headquarters for Admiral Horatio Nelson. Today you can retrace the history of this site at the Dow's Hill Interpretation Centre or at the complex's two museums: Admiral's House and Clarence House, former home of Prince William Henry, later known as King William IV of Britain.

WHAT CAN I BUY?

The primary shopping area on the island is in St. John's, near the cruise ship terminal. This area doesn't have the charm of many Caribbean shopping districts, and is somewhat littered, smelly, and dirty. Still, it's worth a two- or three-hour excursion to have a look at the goods offered in the small boutiques.

Redcliffe Quay is a scenic place to shop and have lunch. You will find plenty of cool shade, brick courtyards, and restored buildings where you can shop for Caribbean items in a charming atmosphere.

If you'd like to get away from the tourist center, take a walk up to Market Street for shops aimed at the local residents, including many fabric stores offering beautiful tropical prints.

Outside of St. John's, head to Harmony Hall in Brown's Bay Mill. This art gallery, which originated in Jamaica, features work by many Caribbean artists. Original works as well as prints and posters are for sale, accompanied by crafts, books, and seasonings that capture the spice of the island.

PRACTICAL INFORMATION

Currency. The Eastern Caribbean (EC) dollar is the legal tender. It is exchanged at a fixed rate of $1US=2.68EC. American dollars are also accepted.

Driving. Driving is on the LEFT.

Information: Contact the Antigua and Barbuda Department of Tourism, *610 Fifth Avenue, Suite 311, New York, NY 10020 or call Tel. 888/268-4227 or Tel. 212/541-4117.* In Canada, contact the Antigua and Barbuda Dept. of Tourism and Trade, *60 St. Clair Avenue East, Suite 304, Toronto, Ontario MT4 1N5 or call Tel. 416/961-3085.*

Web Site. Another good source of information is the Antigua and Barbuda Department of Tourism Web page at *http://www.antigua-barbuda.org.*

ISLAND REPORT CARD	
Transportation to island	A
Transportation around island	B+
Family Resorts	B
Family Restaurants	B-
Friendly atmosphere	B-
Activities for kids	B+
Weather	A
New cultures for kids to experience	B
Safety	B+

ARUBA

Aruba is not the tropical paradise found on islands like Jamaica or St. Lucia. Palm trees and tropical flowers cluster only around well-groomed resorts and desert landscapes.

But that's not to say Aruba is without beauty—you just have to know where to look, that's all. You'll have to venture to the rugged Atlantic shore and watch the tumultuous waves carving the natural bridge, continually changing the demarcation line where the land meets the sea. Or you can hike to some of Aruba's highest hills, curious bumps on the landscape, and look out at the *cunucu* or countryside for traditional Dutch-style houses with their sun-baked orange tile roofs.

But perhaps the best way to see the beauty of Aruba is to look into the faces of the Aruban people, the island's greatest asset. This tiny island, a mere 70 square miles, truly is a melting pot of cultures. Over 43 nationalities are represented here, and with them a melange of languages. Arubans learn from an early age the benefits and necessity of working with other nations and learning different languages is a skill that most young Arubans master. This island is the perfect place to bring your young linguist to inspire the desire to learn.

The language of the Aruban home is Papiamento, a mixture of Spanish, Portuguese, French, Dutch, Indian, English, and even some African dialects. When youngsters head to school, they receive instruction in Dutch, because of Aruba's continuing ties to the Kingdom of Holland. Once they reach third or fourth grade, instruction in English begins. Spanish is introduced during the junior high years, and in high school students select from French or German.

That familiarity with many languages translates into a welcoming atmosphere for visitors of any nationality. There is no hostility to tourists on this island; no language barrier to overcome. There is just a spirit of "Bon Bini" or "Welcome" which greets visitors from the moment they arrive in the airport and continues throughout their visit.

PAPIAMENTO

Papiamento is the language of the streets. To the ear, it resembles Spanish. Here are some common Papiamento phrases:

Bon Bini. Welcome.
Con ta bai? How are you?
Mi ta bon. I am fine.
Bon dia. Good morning.
Bon nochi. Good evening.
Pasa bon dia. Have a good day.
Hopi bon. Very good.
Ayo. Good-bye.

ARE WE THERE YET?

By Air

Aruba is a 2-1/2 hour flight from Miami or four hours from New York. Service into Queen Beatrix International Airport is available from American, *Tel. 800/433-7300*, (from New York, Miami, and San Juan). Air Aruba, *Tel. 800/882-7822*, is the national carrier, and offers non-stop flights from Newark, Miami, Baltimore, and Tampa. Nonstop service from Houston is also available twice weekly aboard Viasa, *Tel. 800/GO-VIASA*. ALM, *Tel. 800/327-7230*, offers service from Miami.

Entry Requirements

American and Canadian citizens need to present a current passport or an official birth certificate and a photo ID.

Getting Around the Island

Taxis are available in resort areas or you can have one dispatched by calling 22116 or 21604 on island. Rates are fixed (no meters), so check with your driver before the ride. Rental cars are widely available.

WHICH ONE IS MY ROOM?
Oranjestad
ARUBA SONESTA SUITES AND CASINO, *L. G. Smith Boulevard, #9, Oranjestad, Tel. 011/297-8-25317, Fax 011/ 297-8-34389. Toll-free reservations Tel. 800/SONESTA. Winter rates from $300-$400, Summer from $205-$305. Credit cards accepted.*

The Sonesta Suites are located just a block from the Resort, but it is a beachfront (albeit a small beach) property. This hotel includes suites with all the comforts of home: a full, furnished kitchen, dining area, and bedroom. As you might expect, it's an especially popular property for those traveling with kids. The free-form swimming pool is the focal point for the property, which also includes a slightly less elegant casino than its nearby cousin.

Guests at the Sonesta Suites also have full use of the Sonesta Island.

Both the Aruba Sonesta Suites and the Aruba Sonesta Resort offer the "Just Us Kids" program. Children 5-12 enjoy the complimentary program available from 10am to 5pm and upon request from 6pm to 9pm. Daily activities such as movies, beach Olympics, horseback riding, museum visits, and miniature golf keep the youngest vacationers happy. Field trips to Baby Beach, Casibari Rock, Natural Bridge, and other sites introduces young travelers to the island; a $6 fee for transportation is charged. Baby-sitting can be arranged for younger children; $7.50 for one child to $10 per hour for three or more kids in the same room. After midnight, baby-sitting is charged at $12.50 per hour.

The Sonesta Suites Kids Center is open from 10am to 9:30pm and here kids can drop in for supervised games, coloring, arts and crafts, and movies. There is no charge for use of this facility.

Teenagers are offered special snorkel trips, water sports, and a resort scuba diving course with others their own age.

ARUBA SONESTA RESORT AND CASINO, *L.G. Smith Boulevard #9, Oranjestad, 011/297-8-36000, Fax 011/297-8-34389. Toll-free reservations Tel. 800/SONESTA, Winter rates from $215-$330, Summer from $145-$235. Credit cards accepted.*

Sonesta Island, located less than ten minutes away by private launch. And this isn't just any boat ride. Venturing up into the hotel via a canal that slices into the shopping mall, guests are transported to a private world where the can dine at the open-air restaurant. Children enjoy the calm, protected waters off the beach and older kids can partake in watersports at the Red Sail Sports concession. Complimentary shuttles run between the hotel and the island ever 20 minutes.

Eagle and Palm Beaches

AMERICANA ARUBA BEACH RESORT AND CA-SINO, *J.E. Irausquin Boulevard, #83, Palm Beach, Tel. 011/297-8-64500, Fax 011/297-8-63191. Toll-free reservations Tel. 800/203-4475. Winter rate from $340, summer from $200, EP. Credit cards accepted.*

The swimming pool is the centerpiece of this 419-room resort. The pool has its own current, so you can just float along the stream or swim against it to work off that Aruban food and drink. The pool also features "Spa Island," which has two whirlpools and a rock waterfall.

Enjoy some family time together while the kids have fun at the Americana Aruba Adventure Club for ages 4 to 13. Activities range from arts and crafts to merengue dance lessons and pool Olympics.

This hotel offers either a European (no meals) or all-inclusive plan.

Children under two stay free; children two to 12 years pay $50 per day in the all-inclusive plan.

HYATT REGENCY ARUBA RESORT AND CASINO, *J.E. Irausquin Boulevard, #85, Palm Beach, Tel. 011/297-8-61234, Fax 011/297-8-65478. Toll-free reservations Tel. 800/233-1234. Winter rates $340-$430, Summer rates $190-$245. Credit cards accepted.*

One of Aruba's most luxurious properties, the 365-room Hyatt is located on the northern end of Palm Beach. Like other Hyatts, this property is for anyone looking for a body holiday: be pampered in the health and fitness facility, slice across the clear Caribbean on a sailboat at the watersports facility, or just luxuriate in the warmth of the sun at the three-level pool complex. Camp Hyatt, for children age three to 12 years, includes activities such as Papiamento lessons, local arts and crafts, and nature hikes. Family Camp, with fun for all members of the family, includes activities such as glass-bottom boat rides, photography classes, and watersports. Kids under 18 stay free in room with parents.

ARUBA MARRIOTT RESORT AND STELLARIS CASINO, *L.G. Smith Boulevard, Palm Beach, Tel. 011/297-8-69000, Fax 011/297-8-60649. Toll-free reservations Tel. 800/223-6388. Winter rates $335-$375, Summer rates $150-$170. Credit cards accepted.*

This 413-room hotel is one of the newest on Palm Beach, a flashy property with a free-form pool, oversize guest rooms, and just about any activity a family could want.

RADISSON ARUBA CARIBBEAN RESORT AND CASINO, *J.E. Irausquin Boulevard, #81, Palm Beach, Tel. 011/297-8-66555, Fax 011/297-8-63260. Toll-free reservations Tel. 800/333-3333. Winter rates $245-$365. Credit cards accepted.*

This 372-room hotel has plenty to keep families busy on the beach with water-skiing, wave runners, catamarans, scuba instruction, the list goes on and on. The kids' program includes a myriad of activities ranging from volleyball to bocce ball to beach Olympics. Baby-sitting available. The whole family can enjoy the 1500-foot-wide beach and the Olympic-sized pool.

HOLIDAY INN ARUBA BEACH RESORT AND CA-SINO, *J.E. Irausquin Boulevard #230, Tel. 011/297-8-63600, Fax 011/297-8-65165. Toll-free reservations Tel. 800/GO-BOUNTY in US, Toll-free reservations Tel. 800/GET-BOUNTY in Canada and Puerto Rico. $235 in high season for all-inclusive program in high season, $145 per person off season. Credit cards accepted.*

The 600-room Holiday Inn Aruba Beach offers the Bounty all-inclusive Vacation program. The package includes room (with air-conditioning and satellite TV), buffet breakfast daily, full service lunch and dinner daily in a choice of indoor and outdoor restaurants, snacks, unlimited liquor, beer, wine, and soft drinks, theme parties, watersports, tennis, hotel tax, tips, and, especially for families, a supervised kids' program.

Camp Bounty, the program for children age 4-12 (although the program can be adjusted for toddlers 2-4 and teens 12-15), runs daily from 9am to 5pm. The program includes breakfast and lunch with program coordinators, daytime snacks, arts and crafts, and plenty of activities. Children enjoy kite flying contests, drawing and coloring contests, sand sculpting, hoola hoop contests, pool and beach Olympics, shell hunting, talent shows, face painting, dance lessons, scavenger hunts, and more. After program hours, baby-sitting is available.

Check for special promotions during summer and fall months; recently the hotel ran a "kids' stay free" promotion where children stayed in the same room as parents without charge.

LA CABANA ALL SUITE BEACH RESORT AND CA-SINO, *J.E. Irausquin Boulevard #250, Eagle Beach, Tel. 011/ 297-8-79000, Fax 011/297-8-77208. Toll-free reservations Tel. 800/835-7193 in US and Canada. Winter rates from $210 double occupancy, Summer rates $120 double occupancy. Credit cards accepted.*

Located across the street from Eagle Beach, this orange sherbet-tinted property has plenty of action, including a huge casino. All guest rooms are suites—from studios for families to three bedroom suites for families, and all include a fully equipped kitchenette.

La Cabana offers kids' programs for every age. The Club Cabana Nana program for children 5 to 12 offers activities from 10:30am until 3:30pm daily, except Wednesdays when the program runs from 5pm to 8:30pm. Priced at $80 per child per week, the program runs year around. Kids receive a Club Cabana Nana T-shirt, lunch daily (pizza on Wednesday nights), and plenty of activities from which to choose: scavenger hunts, mini-golf, sandcastle building, talent show, and more. Papiamento lessons are a fun and educational part of the program, along with a botanical tour of the property and lessons on the island's history and culture.

Teens aren't forgotten either. The Teen Cabana Culture Club entertains ages 13 to 17 with windsurfing, snorkeling, billiards, mini-golf, beach disco parties, and more.

THE CONCIERGE RECOMMENDS...

Concierge Celia Nagtegaal at Aruba Sonesta Resorts at Seaport Village suggests these family activities on Aruba:

1. Take a ride on the Atlantis Submarine.
2. Enjoy miniature golf at Adventure Golf, also includes bumper boats and restaurant.
3. Go horseback riding to the Natural Pool (accessible only by hiking or horseback).
4. Go to Baby Beach for a family picnic and snorkeling.
5. Rent a car or a jeep for island tours.
6. Visit the sand dunes at the Light House.
7. Climb the Casibari rock formation.
8. Climb the Haystack.
9. Visit the caves to see Indian drawings.
10. Take a long walk along the beaches and look for shells.
11. Visit the ruins of the gold mine.
12. Take a walk through the national park.
13. Go snorkeling and enjoy the activities at Sonesta Island.
14. Take a sunset sail on a catamaran.
15. Take a snorkel trip.
16. Enjoy a glass bottom boat trip out to see the German tugboat wreck.
17. Take a Papiamento lesson.
18. Take a Caribbean dance lesson.
19. Try your luck at a bingo game at the Sonesta or on Sonesta Island.

WHAT ARE WE DOING NEXT?

As home to both the cruise port and the airport, your first look at Aruba will probably be in the city of **Oranjestad**. This beautiful city, where nearly every building sports a fresh coat of paint and a distinct Dutch style, is well worth spending an afternoon wandering the safe, clean streets and enjoying the friendly atmosphere.

114 CARIBBEAN WITH KIDS

Also make sure to have a look at the rest of the island. The biggest tour operator is DePalm Tours, with desks in every major hotel. This firm offers an excellent half-day tour aboard air-conditioned motor coaches with hotel pick-up. At the conclusion of the tour, you can return to your hotel or get off in downtown Oranjestad for an afternoon of shopping.

Island tours reveal a terrain with a windswept family beauty that families learn to love for its contrast of ochre colors against the turquoise sea and for its rugged beauty. You'll have an excellent view of the *cunucu*, or countryside, atop **Casibari Rock Formation**. It's a fairly easy climb (although you'll find yourself bent over and squeezing between rocks a few times), but wear good shoes for this trek.

Families also should visit the **natural bridge**, like the divi-divi tree, a symbol of Aruba. This bridge was carved by the tumultuous sea waves that continue to crash on the rocks and spray visitors. You'll always find a crowd at the natural bridge, which is somewhat touristy with a bar and souvenir shop, but it's still worth a visit, especially if you're doing some photography along the way.

A favorite family activity is a ride aboard the **Atlantis Submarine**, *Tel. 297-8-36090*. This 65-foot vessel is a real submarine and take travelers on a one-hour excursion to see what lies below Aruba's waves. Photo tip: Bring fast film (ASA 400 or higher) for this excursion. You won't be able to use your flash inside the sub but there are many good photo opportunities, especially of your children looking through the portholes at the coral reefs beyond.

> ## THE CONCIERGE RECOMMENDS...
>
> Concierge Bernadette Davis at La Cabana Resort recommends several Aruba activities for families:
>
> 1. Tiri Kochi Park: a playground park where kids can play.
> 2. Kibaima Park: A mini zoo and recreational park. They have miniature Aruban village houses, a replica coin house, a replica stamp house, redesigned miniature houses of children's classic stories such as Cinderella, the Seven Dwarfs, and the Three Bears. This park is good for children age nine and under.
> 3. Baby Beach: A perfect beach for children with no current or tide. It's a family beach that's calm and shallow. There are picnic huts and lots of shade; all ages will enjoy.
> 4. Adventure Golf. Great for kids with arcade machines, a boat ride for children age five and up. Mini golf for all ages with an Italian restaurant on premise.

Sports and Recreation

Guided **horseback rides** at Rancho Del Campo are popular with many families. On tours, you can ride through Aruba's only national park: **Arikok National Wildlife Park**, home of Indian rock markings, gold digging ruins, and a restored cunucu home. Don't forget to bring long pants for the horseback ride!

Of course, much of Aruba's allure is the sea, both for its beaches and the action in the water. On the southwest end of the island, **Palm and Eagle beaches** are some of the most popular because of their proximity to the major hotels, but for the calmest waters head to **Baby Beach**. Located on the far southern tip of the island near the town of San Nicolas, it is well-known for its lake-calm waters and a favorite with families. Swimmers should avoid the waters of the island's north shore, which are rough and often plagued by undertow.

Aruba offers some of the Caribbean's top **windsurfing**. Fisherman's Hut is an ideal beginner's site because of its calm, shallow waters, and most resorts offer beginners lessons so your teens and preteens can get a taste of a new sport.

WHAT CAN I BUY?

Crafts are few, and most are imported from South America. Kids will find some inexpensive craft items at the mall and also at a small market (filled with picturesque displays of tropical fruit) near the cruise dock in Oranjestad. Here you can also find a true souvenir of the island: an Aruba license plate for US $4.

Aruba definitely ranks as a top Caribbean shopping destination. International goods — perfumes, china, crystal, jewelry, cameras, and clothing—are best buys. Unlike the practice of many islands, bargaining is not customary in Aruba.

Stores are open 8am to 6:30pm, Monday through Saturday, and usually close for two hours during lunch. If a cruise ship is in port, you may find some shops open on Sunday.

The primary shopping district stretches along Oranjestad's waterfront. Malls as colorful as sherbet line this route, tempting shoppers with goods that range from T-shirts and Delft Blue salt and pepper shakers to European *tres chic* designer outfits and fine jewelry.

Seaport Mall and Seaport Marketplace have the lion's share of the mall business. The Mall is located adjacent to Sonesta Resort and includes high-priced shops on its lowest level. Upstairs, boutiques offer moderately priced resort wear, jewelry, china, and more for a total of over 65 shops. At Sonesta Suites, the Seaport Marketplace is an outdoor gallery of nearly 60 shops specially targeted for vacationers.

If you forget someone special on your list, you'll also find shops at the Queen Beatrix International Airport.

PRACTICAL INFORMATION

Banks. Hours are 8am to 4pm. ATMs are found at the Caribbean Mercantile Bank and the ABN-AMRO Bank. Either major credit cards or Cirrus network bank cards may be used.

Currency. The Aruban florin is the official currency although US dollars are also widely accepted. At press time the exchange rate was $1US to A.Fl. 1.78 although this fluctuates.

Driving. Driving is on the right side of the road.

Electricity. North American appliances may be used without adapters. Voltage is 110 volts, 60 cycles.

Hospitals. The Dr. Horacio Oduber Hospital near Eagle Beach is a modern facility with 280 beds. The local number is 74300.

Information. The toll-free number for Aruba information is 800/TO-ARUBA. For additional information, contact the Aruba Tourism Authority office nearest to you:

Florida office:
2344 Salzedo Street
Miami, FL 33144-5033
Tel. 305/567-2720

Georgia office:
199 14th Street NE
Suite 2008
Atlanta, GA 30309-3688
Tel. 404/89-ARUBA

New Jersey office:
1000 Harbor Boulevard
Weehawken, NJ 07087
Tel. 201/330-0800

Texas office:
12707 North Freeway
Suite 138
Houston, TX 77060-1234
Tel. 281/87-ARUBA

Canada office:
86 Bloor Street West
Suite 204
Toronto, Ont.
M5S 1M5 Canada
Tel. 416/975-1950

On Island Information: While on Aruba, contact the local office:

Aruba Tourism Authority
L.G. Smith Boulevard 172
Aruba, Dutch Caribbean
Tel. 011/2978-21019

Web Site. Check out the official Web site at: *http:// www.interknowledge.com/aruba.*

For More Information: Call the Aruba Tourism Authority, *Tel. 800/TO-ARUBA.*

ISLAND REPORT CARD

Transportation to island	A
Transportation around island	A
Family Resorts	A-
Family Restaurants	A
Friendly atmosphere	A+
Activities for kids	A-
Weather	A+
New cultures for kids to experience	A
Safety	A+

BAHAMAS

For family travelers, the most popular stop in the Bahamas is Grand Providence Island, home of the capital city of Nassau. Located just a half hour flight from Miami, this island may be just a stone's (or a conch shell's) throw from the U.S. mainland, but it gives visitors a wonderful taste of Caribbean life.

The atmosphere in Nassau is a delightful combination of the British and the Caribbean. The Parliament House, a pink building from which the British ruled the Bahamas until 1972, still stands in the middle of the bustling city. The country still retains many British influences, with the Royal family smiling back from the currency and postage stamps. Driving is on the left side of the road.

The heart of Nassau is Rawson Square. Make your first stop at the Visitors Information Center for brochures and maps before starting off on busy Bay Street, the shopping district. Here gold and gems are sold down the street from straw baskets and T-shirts at the Straw Market, one of the most popular souvenir stops. Be sure to look out the back of the Straw Market for a glimpse at the cruise ships that dock at Prince George Dock.

From the cruise port you'll also see a tall, curving bridge. This leads to Paradise Island, the most luxurious area of Grand Providence Island. Once named Hog Island, this area was revitalized by investments by Donald Trump and Merv Griffin and now by South African businessman Sol Kerzner.

Another plush area is Cable Beach, located 10 minutes by cab from downtown Nassau. This stretch of sandy beach is lined with high-rise hotels. Shuttles take guests at these resorts to Nassau several times daily.

Technically, the Bahama islands lie outside the boundaries of the Caribbean. But, except for a few days when the islands are cooled by winter's chill, you'll have a hard time telling the difference. These 700 islands, sprinkled like seashells across shallow water, share the same sun, sand, and festive atmosphere as their southern neighbors.

Beyond these two resort areas, the island moves at a quieter pace. If you crave tranquillity, head to the south shore, about a 30-minute ride from downtown. Here, beneath willowy casuarina trees, families can enjoy privacy and beautiful beaches that give way to a shallow sea.

You may want to book your visit in spring, summer, or fall to be assured of a warm weather vacation. Winter temperatures are usually balmy, but occasionally a cold front reaches its chilly fingers into these waters and drops temperatures to spring-like levels. On an early March visit, we dug into our luggage for sweatshirts and, although temperatures were perfect for island touring, found that it too chilly for comfortable swimming.

While we're warning you, be careful of March and April bookings for another reason: spring breakers. Those low-cost downtown properties (and even some of the Paradise Island and Cable Beach resorts) swell with students during these weeks. Because of the charter packages, Nassau is the Caribbean for the masses and, during this time, that means raucous students. For a quiet, family getaway, consider an alternate month or a different destination.

ARE WE THERE YET?

By Air

Most visitors arrive via the Nassau International Airport. Delta, American Eagle, USAirways, Bahamasair from Miami, *Tel. 800/222-4262*, Carnival from New York and Fort Lauderdale, *Tel. 800/8-AIR-FUN*, Comair from Orlando, *Tel. 800/241-1212*, and Air Canada provide service to this airport. Paradise Island also has a small airport with flights from Miami, Ft. Lauderdale, and West Palm Beach aboard Paradise Island Airways from Miami, Fort Lauderdale, and West Palm Beach, *Tel. 800/SUN-7202*.

Departure tax is US $15 per person, although children under six years of age are exempt with proof of age.

By Ship

Cruise ship passengers arrive right in town at the Prince George Dock. Located just off Bay Street between the island and Paradise Island, cruise passengers find they're right in the heart of the action.

Getting Around the Island

You'll find plenty of taxis throughout Nassau. Public minibuses, called jitneys, are widely available and run during business hours. They're slower and more crowded than a taxi ride, but an inexpensive option if you're not in a hurry. Catch jitneys on Bay Street next to the Best Western British Colonial. Be sure to check the destination with the driver before you board, and have correct change (drivers don't give change).

Car rental desks are available at the airport and major hotels. Plan on plenty of traffic within Nassau, however, and don't forget that you'll be driving on the left.

Entry Requirements

US and Canadian citizens must carry proof of citizenship (passport or certified birth certificate and photo identification). Voter registration cards are not accepted as a proof of citizenship. Visas are not required for stays shorter than eight months.

You will be issued an immigration card when entering the Bahamas. Hold onto it; you will need to present the card upon departure. When departing, you'll clear US Customs and Immigration in Nassau, a real time-saver.

WHICH ONE IS MY ROOM?

RADISSON CABLE BEACH CASINO AND GOLF RESORT, *West Bay St., Tel. 242/327-6000, Fax 242/327-5969. Toll-free reservations Tel. 800/333-3333. Winter rates $205-$245, Summer rates $165-$205. Credit cards accepted.*

Sporting a new $15 million renovation, the Radisson Cable Beach offers round-the-clock action both on and off the beach. Every room in the high-rise hotel offers an ocean view. For real luxury, splurge with a junior suite located at the end of each floor. We did and enjoyed sunrise from the bedroom balcony and sunset from the living room balcony.

A shopping arcade (with surprisingly good prices, we found) connects the Radisson with the neighboring Marriott Crystal Palace Casino.

The hotel's all-inclusive program is available. Participants wear a wristband that allows them unlimited use of all sports, plus all meals, drinks, snacks, and tips.

As part of the all-inclusive program, kids under 12 stay, eat, and play free when sharing a room with one full paying adult (one child per adult, two children per room maximum).

Camp Junkanoo offers daily supervised fun on a half- or full-day basis. Children are divided into two age groups: four to six and seven to 11. The ratio of children to child coordinators is six to one and children are always monitored and kept in a secure area. Typical activities include a treasure hunt, beach Olympics, arts and crafts, pool and lagoon games, ice cream contests, candy bar bingo, movies, and field trips such as to the Crystal Key Underwater Observatory and Marine Park or Ardastra Gardens and Zoo.

Complimentary cribs are offered and baby-sitting is available at nominal charge.

TYPICAL DAY AT CAMP JUNKANOO

9:30-10am	Register
10am	Nature Walk
11am	Treasure Hunt/Face Painting
12noon	Lunch time
1:30	Afternoon registration
2:30	Arts and Crafts/Ping Pong
3:30	Water Balloon relay
4pm	Relaxing hour
4:30	Pick up time

NASSAU MARRIOTT RESORT AND THE CRYSTAL PALACE CASINO, *Cable Beach, Tel. 242/327-6200, Fax 242/327-6801. Toll-free US phone number 800/222-7466. Winter rates from $159, summer from $109. Credit cards accepted.*

With 867 rooms, Cable Beach's largest hotel is tough to miss. The large room property literally glows in the dark, with colored lights over each balcony giving the hotel the look of a seaside candy cane. This is one of the liveliest nightspots in town, thanks to its super-sized casino and glitzy revue.

The Marriotter Kids Club welcomes children with services including baby-sitting with tuck-ins, bedtime stories, and a complimentary photo. Tuck in charge is $10 per child or $15 per family.

Kids Club operates from 9am to 5pm (11pm Thursday through Saturday). A four-hour program includes lunch and a prize for $25 per child ($15 for each additional child in the family). The five- to eight-hour program costs $5 more and includes dinner. Activities range from Sega games to pool relays to scavenger hunts.

BEST WESTERN BRITISH COLONIAL, *downtown Nassau, Tel. 242/322-3301, Fax 242/322-2286. Toll-free reservations Tel. 800/528-1234. Winter rates $139-$179, Summer rates $99-$114. Credit cards accepted.*

This pink behemoth sits at the head of Bay Street, a reminder of Nassau's early hotel days. It's a warm reminder of our early hotel days as well, as the scene of our first visit to the Caribbean.

Sadly, the British Colonial (or BC, as the taxi drivers say) is looking a little tired these days. Still, it's a bargain hotel situated in a great location. It has a small beach of its own, and it is just steps away from the duty-free shops (and the fast food restaurants if you're watching your pennies). Skip this property during spring break if you don't want your teens caught up in an around-the-clock party atmosphere. This is one of the most popular hotels with student tour groups.

ATLANTIS RESORT, *Paradise Island, Tel. 242/363-3000, Fax 242/363-2593. Toll-free reservations Tel. 800/321-3000. Winter from $195, summer from $130. Credit cards accepted.*

See "Best Places to Stay with Kids" chapter for resort review.

WHAT ARE WE DOING NEXT?

The heart of Nassau is Rawson Square. Make your first stop here at the **Visitors Information Center** for brochures and maps before starting off on busy Bay Street, the shopping district. Here gold and gems are sold down the street from straw baskets and T-shirts at the Straw Market, one of the most popular souvenir stops. Be sure to look behind the Straw Market for a glimpse at the cruise ships that dock at Prince George Dock. At Rawson Square, horse-drawn **surreys** wait for passengers, who pay $10 (be prepared to negotiate) for a two-person, half-hour ride along picturesque Bay Street.

Landlubbers who are curious about the creatures of the deep should consider a ride on the **Atlantis submarine**. Following an island tour, visitors board the submarine for a look at marine life 80 feet below the surface. For 50 minutes, the submarine views coral reefs, tropical fish, a Cessna aircraft wrecked for the filming of Jaws 2, and even the Tongue of the Ocean, a wall that drops 8,000 feet into liquid darkness. The submarine departs from the far west end of the island near Lyford Cay at a dock built for the recent Flipper movie.

You can also see colorful marine life at **Coral Island**, *Silver Cay,* a white tower easily spotted just west of downtown. Twenty feet below the surface, visitors view what Coral Island calls the world's largest man-made living reef, dotted with coral and colorful fish. At Coral Island you can also view sharks, sea turtles, and stingrays in pools.

Another popular attraction is the **Ardastra Gardens and Zoo**, *Tel. 242/323-5806.* The only zoo in the Bahamas, Ardastra features 300 species of animals and 50 species of birds including monkeys, iguanas, and marching pink flamingos. Stop here if you have time, but we felt that this is one stop that can be cut from busy itineraries. The caged animals are depressing to view, and the personnel here are far from friendly.

History buffs should head over to **Fort Charlotte** for a free guided tour of the largest fort in the Bahamas. Perched high on a hill overlooking Cable Beach, this fort never saw action but today sees plenty of activity as tourists come to enjoy a bird's eye view and a look at the fort's dungeons, cannons, and exhibits.

Sports & Recreation

One of the most popular activities in Nassau is a day at **Blue Lagoon Island,** *Tel. 242/363-3577.* This "uninhabited" island lies about half an hour from the dock at Paradise Island and offers some beautiful beaches, hammocks beneath towering palms, and plenty of watersports activity. For additional charges, visitors can parasail, swim with stingrays, or meet dolphins (make reservations early for this choice). One option includes feeding, petting, and swimming with the friendly mammals. (The dolphin encounters can also be booked as a separate attraction without a day at Blue Lagoon Island by calling Tel. 242/363-1653.) If you make this trip, bring a towel for everyone in the family and, to save money, your own snorkel gear.

A fun way to view the sea creatures of the Bahamian waters is by participating in **Hartley's Undersea Walk**, *Tel. 242/393-8234*. The procedure is simple: put on a watertight diving helmet (yep, the old-fashioned brass kind) and off you go. Be sure to call for reservations for this one because the excursions fill up fast.

WHAT CAN I BUY?

For authentic Bahamian souvenirs, head down Bay Street to the frenzied, open-air Straw Market. Every imaginable straw good is sold here, and if you don't see it, the nimble-fingered women will make it for you. Expect to haggle over prices here, but overall, prices and goods vary only slightly from booth to booth. Upstairs, wood carvers chip away at logs to produce sculptures of animals, birds, and anything else you might request. Children will find many inexpensive items here at the market including T-shirts (the best bargain is the three for $10 offer in some stands), seed necklaces for $1, small straw purses, and straw hats. Kids can also get their hair, or even just a small section, braided. For just a few braids, expect to pay about $1 per braid including beads.

Perfume prices are regulated by the government, so you will find the same prices at any of the "perfume bars" which are frequent in Nassau. Everything from French to American perfumes, colognes and aftershaves are sold in the perfume bars, as well as in many clothing stores.

Americans may take home up to $600 in goods duty-free. You may also mail home gifts (marked "unsolicited gift") up to $50 in value duty free. Items manufactured in the Bahamas are not dutiable. Travelers may also take back two liters of liquor provided that one of the liters is a Caribbean product.

PRACTICAL INFORMATION

Currency. The currency is the Bahamian dollar, equivalent to the US dollar.

Driving. Driving is on the LEFT side of the road.

Electricity. The current is 120 volts.

Information. For information on the Bahamas, call toll-free 800/8-BAHAMAS within the United States. From Canada, the toll-free number is 800/677-3777. For additional information, contact the office nearest you:

Chicago office:
8600 Bryn Mawr Avenue, Suite 820
Chicago, IL 60631
Tel. 773/693-1500

Dallas office:
World Trade Centre, Suite 116
2050 Stemmons Freeway
P.O. Box 581408
Dallas, TX 75258-1408
Tel. 214/742-1886

Los Angeles office:
3450 Wilshire Boulevard, Suite 208
Los Angeles, CA 90010
Tel. 213/385-0033

Miami office:
One Turnberry Place
19495 Biscayne Boulevard, Suite 242
Aventura, FL 33180
Tel. 305/932-0051

New York office:
150 East 52nd Street
28th Floor North
New York, NY 10022
Tel. 212/758-2777

Toronto office:
121 Bloor Street East
Suite 1101
Toronto, Ontario M4W 3M5
Tel. 416/968-2999

Language. English, with a Bahamian lilt, is spoken throughout the Bahamas islands.

Time. The islands are in the Eastern time zone. From April through October, daylight savings time is observed.

Web Site. Check out the official Web site at: *http:// www.interknowledge.com/bahamas.*

```
ISLAND REPORT CARD

Transportation to island              A+
Transportation around island          A
Family Resorts                        A
Family Restaurants                    A
Friendly atmosphere                   B+
Activities for kids                   A+
Weather                               B+
New cultures for kids to experience   B+
Safety                                A-
```

BARBADOS

Barbados is a pear-shaped island with gentle rolling hills. Agriculture still rules much of the landscape, and cane is still king. Although sugar prices have dropped severely in recent years, the crop is a Barbadian mainstay. A drive through the island will take you through a jungle of cane, often with nothing but the road before and behind you visible during the peak of the growing season.

The most easterly of the Caribbean islands, Barbados has strongly differentiated east and west sides. On the Atlantic side, currents are strong, and jagged cliffs and sea caves are carved by the water's force. In contrast, western beaches offer placid Caribbean waters with excellent visibility, little current, and a gentle trade breeze.

This island has welcomed tourist for hundreds of years, as far back as George Washington who came here to enjoy the healthful climate (much needed by his tuberculosis-stricken brother, Lawrence).

Today Barbados has the most proper British atmosphere found in the Caribbean. As you drive through the island, look for both men and women in cool white suits on the cricket fields. In the afternoons, take time to enjoy high tea. And listen to the voices of the Barbadians or Bajans (rhymes with Cajun): their accent is almost British.

ARE WE THERE YET?

By Air

American Airlines, BWIA, and Air Canada offer service from the US and Canada.

By Ship

Cruise ship passengers arrive at the Bridgetown port facility, recently renovated for $6 million. The enhanced terminal, designed to resemble an island street, now offers 19 duty-free shops, 13 local retail stores, and many vendors as well as tourist information booths, car rentals, and dive shops.

Entry Requirements

A passport or birth certificate and driver's license or identification card is required of US and Canadian citizens.

Getting Around the Island

Taxis are prevalent, but not inexpensive. A drive from the airport to the Speightstown-area hotels will run you close to US $30.

Rental cars are available; a Barbados drivers license (US $5) is required. Many visitors rent "Mini-Mokes," a cross between a jeep and a dune buggy for about $50 US daily. And, don't forget, driving is on the left side of the road.

Island tours are offered by several operators. Highland Outdoor Tours, Inc. offers adventure excursions, including a horseback trek across the island, safari rides, and plantation tours. Bajan Tours, *Tel. 407/437-9389*, offers a complete island tour with stops at Holetown, Speightstown, the East Coast, Sam Lord's Castle, and other places of interest.

WHICH ONE IS MY ROOM?

SANDY LANE HOTEL AND GOLF CLUB, *Tel. 246/ 432-1311, Fax 246/432-2954. Toll-free US phone number 800/ 223-6800. Winter from $695. Credit cards accepted.*

One of the Caribbean's most expensive resorts, Sandy Lane is for those looking for the highest level of luxury and style.

ROYAL PAVILION, *Tel. 246/422-5555, Fax 246/422-3940. Toll-free US phone number 800/283-8666. Winter rates from $485. Credit cards accepted.*

This elegant property is designed for guests looking for the finest money can buy: from a grand entrance lined with the finest boutiques such as Cartier, to the 72 junior suites that overlook the sea. In your room, you'll be pampered as well with twice daily maid service, a private terrace or patio, and a decor that combines elegance and tropical splendor. Children aren't permitted at Royal Pavilion during high season.

The sister property of this resort is Glitter Bay, and guests share facilities and services with that property. Guests also enjoy golf privileges at the Robert Trent Jones, Jr.-designed course, the Royal Westmoreland.

ALMOND BEACH VILLAGE, *Speightstown, Tel. 407/872-2220, Fax 407/872-7770. Toll-free reservations Tel. 800/425-6663. Winter rates from $460, summer from $375. Credit cards accepted.*
See "Best Places to Stay with Kids" chapter.

GLITTER BAY, *St. James, Tel. 246/422-5555, Fax 246/422-3940, Fax 809/111-1112. Toll-free reservations Tel. 800/223-1818. Winter from $395, summer from $215. Credit cards accepted.*
You'll feel the elegance and refinement of Barbados and Britain at Glitter Bay, constructed as the home of shipping magnate Sir Edward Cunard. The Mediterranean-style structure, with white stucco walls and Spanish clay roofs, is located on a half mile long beach. Glitter Bay's sister resort is the Royal Pavilion (see below), so guests enjoy reciprocal privileges and services of both resorts. You can also golf at the island's golf course, the Royal Westmoreland.

For all its elegance, Glitter Bay welcomes families with a special program. From early April through mid-December, children 12 and under stay free when sharing a room with one or two adults (maximum two children) and receive complimentary meal plan from the children's menu for each adult meal plan purchased.

During peak summer weeks, kids also have use of the Cub's Club, aimed at children 3-12. The daily program includes a variety of activities and children receive a T-shirt; there is a one-time $25 registration fee per child.

SAM LORD'S RESORT, *Long Bay, St. Philip, Tel. 246/ 423-7350, Fax 246/ 423-5918. Toll-free US phone number 888/ 765-6737. Winter from $210, summer from $145. Credit cards accepted.*

This resort is more than a hotel, it's a regular tourist attraction. Built in the 19th century, this castle was the property of the pirate Sam Hall Lord who, according to legend, lured passing ships onto the east coast rocks. Of course, no real castle would be complete without its resident ghost, and at Sam Lord's they say his truly still rests on his four-poster bed.

WHAT ARE WE DOING NEXT?

Barbados is home to many **beaches** where families can snorkel in calm Caribbean waters or enjoy windswept vistas on the Atlantic shoreline. Swimmers should definitely head to the Caribbean coast; precautions should be taken not to get over waist deep in the often-dangerous Atlantic currents. These Atlantic waters are preferred by windsurfers and sailors, but swimmers are better off with the calm waters found on Mullins Beach, Crane Beach, and Dover Beach.

The natural beauty of Barbados can also be enjoyed in many of its other attractions. Hold hands and enjoy a ride into **Harrison's Cave**, where damp rooms reveal their hidden formations, waterfalls, and pools. A sea cave rather than a cavern, the **Animal Flower Cave** is named for the sea anemones found in its pools.

If you're wondering what lies beneath the ocean's depths, take a cruise aboard the **Atlantis Submarine,** which cruises to a depth of 150-feet below sea level. It's an excellent way for non-divers to see the rich marine life and the wrecks that surround this island.

If the two of you will be enjoying many excursions, check out the **Heritage Passport Program**, sponsored by the Barbados National Trust. Sixteen sites are included on the pass, which offers about a 50% savings on admission (a mini passport is available for fewer stops). The passport includes admission to Harrison's Cave, St. Nicholas Abbey, Mount Gay, and many other sites.

WHAT CAN I BUY?

The primary shopping area on the island is found in Bridgetown along Broad Street. Here the two of you will find fine goods of every variety: luggage, designer clothing, china, crystal, silver, cameras, the list goes on. Barbados is a tax free haven, so you'll enjoy savings. Only liquor must be delivered to the airport or the cruise port; other purchases can be carried out from the store.

In Bridgetown, Cave Shepherd shop offers china, crystal, fine clothing, electronics, and perfumes. Located on Broad Street, this shop has been serving Barbados visitors and residents since 1906. Today it includes a Columbian Emeralds International outlet with fine jewelry as well as two restaurants, an activities desk for island tours, photo lab, and American Airlines office. Other Bridgetown shopping malls include Sunset Mall and DaCostas Mall, with over 35 shops offering everything from perfumes to china to cameras.

For island crafts, drop by the Medford Craft Village in St. Michael. Hand-carved items such as birds, boats, clocks, and fish are made here from local mahogany.

PRACTICAL INFORMATION

Currency. The Barbados dollar (BDS) is the official currency. Bd converts at 1.98BDS=$1US, 1.48BDS=$1CAN. The rate does not fluctuate but is fixed to the US dollar. Both US and Canadian dollars are widely accepted.

Electricity. The current on the island is 110 volts/50 cycles.

Information. Contact the Barbados Tourism Authority, *Tel. 800/221-9831.* In Canada, the Barbados Tourism Authority can be reached at *Tel. 800/268-9122* in Ontario.

Time. Barbados is on Atlantic Standard Time, one hour ahead of Eastern. Daylight savings time is not observed.

Web Site. Check out the official web site for more information: *http://www.barbados.org/.*

ISLAND REPORT CARD

Transportation to island	B+
Transportation around island	A
Family Resorts	B+
Family Restaurants	B+
Friendly atmosphere	A-
Activities for kids	B+
Weather	A
New cultures for kids to experience	B+
Safety	A

BRITISH VIRGIN ISLANDS

Hoist the sails and gather way. Grip the wheel in your hands and cut a feather through aquamarine waters to a quiet Caribbean cove. Drop anchor and motor a small launch to an empty beach for a gourmet picnic lunch on white sand.

Sound like a boating fantasy? It is, but in the British Virgin Islands, it is also reality. Year around, skippers and would-be boaters come from around the world to sail these calm waters and take advantage of a group of 50 islands that call themselves "Nature's Little Secrets." Unlike their nearby American cousins, these Virgin Islands are not a shopper's paradise, but one for nature lovers looking for quiet getaways, empty beaches, and a maritime atmosphere. Families will find that kids can romp and enjoy local life on some of the safest islands in the Caribbean.

Boats of every description come to this capital of the Caribbean boating world. But long before today's sleek vessels made the BVI a popular port of call, Christopher Columbus plied these waters. The explorer landed on the island of Tortola in 1694. The multitude of surrounding tiny islands reminded Columbus of the tale of Saint Ursula and her 11,000 virgins so he named these the Virgin Islands.

Although there are over 50 islands in the chain, only a handful have facilities for travelers. **Tortola**, named for the turtle doves found here, is the largest island with only 21 square miles. Don't let distance fool you, however. Because of steep hills, a car trip around or across the island is a slow undertaking.

One of the best ways to see Tortola, and all the British Virgin Islands, is by boat. Even if you don't know a rigging from a rudder, you can enjoy a vacation at sea thanks to skippered boat programs. For about the same cost as a stay at a luxury resort, you can enjoy a week aboard a vessel with a skipper to man the wheel and a cook to prepare local dishes like fried conch or rice and peas.

Tortola's largest community, **Road Town**, is the home office of the largest charter yacht company in the world. Visit The Moorings to view the huge fleet of yachts managed by the company and owned by sailors around the globe.

Set your course for **Jost Van Dyke**, an island named for a Dutch pirate. Jost (pronounced Yost) Van Dyke is a real getaway, a Robinson Crusoe kind of place without luxury hotels, gourmet restaurants or pricey shops. What Jost Van Dyke does have are nearly deserted beaches, coral reefs teeming with colorful fish, and a place called Foxy's.

Foxy's Tamarind Bar is a landmark in the world of Caribbean boaters. It is located beneath palm thatched roofs plastered with boat flags, skippers hats, and business cards left here by visitors. The restaurant serves West Indian specialties like curried chicken *rotis*, but the real treat is Foxy himself. Foxy, a.k.a. Philicianno Callwood, is a one-man show greeting incoming guests with impromptu songs sung to a calypso beat.

Jost Van Dyke may be named for a pirate, but the best known pirate connections in the BVI are **Norman Island** and **Dead Chest**. Norman Island is thought to have been the inspiration for Robert Lewis Stevenson's *Treasure Island*. Dead Chest is the island where the pirate Blackbeard allegedly marooned 15 men and one bottle of rum, starting a fight that left no survivors. The incident inspired the mariners' ditty: "Fifteen men on a dead man's chest. Yo ho ho and a bottle of rum."

A popular port of call is **Virgin Gorda** (the fat virgin), the second largest island in the BVI. The Baths, Virgin Gorda's most photographed attraction, can be reached by land or sea. Left by volcanic upheaval, The Baths are formed by giant boulders that provide a picturesque contrast to the white beach. Duck between boulders to enter the sea cave where you can wade in the cool, shady baths.

Although some hotels feature local musicians, don't look for casinos or nightclubs in these Caribbean islands. The BVI makes no claim to being a swinging destination, and even in the large resorts most activity stops by 11pm.

The reason is simple. Only hours away, the sun will again rise on another Caribbean day. And across the British Virgin Islands, boaters want to be ready.

ARE WE THERE YET?

By Air

Service to Tortola's Beef Island International Airport is available from San Juan on American Eagle. Other vacationers prefer to fly directly into St. Thomas and ferry over to Tortola. Service into St. Thomas is available from American Airlines with flights from JFK/New York, Miami, and Washington/Dulles via San Juan. Direct service from Baltimore/Washington is available aboard USAirways, and service from Atlanta is available on Delta. Direct flights from Miami are also available on Prestige Airways.

By Ferry

Island hopping is a way of life in the BVI and the most common way is aboard ferries. One-hour service from St. Thomas is available daily to Road Town and West End in Tortola aboard Smith's Ferry Service, *Tel. 284/495-4495*. Service from West End to Cruz Bay, St. John is available from Inter-Island Boat Service, *Tel. 284/495-4166*.

Entry Requirements

US and Canadian citizens should bring a current passport or original birth certificate with photo ID. You'll also have to show a return or onward ticket.

WHICH ONE IS MY ROOM?

BIRAS CREEK, *Virgin Gorda, Tel. 284/494-3555, Fax 284/494-3557. Toll-free reservations Tel. 800/608-9661. Winter: $495-$795, Summer: $350-$600. Credit cards accepted.*

Tucked on the north end of Virgin Gorda on a 140-acre peninsula, this recently renovated resort is a favorite with families looking for a relaxing getaway. The 32-suite property recently was purchased by Bert Houwer, who had vacationed at the hotel for 14 years. You can't get a much better guest recommendation than that.

Biras Creek makes a good getaway for family vacationers looking to spend time at the private beach, walking on nearby nature trails, and exploring Virgin Gorda. Each suite includes bicycles (and children's bikes for the youngest travelers) so your family can explore. Families also enjoy use of two tennis courts, and complimentary use of snorkel fins, windsurfers, sailboats, and motor dinghies, including free instruction. Complimentary snorkel trips to the surrounding islands are also offered.

When you're ready to take a break, guest assistants (GA's) can entertain the children with an afternoon filled with treasure hunts or crab races.

Consideration for young visitors encompasses the restaurants as well. The restaurant offers early dinners with a special children's menu.

A family break seven-night package is aimed at family travelers (two adults and two children ages 6 to 12) and offers two oceanview suites, a reef tour in a glass-bottom boat, and a sunset sail for the parents for $4,200. The Family Break package is available from June 1 through early November.

BITTER END, *Virgin Gorda, Tel. 284/494-2746, Fax 284/494-4756. Toll-free reservations Tel. 800/872-2392. From $480 in winter, from $370 in summer. Credit cards accepted.*

This 100-room resort is located at the "bitter end" of the BVI on the North Sound. Reached only by boat, this resort gives you the feeling of staying at a yacht club, where days are spent in close connection with the sea. The resort boasts 150 vessels, the largest fleet of recreational boats in the Caribbean. Many guests arrive via their own craft and simply dock for their stay. Those without a boat can stay in a resort room or aboard one of the club yachts. Spend the day in your "room" boating among the islands, then return to port at night and enjoy a quiet meal in the resort's elegant restaurant.

Children are an important part of the clientele at the Bitter End. Families have complimentary use of over 100 watercrafts, from sailboats to windsurfers to Boston Whaler tenders. Children can also participate in the Bitter End's Nick Trotter Sailing and Windsurfing Class. The Junior Sailing Program offers half-day lessons for young mariners age seven to 12 on a year around basis. (Lessons are complimentary during the summer months as well as during school holidays.)

Other family oriented activities at the resort include snorkel lessons with the watersports staff, guided nature hikes or striking out on your own on the hiking trails, and cruises to the Baths and Anegada in the BVI. Families can also take out a Boston Whaler skiff to a nearby private island for a quiet picnic.

LITTLE DIX BAY, *Virgin Gorda, Tel. 284/495-5555, Fax 284/495-5661. Toll-free reservations Tel. 888/ROSEWOOD or 800/767-3966. From $450 in winter, from $250 in summer. Credit cards accepted.*

We have fond memories of our stay at Little Dix: lazing beneath a palm palapa, snorkeling just offshore, enjoying our rondoval guest room with a wonderful view in every direction, dining outdoors to the music of whistling tree frogs.

Apparently plenty of other families also have good memories of Little Dix; it boasts a wonderful repeat business. Many customers have been coming since the days Laurance Rockefeller first developed this property in 1964. Today the hotel still has the same attention to service as it did in its Rockresort days; you'll find that the ratio of employees to guests is one to one.

PETER ISLAND, *Peter Island, Tel. 284/495-2000, Fax 284/ 495-2500. Toll-free reservations Tel. 800/346-4451 in US. From $415 in winter, from $380 in summer. Credit cards accepted.*

This is true luxury: a resort that occupies an entire island. Owned by the Amway Corporation (a fact that most visitors are unaware of except for the can of Amway spot remover in the closet), Peter Island is truly a place where relaxation can flourish like the bougainvillea, hibiscus, and sea grapes that dot its hills. This 1,800-acre island is paradise for families. It starts with your arrival by private launch from Tortola, and continues as you check in and see your guest room: a combination of Scandinavian and Caribbean styles. This resort was recently refurbished and sports a fresh face.

LONG BAY BEACH RESORT, *Tortola, Tel. 284/495-4252, Fax 284/495-4677. Toll-free reservations Tel. 800/729-9599. Winter from $260. Credit cards accepted.*

They call this resort Long Bay but we found that they might as well change the name to Long Beach. A mile-long white sand beach is the central focal point of this 105-room resort located near West End. All rooms, both hilltop and beachside, have views of the beach and the quiet waters of Long Bay.

THE MOORINGS, *Road Town, Tortola, Fax 284/494-2507. Toll-free reservations Tel. 800/437-7880 or 888/952-8420.*

Price varies with size of yacht and number of passengers. Credit cards accepted.

Ahoy mates, here's your chance to take to the seas on your own yacht. Well, maybe the yacht's not technically yours, but for a few days it will be home to yourselves and usually two or three other families. You can rent a stateroom aboard a yacht and enjoy a luxurious trip around the islands (or for true luxury you can rent the entire boat, complete with the services of a captain and a cook.) The Moorings is the world's largest charter yacht company, an operation that started right in tiny Road Town.

WHAT ARE WE DOING NEXT?

One top destination in the BVI (or, for that matter, in the Caribbean) is **The Baths.** This 682-acre park is located on Virgin Gorda, and it's so unique that once you visit it you'll be able to spot this park in any Caribbean video or magazine. Unlike most Caribbean beaches which are mostly flat, this site is scattered with massive granite boulders. As smooth as riverbed stones, these gargantuan rocks litter the sea and the beach. They also form shadowy caves where you can swim in water that's lit by sunlight filtering through the cracks. This unique site is unspoiled (just one or two concessionaires and no hagglers) and a fun snorkeling spot as well.

Hikers should save time for a visit to **Sage Mountain National Park** on Tortola. The BVI's highest point has an altitude of 1,780 feet and is lush with greenery that can be viewed from its many gravel walkways.

Sports & Recreation

Divers will find plenty of activity in the waters off any of the British Virgin Islands. The best known **dive spot** is the wreck of the *RMS Rhone*, a mail steam packet that broke up in a storm. You may be familiar with this wreck—it was used in filming *The Deep*. The bow lies just 80 feet below the surface, making it an easy wreck dive (and usually even visible for snorkelers). Other top dive sites include Alice in Wonderland, a deep dive with mushroom-shaped corals, the *Chikuzen* wreck, a 246-foot fish-filled wreck just 75 feet below the surface, and Santa Monica Rock, located near the open ocean and a good place to spot large fish.

WHAT CAN I BUY?

Unlike the "other" Virgin islands, shopping is not a major attraction of the BVI. However, you will find a good variety of shops in Road Town and West End at Soper's Hole. Spices are also popular buys, from hot sauces to West Indian mustards to chutney. One of the best selections is found at Sunny Caribbee, *Main Street, Road Town, Tel. 284/494-2178*, has a good collection of things Caribbean, including local crafts, cookbooks, and art prints.

For inexpensive buys, visit the open-air market on Main Street. Here you can haggle for jewelry, T-shirts, calabash bags, and straw hats. The mood is friendly, and you'll be entertained most days by steel band musicians.

PRACTICAL INFORMATION

Currency. The US dollar is legal tender in the British Virgin Islands.

Driving. Driving is on the LEFT side of the road.

Electricity. The BVI uses 110 volts, 60 cycles throughout the islands.

Information. Contact the British Virgin Islands Tourist Board, *Tel. 800/835-8530* in the eastern US or *Tel. 800/232-7770* in the western US. For additional information, contact the tourist office nearest you:

New York City office:
B.V.I. Tourist Board
370 Lexington Avenue
Suite 313
New York City, NY 10017
Tel. 800/835-8530 or 212/696-0400
Fax: 212/949-8254

San Francisco office:
B.V.I. Tourist Board
1804 Union Street
San Francisco, CA 94123
Tel. 800/835-8530 or 415/755-0344
Fax 415/755-2554

Information on Island. Call the B.V.I. Tourist Board in Road Town, *Tel. 284/494-3134.*

Web site. Check out *http://www.city.net/countries/ british_virgin_islands/*and *http://www.Britishvirginislands. com* for a variety of island information.

ISLAND REPORT CARD	
Transportation to island	B
Transportation around island	A
Family Resorts	B-
Family Restaurants	B-
Friendly atmosphere	A
Activities for kids	B
Weather	A
New cultures for kids to experience	B+
Safety	A+

CAYMAN ISLANDS

Ready, set, dive.

Whether you're a certified diver or a non-swimmer, the Cayman Islands are the place for you to act out your Jacques Cousteau fantasies. Grab some sunscreen and make your way to the luxurious Grand Cayman, one of the easiest Caribbean destinations for vacationers to reach. Less than two hours from Houston and just over an hour from Miami, visitors will find it a place where crime is low, public peddling is prohibited, and the living is definitely easy. The islands have one of the highest standards of living in the world. Boasting an average household income is $56,000CI (US $68,292), a status as one of the top financial centers in the world, and a low unemployment rate, this destination is one that is a natural magnet for vacationers looking for a luxurious getaway.

Just 80 miles northeast of Grand Cayman but worlds apart in terms of atmosphere, **Little Cayman** is tailor made for families looking for secluded scuba diving, fly or tackle fishing, and nature appreciation. Appropriate to its name, Little Cayman spans only 11 miles in length and two miles at its widest point. Boasting none of the glitz of Grand Cayman, Little Cayman does greet guests with all the basic comforts, including several small lodges and condominiums with air-conditioning, satellite television, and telephone service.

With just over 100 permanent residents, the island's largest population is that of birds and iguanas. Over 2,000 Little Cayman Rock Iguanas inhabit the island, so many that "Iguana Crossing" and "Iguana Right of Way" signs are posted throughout the island to protect the five-foot long lizards.

If Grand Cayman is the flashy big brother of the Cayman Islands, swelled with pride about its lavish condominiums, full-service resorts, international dining, and top-notch diving, and Little Cayman is the family's youngest sibling, favored for its petite size and almost shy demeanor, then **Cayman Brac** is the middle child.

This middle sibling, however, is far from overlooked. Cayman Brac has its own special qualities, assets that include world-class diving along undersea walls, hiking in the most rugged terrain found in the Cayman Islands, caves that tempt exploration, birdying, and much more.

The island is named for the "brac," Gaelic for bluff, which soars up from the sea 140 feet on the island's east end. It's the most distinct feature of this 12-mile long, one mile wide island located 89 miles east-northeast of Grand Cayman and just five miles from Little Cayman.

With a population of only 1,300 residents, Cayman Brac is closer in pace to Little Cayman than its big brother, Grand Cayman. Residents, or Brackers, are known for their personable nature and welcome vacationers to their sunny isle.

By far, though, the most popular family destination among these three is **Grand Cayman**. Although it has been a popular destination for many years, Grand Cayman drew the attention of moviegoers across the country because of its prominent role in the movie *The Firm*, an adaptation of the John Grisham book starring Tom Cruise and Gene Hackman. Much of the movie was filmed at the Hyatt Regency and at popular dive sites just offshore. (And, yes, the stars actually did dive the coral reefs for many scenes.)

Hackman and Cruise may have starred in their dive scenes, but at Stingray City the stingrays definitely receive the leading role. Enjoyed by both divers and snorkelers, Stingray City is a shallow sandbar located offshore where numerous operators take vacationers to enjoy what is one of the most unique experiences in the Caribbean. Accustomed to being fed, the stingrays (which range is size from about one to six feet across) are docile and friendly, brushing against swimmers and even allowing themselves to be held and petted. About 30 stingrays frequent this area.

Little Cayman

Little Cayman's chief draw is its **ecotourism**: diving, fishing, and bird watching. The late Phillipe Cousteau called the island's Bloody Bay Wall one of the best dives of his life; today its still a favorite with divers.

Anglers come to this tiny isle for its excellent **bonefishing**. Bonefish and permit, both caught in the flats, and tarpon, reeled in from brackish Tarpon Lake, draw fishermen. The Southern Cross Club fishing lodge first attracted anglers to these waters; today McCoy's Diving and Fishing Lodge also caters to fishermen. Guests at other island resorts can arrange fishing guides from these lodges.

Birders enjoy the **Booby Pond Visitors Centre**, open Monday through Saturday 2-5pm. Operated by the National Trust, this pond is the home of the Caribbean's largest breeding colony of Red-Footed Bobbies and a breeding colony of Magnificent Frigate Birds. Visitors can view the birds from two telescopes (available for use any time) and see exhibits on the birds of Little Cayman in the visitors center. Admission is free although donations are welcomed.

An overview of Little Cayman's attractions is available for day trippers through Island Air and local guide Chip McCoy. The package includes round-trip air, an island tour, snorkeling along Bloody Bay Wall, and lunch at uninhabited Owen's Island; the cost is US $170. Bookings are made through Island Air, *Tel. 345/949-5252.*

Small resorts, condominiums, and an efficiency apartment complex make up the accommodations offerings.

The largest complex is the 40-room **LITTLE CAYMAN BEACH RESORT**, *Tel. 800/327-3835 or 345/948-1033, Fax 345/948-1040.* A favorite with divers, the resort includes a resort-owned and managed dive center and the Reef Photo and Video Center for on-site processing of underwater shots.

Another choice of divers is the all-inclusive **PIRATES POINT**, *Tel. 800/327-8777, 345/948-1010, Fax 345/948-1011,* a 10-room property that includes four dive instructors as well as fishing guides. **MCCOY'S DIVING AND FISHING LODGE**, *Tel. 800/626-0496 or 345-948-0026*, offers two dive boats to transport visitors to the 22 dive sites around the island.

A small motel property, **THE VILLAGE INN**, *Tel. 345/948-1069, Fax 345/948-0073*, includes kitchens and full baths without televisions or telephones.

Several condominium and villa properties provide self-sufficiency for family vacationers. **CONCH CLUB CONDO-MINIUMS**, *Tel. 800/327-3835 or 813/323-8727, Fax 813/323-8827*, are the island's newest development; the 12-unit complex offers two- and three-bedroom units. **PARADISE VIL-LAS**, *Tel. 345/948-0001, Fax 345/948-0002*, features one bedroom villas with living room, kitchen, and a seaside deck; the Hungry Iguana restaurant is located on property. For vacationers looking for seclusion and privacy, good choices are rentals available through **MCLAUGHLIN PROPER-TIES**, *Tel.345/948-1000, Fax 345/948-1001*. Sunset Point Condo offers four units with screened porches; Bloody Bay House is a favorite with divers because of its location across the road from the Bloody Bay Wall.

The only stand-alone **restaurant** on the island is the Hungry Iguana, located near the airport. The seaside eatery, named for an iguana often seen at the airport, now sports a 40-foot mural of its namesake. Continental buffet breakfasts start the day; lunch and dinner feature jerk chicken, grouper sandwiches, prime rib, and burgers.

Getting There: The dirt airstrip of Edward Bodden Airport has service twice daily from Grand Cayman. Island Air, *Tel. 800/9-CAYMAN or 345/949-5252, Monday through Sunday 9am to 5pm* , departs on the 45-minute flight at 8am and 3:50pm; return flights depart at 9:55am and 5:45pm. Round trip tickets are US $122 (US $98 for passengers under 12); a day trip package is also available for US $105 (US $84 for travelers under 12).

Passengers may check up to 55 pounds of baggage free of charge; excess baggage is charged US 50 cents per pound. Service is also available from Little Cayman to Cayman Brac twice daily.

Only one rental car agency operates on the island. McLaughlin Jeep Rental, *Tel. 345/948-1000, Fax 345/948-1001*, offers daily and weekly rates for jeeps; only standard transmission jeeps are available. To call the rental agency on arrival, visitors pick up the phone located on the side of the airport building. Vehicles are left drive; driving is on the left side of the road. Rates start at US $59 daily.

Cayman Brac

The most recognized site on the island is the Brac, the sheer bluff that is visited by hikers and non-hikers alike. This area is a favorite for birdwatching, one of the most popular activities on Cayman Brac. Here the 180-acre **Parrot Reserve** is home to the endangered Cayman Brac Parrot. Only 400 of the birds remain in the wild on this island.

Among Cayman Brac's most unique features are its many **caves**. The Bluff is pocked with caves that frame beautiful seaside views. Several of the 18 caves on Cayman Brac have been explored and five are frequently visited by vacationers. Rebecca's Cave, east of Divi Tiara Hotel, is marked with signs. The best known of the island's caves, sadly this one is named for a young child who died here during the Great Hurricane of 1932.

Without a doubt, **diving** is one of the island's prime attractions. Over 50 excellent dive sites tempt all levels of divers. The latest attraction is a Russian frigate deliberately sunk in September 1996. Renamed the **M/V Captain Keith Tibbbets**, this 330-foot freighter was built for use by the Cuban navy. It lies approximately 200 yards offshore northwest of Cayman Brac. The bow rests in about 90 feet of water; the stern is just 40 feet below the surface. The sinking of the vessel was recorded by Jean-Michel Cousteau Productions in a documentary film "Destroyer at Peace."

Bonefishing is another top draw for many Cayman Brac vacationers. Guides lead anglers on half- and full-day excursions to seek bonefish in the shallows; deep sea fishing is another popular option and groups of up to four can book a charter for a chance at a trophy catch.

Small resorts, condominiums, and an efficiency apartment complex make up the accommodations offerings. Cayman Brac's largest resort is the 59-room **DIVI TIARA BEACH RESORT**, *Tel. 800/367-3484, or 345/948-1553, Fax 345/948-1316.* A favorite with scuba divers, the resort includes a dive shop, underwater photo center, and more.

Another popular property with divers is the 40-room **BRAC REEF BEACH RESORT**, *Tel. 800/327-3835, reservations office 813/323-8727.* Located off Channel Bay on the island's southeast shore, this resort includes a pool, Jacuzzi, restaurant, bar, dive shop, snorkeling, fishing, tennis, underwater photo center and gift shop. The 16-room Brac Caribbean Beach Village at Stake Bay offers a dive shop, snorkeling, and tennis.

Getting There: Direct flights to Cayman Brac Gerrard Smith Airport are available from Miami, Tampa, Atlanta and Houston or from Grand Cayman aboard Cayman Airways , *Tel. 800/422-9626 from US, from Canada Tel. 800/441-3003.* Twice daily service from Grand Cayman is provided on small prop planes with Island Air, *Tel. 345/949-5252, Monday through Friday 9am to 5pm; Fax 345/949-7044.* Flights depart at 8am and 3:50pm ; return flights depart at 9:30am and 5:20pm. The flight takes one hour and ten minutes, making a brief stop in Little Cayman. Round trip tickets are US $122 (US$98 for passengers under 12); a day trip package is also available for US $105 (US $84 for travelers under 12).

Flights are also available on Island Air from Cayman Brac to Little Cayman and cost US$40 round trip. Special fares are available for children under age 12.

While on the island, rentals are available from Avis/Cico, *Tel. 345/948-2847*, Brac-Hertz Rent-a-Car, *Tel. 345/948-1515*, and Four D's Car Rental, *Tel. 345/948-1599*.

ARE WE THERE YET?

By Air

You'll arrive in the Cayman Islands at Owen Roberts International Airport, a stylish facility that resembles a Polynesian structure. The principle carrier into this port of entry is Cayman Airways, *Tel. 800/G-CAYMAN*, the national carrier with flights from Miami, Tampa, Atlanta, and Houston. Air/land packages are also available from Cayman Airtours, *Tel. 800/247-2966*. Service is also available from American Airlines from Miami (and Raleigh-Durham during high season), Northwest Airlines from Miami, USAirways from Charlotte and Tampa, and America Trans Air from Indianapolis.

Direct flights to Cayman Brac are available from Miami, Tampa, Atlanta and Houston or from Grand Cayman.

By Ship

Cruise ship passengers arrive in George Town, a wonderfully charming community brimming with shops and restaurants along its clean waterfront.

Entry Requirements

US and Canadian citizens need to show proof of citizenship in the form of a passport, birth certificate or voter registration card. Visitors must also show a return airline ticket.

Getting Around the Island

Transportation around Grand Cayman is easy. Take your pick from taxis and group tours as well as rental cars, vans, jeeps, and scooters (a scary option to us, considering the left side driving and traffic in George Town).

WHICH ONE IS MY ROOM?

Most visitors to Grand Cayman stay along Seven Mile Beach just outside of George Town.

Along this busy stretch you'll find luxurious hotels, fine restaurants, nightclubs, and most of the activity on the island.

SEVEN MILE BEACH RESORT AND CLUB, *Seven Mile Beach, Tel.345/949-0332, Fax 345/949-0331. Rates for one to four people (children under 12 free) are $350 per room in high season ($450 during Christmas week), and $210 during low season. Credit cards accepted.*

Located inland but with private beach facilities, this condominium property offers two-bedroom, two-bath units. Each has private balcony, air-conditioning, telephone, cable TV, VCR, and a fully equipped kitchen. The complex includes a freshwater pool, Jacuzzi, lighted tennis court, outdoor grills, and children's play area. Seven Mile Watersports arranges trips to Stingray City and has complete dive facilities, including resort and certification courses.

WESTIN CASUARINA RESORT, *Seven Mile Beach, Tel.345/945-3800, Fax 345/949-5825. Toll-free reservations Tel. 800/228-3000. Winter rates start at $330, Summer rates begin at $205. Credit cards accepted.*

The newest hotel in Grand Cayman is built on a strip of beach bordered by willowy casuarina trees. The hotel has 340 guest rooms, most with breathtaking views of the sea from step-out balconies. The hotel has the feel of a conference property, with a slightly dress-up atmosphere in the main lobby.

Facilities include beachfront, casual and fine dining restaurants, pools, whirlpools, tennis, fitness facilities, beauty salons, masseuse and masseur.

GRAND PAVILION, *Seven Mile Beach, Tel.345/945-5656, Fax 345/945-5353. Toll-free reservations Tel. 800/HERITAGE. Winter rates $300-$425, Summer rates $160-$280. Credit cards accepted.*
One of Grand Cayman's most lavish hotels, resembling a Southern plantation, this hotel might be a little stuffy for some vacationers. The hotel includes two restaurants, two bars, a gym, 24 hour room service, and other services aimed at business and convention travelers. Not the place you want to drag into with the impression of a snorkel mask stamped into your face, dripping seawater and sand.

VILLAS OF THE GALLEON, *Seven Mile Beach, Tel.345/945-4433, Fax 345/945-4705. Rates range from $300-$555 (2 to six guests) in high season, $235-$405 during off peak months. Credit cards accepted.*
Located within walking distance of the Holiday Inn for those looking for nightlife, this 74-unit complex is popular for its well-furnished units. Rooms include air-conditioning, telephone, TV, VCR, kitchen, laundry facilities, maid services.

HYATT REGENCY GRAND CAYMAN, *Seven Mile Beach, Tel. 345/949-1234, Fax 345/949-8528. Toll-free reservations Tel. 800/233-1234. Winter rates from $295, Summer rates $190-$315. Credit cards accepted.*
One of Grand Cayman's most beautiful resorts, the Hyatt is not located directly on the beach but does offer its guests use of a private beach club across the street with full watersports. You may recognize parts of this resort from the movie *The Firm* (it's the place where Gene Hackman

and Tom Cruise stayed). The 235-room hotel includes many levels of rooms and suites plus luxury villas. Landscaping as beautiful as a botanical garden, the hotel flows from a great main house to grounds dotted with royal palms and ponds filled with colorful koi, and a freeform swimming pool, complete with bridges and pool bar.

All rooms include air-conditioning, mini-bar, satellite TV, coffee makers, telephones, and more. Resort facilities include four restaurants and five bars, private beach club, pool and hot tub, dive shop, 24-hour room service, watersports, dive shop, golf, health club, beauty spa, and more.

The Hyatt Regency Grand Cayman offers guests a unique cultural program to introduce guests to the island's history, culture, and flora and fauna. Horticultural tours led by the resort's landscaping experts point out sea grape, travelers' palm, silver thatch palm, and more. For a peek at the island's past, visitors can talk with a local historian. For more hands-on experiences, a coconut husker can teach the secrets of obtaining the edible portions of this thick fruit, while local artists show the skills needed to make rope, baskets and hats from silver thatch palms.

PLANTANA CONDOMINIUMS, *Seven Mile Beach, Tel.345/945-4430, Fax 345/945-5076. Winter rates start at $260, summer rates at $175. Credit cards accepted.*

This 49-unit complex offers elegant condo accommodations just steps from the beach. Two and four guest units are available, all with air conditioning, ceiling fans, telephones, television, kitchens, maid service, laundry facilities.

INDIES SUITES, *Seven Mile Beach, Tel.345/947-5025, Fax 345/947-5024. Toll-free reservations Tel. 800/654-3130. Winter rates $255, $170 in summer. Credit cards accepted.*

Although it doesn't have a beachfront location, Indies Suites is a good choice for those looking for suite accommodations. All rooms include either a king-size or two double beds and a full-size kitchen equipped for four. All rooms also include satellite TV, telephone, storage locker for dive gear, and convertible sofa bed. The family-operated all-suites hotel includes a dive shop and a resort course for an introduction to scuba diving, free. The resort includes a pool, hot tub, cabana bar, boutique, mini-mart, and complimentary continental breakfast daily.

TREASURE ISLAND RESORT, *Seven Mile Beach, Tel.345/949-7777, Fax 345/949-8489. Toll-free reservations Tel. 800/327-8777. Winter rates start at $220, summer rates begin at $155. Credit cards accepted.*

This 280-room resort includes an offshore snorkel trail. Now starting to look a little tired around the edges, the hotel nonetheless has a pretty pool area with waterfall cascading down from the third floor restaurant. Facilities include two freshwater pools, 2 whirlpools, tennis, dive operation, shopping, informal dining, bar, and lounge.

DISCOVERY POINT CLUB, *Seven Mile Beach, Tel.345/ 945-4724, Fax 345/945-5051. Winter rates start at $200, summer rates start at $175. Credit cards accepted.*

This beachside condominium complex offers 45 suites. The one- and two-bedroom apartments include air-conditioning, screened porches or balconies, telephone, and TV. Units have kitchens, but some gardenview hotel-type units are available without kitchens. Facilities include Jacuzzi, pool, and tennis. Children under six stay free.

MARRIOTT GRAND CAYMAN, *Seven Mile Beach, Tel.345/949-0088, Fax 345/9949-0288. Toll-free reservations Tel. 800/223-6388. Winter rates $195-$290, summer rates $190-$290. Credit cards accepted.*

Located two miles from George Town and about four miles from the airport, this convenient property (formerly the Radisson) is located on a beautiful stretch of Seven Mile Beach. Swimmers and snorkelers can enjoy calm waters and a small coral reef just offshore or learn scuba diving. Booking dive trips is through the on-site shop. Oceanfront rooms include private balconies with good beach views and are worth a somewhat long walk to the elevators in this 315-room hotel. Facilities include casual and fine dining, pool and hot tub, dive shop, wave runners, windsurfing, shopping arcade, and full service spa.

Luxury Properties

If you're lucky enough to vacation without an eye on the budget, you'll find plenty of pampering hotels and condos for your family to enjoy.

THE GREAT HOUSE, *Tel. 800/235-5888, 345/945-4144, Fax 345/949-7471*, on Seven Mile Beach was used by *The Firm* filmmakers, and includes three bedrooms and a den that can become a private fourth bedroom. Three and a half baths, satellite TV and VCR, kitchen with microwave, dishwasher, icemaker, wine cellar, and washer/dryer, dining room, and beachfront balcony are found in the apartment as well. This luxury accommodation is rented with a minimum of one month stay; the winter rate (including daily maid service, tax, and gratuity) is US $30,975 per month.

THE GREEN HOUSE, *Spotts Beach, Tel. 800/235-5888, 345/945-4144, Fax 345/949-7471*, is a new private home located on the beachfront about five minutes from the airport in George Town. The house includes four oceanview bedrooms (two masters each with king bed), four full ensuite bathrooms and a half guest bath, living and dining room, freshwater pool, and housekeeping services. During winter months, the per night rate is $1475.

Grand Cayman offers almost twice as many condominium properties as hotels, and an increasing number are aimed at the luxury traveler. On Seven Mile Beach, **THE AVALON CONDOMINIUMS**, *Tel. 345/945-4171, Fax 345/ 945-4189*, each offer three bedrooms and three baths. Overlooking Seven Mile Beach, the condos each include cable TV, fully equipped kitchens, and laundry facilities; guests have use of a fitness center, lighted tennis courts, freshwater pool, and Jacuzzi. Winter rates for one to four persons runs US $600 and a maximum of five to six persons can be accommodated for $670. Children under two stay without charge.

WHAT ARE WE DOING NEXT?

To experience the entire island, consider an **island tour**. We signed up for a tour with Burton Ebanks, *Tel. 345/949-7222*, a local with an extensive knowledge of the entire region. We headed off for the day to view the 76 square-mile island.

Outside the city of George Town, the population is sparse and the atmosphere is rural. Located about 25 minutes from George Town, the **Queen Elizabeth Botanic Park**, *Tel. 345/ 947-9462*, is a 65-acre park filled with native trees, wild orchids, as well as birds, reptiles, and butterflies. Here our family enjoyed a self-guided tour and a quiet look at the flora and fauna that make the Cayman Islands special.

From the North Side most tours travel to the East End, home of the **Blow Holes**. Park and walk down to the rugged coral rocks that have been carved by the rough waves into caverns. As waves hit the rocks, water spews into the air, creating one of the best photo sites on the island.

Just under 30,000 people populate the island, and almost half live in the capital city of **George Town**. Save a few minutes for a tour of the **Cayman Islands National Museum**, *Harbour Drive, Tel. 345/949-8368*. This excellent two-story museum traces the history of the Cayman Islands, including the islands' natural history. George Town bustles with life any time of day as a center for shoppers and diners. Among historic government buildings, you'll find plenty of shops selling Cayman souvenirs and restaurants featuring both Caribbean cuisine and international dishes.

Continuing past George Town lies the world's only **Turtle Farm**, *West Bay, Tel. 345/949-3893*. Here you'll have a chance to get up close and personal with green sea turtles, viewing them as eggs, hatchlings, and in various sizes as they work their way up towards adulthood. Some reach 600 pounds, and can be viewed slowly swimming in an open-air tank in the center of the farm.

The Turtle Farm is one of the Caribbean's most popular attractions for children. They can learn a great deal about these marine creatures as well as other wildlife found on Grand Cayman at this farm. The favorite part for children is the holding tank, where they can pick up a turtle. (A tip: Have your child hold the turtle vertically. As long as he's held horizontally, he'll flap around and try to "swim" away.) This is a great place for some terrific vacation photos.

There's no visiting Grand Cayman without seeing what lies beneath the water's surface. But you don't even have to get wet to enjoy the underwater sights of the Caribbean. The **Atlantis submarine**, *George Town, Tel. 800/253-0493*, offers hourly dives six days a week. For 50 minutes, you'll feel like an underwater explorer as you dive to a depth of 100 feet below the surface. It's a unique opportunity to view colorful coral formations and sponge gardens, and identify hundreds of varieties of tropical fish. The submarine has individual porthole windows for each passenger, plus cards to help you identify fish species. A pilot and co-pilot point out attractions during the journey.

Although Grand Cayman has long been the home of the Atlantis submarine, it is now home base for the **Nautilus**, *Tel. 345/945-1355*. This new 80-foot semi-submersible submarine, docked at Calico Jack's in George Town, has provided a one-hour tour to view the rich marine life of the bay. The sub goes out about three-fourths of a mile offshore offering visitors a chance to view two shipwrecks and to watch a diver feed a variety of tropical fish. Good for families with children and for anyone claustrophobic, travelers sit in a glass hull six feet beneath the surface but can go up on deck anytime during the trip. Tours are offered at 10:30am and 2:30pm daily, with additional tours scheduled on Tuesday, Wednesday, and Thursday mornings as needed to accommodate cruise ship travelers. The tours are priced at $35 per person and $19 for children.

To feel like one of the pirates of the Caribbean, consider a cruise aboard the **Jolly Roger**, *Tel. 345/949-8534*, an authentic replica of a 17th century galleon. Cruises, starting at US $15, take families on a rollicking pirate excursion or an elegant dinner cruise.

A sunset cruise may be pure heaven, but one of Grand Cayman's top tourist spots is pure **Hell**. This odd attraction is actually a community named **Hell**, a moniker derived from the devilishly pointed rocks near town, a bed of limestone and dolomite that through millions of years eroded into a crusty, pocked formation locally called ironshore.

Today, Hell trades upon its unusual name as a way to draw tourists to the far end of west Bay. The Devil's Hangout Gift Shop (open daily) is manned by Ivan Farrington, who dresses as the devil himself to greet tourists who come to buy the obligatory postcard and have it postmarked from Hell.

For a look at native birds, animals, and reptiles **Cardinal D's Park**, *off Courts Road, Tel. 345/949-8855*, is a good stop for families. Over 60 species of exotic birds including Cayman parrots and whistling ducks as well as agoutis, blue iguanas, turtles, miniature ponies, emus, and more are on display. A petting zoo and snack bar make this attraction popular with kids. The park is open daily; guided tours available at 11am and 2pm.

Island Tours

Experienced tour operators offer an in-depth look at the islands. Guides can provide a general overview of the island as well as specialized tours focusing on eco-tourism, plants, history, birding, and shopping.

Overviews of the island range in length from two and a half hours to all day. Typical tours include a drive through look at the capital city of George Town, a photo stop at the Conch Shell House (a private residence made of conch shells), a drive along Seven Mile Beach, a tour of the Cayman Turtle Farm (the world's only such operation), and a visit to the community of Hell where vacationers can stop to mail postcards and have them postmarked from Hell.

Full day tours include the same stops as a brief tour but also take a look at the less visited east side of the island. Tours often drive through Bodden Town, visit the Pirate's Caves, stop for photos of the Blow Holes, and swing around to Rum Point, a popular watersports area overlooking the entrance to the North Sound.

FOR AN ISLAND TOUR, CALL...

Burton's Tours, *Tel. 345/949-7222, Fax 345/947-6222*

Elite Limousine Service, *Tel. 345/949-5963, Fax 345/949-2058*

Evco Tours, *Tel. 345/949-2118, Fax 345/949-0137*

Majestic Tours, *Tel. 345/949-7773, Fax 345/949-8647*

McCurley's Tours, *Tel. 345/947-9626*

Reids Premier Tours, *Tel. 345/949-6531, Fax 949/949-4770*

Tropicana Tours Ltd., *Tel. 345/949-0944, Fax 345/949-4507*

Vernon's Sightseeing Tours, *Tel. 345/949-1509, Fax 345/949-0213*

Sports & Recreation

There's no doubt that one of the top draws of Grand Cayman is the unparalleled **scuba diving** in its clear waters. With visibility often exceeding 100 feet, this is a diver's paradise with over 130 sites to select from near Grand Cayman. Wall and reef dives, many less than half a mile from shore are available as well from many operators including Bob Soto's Diving, *Tel. 800/BOB-SOTO,* Don Foster's Dive Cayman, *Tel. 800/83-DIVER,* Red Sail Sports, *Tel. 800/255-6425,* Treasure Island Divers, *Tel. 800/872-7552,* Tortuga Surfside Divers, *Tel. 800/748-8733,* and many more.

The top attraction on Grand Cayman is **Stingray City**, the place for your family to act out Jacques Cousteau fantasies. It's an area where numerous operators (including many of the scuba operators named above) introduce vacationers to one of the most unique experiences in the Caribbean.

Following a short boat ride, visitors don snorkel gear and swim with the stingrays just offshore on a shallow sandbar. Accustomed to being fed, the stingrays (which range in size from about one to six feet across) are docile and friendly, brushing against swimmers and even allowing themselves to be held and petted. About 30 stingrays frequent this area. Even non-swimmers can enjoy the shallowest stop. Use your own judgment on this attraction. We've seen many school age children participating but you should realize that the rays are large and will come close to the children.

At Calico Jack's, vacationers can now sample the sport of scuba diving with **Snuba**, *Tel. 345/949-4373.* This new addition to Grand Cayman combines snorkeling and scuba diving to give even non-swimmers an opportunity to explore life below the surface. Anyone eight years or older can enjoy this safe activity, which can be experienced by handicapped and senior vacationers as well.

The equipment utilized by Snuba participants is much like that used by certified scuba divers. After a short safety and usage course (about 10 to 15 minutes), Snuba divers swim out from shore and enjoy the spectacle of marine life found just yards away. Five foot-long tarpon are often spotted (every evening the nearby restaurants feed these silvery beggars) as well as crabs and parrotfish. The highlight of the Snuba experience is the chance to dive the wreck of the Cali, a four-masted schooner.

Ticket prices are US $65 per person. Dives are scheduled at 8:30, 10, 11:30, 1, and 2:30 daily. Sports fun also exists on dry land. The Links at Safe Haven, *Tel. 345/947-4155, Fax 947-4001,* is the only championship 18-hole **golf course** in the Cayman Islands. Rates average about US $60 for 18 holes. Shoe and cart rental are available.

If you're looking for a bird's eye view of Grand Cayman take a **flightseeing tour** offered by Seaborne Flightseeing Adventures and Island Air, *Tel. 345/949-6029 or 345/949-5252.* The 25-minute tour includes a look at Grand Cayman from a 19-passenger Twin Otter aircraft. Tours are scheduled only from December through June. Cost is $56.

WHAT CAN I BUY?

The Cayman Islands are a duty-free port, so after 48 hours out of the States, Americans can return home with up to $400 in purchases without paying duty. (Families can pool their exemptions, however. A husband and wife can take an exemption of $800, a family of four $1600.) Also, Cayman crafts are exempt from this allowance, as are works of art, foreign language books, caviar, and truffles.

Duty-free shopping is especially popular in George Town where you can choose from china, perfumes, leather goods, watches, crystal, and more. If you're looking for something uniquely Cayman, check out the Caymanite jewelry. Made from a stone found only on the eastern end of Grand Cayman and on Cayman Brac, Caymanite somewhat resembles tiger's eye.

An excellent shopping spot for families is the museum shop at the Cayman Island Museum in George Town. Look for Caribbean children's books, puzzles, locally made jewelry, crafts, and other inexpensive items with a real Cayman feel.

PRACTICAL INFORMATION
Currency. The official currency is the Cayman Dollar, exchanged at a rate of US $1 equals CI $1.20.

Driving. Driving is British style, on the LEFT.

Information. For general information and reservations, call the Cayman Islands Department of Tourism, *Tel. 800/ 346-3313*. For hotel and condo rates in the Cayman Islands and for special air-accommodation packages, call Cayman Airways Holidays, *Tel.800/G-CAYMAN*.

For additional information, contact your nearest Cayman Islands Department of Tourism Office:

Miami: *6100 Blue Lagoon Drive, Suite 150, Miami, FL 33126-2085, Tel. 305/266-2300, Fax 305/267-2932*

New York: *420 Lexington Avenue, Suite 2733, New York, NY 10170, Tel. 212/682-5582, Fax 212/986-5123*

Houston: *Two Memorial City Plaza, 820 Gessner, Suite 170, Houston, TX 77024. Tel. 713/461-1317, Fax 713/461-4109*

Los Angeles: *3440 Wilshire Boulevard, Suite 1202, Los Angeles, CA 90010, Tel. 213/738-1968, Fax 213/738-1829*

Chicago: *9525 W. Bryn Mawr Avenue, Suite 160, Rosemont, Il 60018, Tel. 708/ 678-6446, Fax 847/678-6675*

Canada: *234 Eglinton Avenue East, Suite 306, Toronto, Ontario, Canada M4P 1K5, Tel. 416/485-1550, Fax 416/485-7578*

Information on Island. When on Grand Cayman, visit the Cayman Islands Department of Tourism office at Elgin Avenue in George Town, *Tel. 345/949-0623.*

Web site. Check out the Cayman Islands web site on the Internet at *http://www.caymans.com* for lots of helpful information, current weather, news, and more.

ISLAND REPORT CARD

Transportation to island	A+
Transportation around island	A
Family Resorts	A
Family Restaurants	A
Friendly atmosphere	A
Activities for kids	A
Weather	A
New cultures for kids to experience	B-
Safety	A+

CURAÇAO

For family travelers in search of something a little off the beaten path, here it is. Curaçao is a magical destination, favored by those looking for beautiful beaches, good snorkeling, and an exotic atmosphere that combines a Dutch heritage with a strong South American influence and a Caribbean beat for a truly unique getaway.

The island is part of the Netherlands Antilles along with the islands of Sint Maarten, Bonaire, Saba, and St. Eustatius. (The Netherlands Antilles, the island of Aruba, and Holland comprise the Kingdom of the Netherlands.) Ruled by a governor appointed by the Queen, each island has autonomy on domestic affairs. Curaçao is the capital of the Netherlands Antilles, and here you'll find most of the governmental, financial, and industrial positions.

Tucked into the far southern reaches of the Caribbean, less than 40 miles from the coast of South America, Curaçao is very much an international destination. Dutch is the official language, and you'll hear many Dutch-speaking vacationers. Many South Americans also enjoy the island where most residents speak Spanish. We found that most Curaçao residents speak an amazing total of five languages: Dutch, Spanish, English, Papiamento, and either French or German.

Papiamento is the local language spoken on the streets, a veritable cocktail of tongues. Spanish, Portuguese, French, Dutch, Indian, English, and some African dialects combine to form the *lingua franca* of the Netherlands Antilles. Even between the islands the language varies slightly, each with its own slang and accent.

That ease with multiple languages also seems to translate into a comfort with many nationalities as well. Over 70 nationalities are represented on the island and, with such a true melting pot on this 184-square mile piece of land, there's a true welcoming spirit for tourists, wherever their home-

166 CARIBBEAN WITH KIDS

land. When Curaçaoans says "Bon Bini," they mean welcome in any language.

On one side of the island lies the capital of Willemstad, a truly international city with streets lined with Dutch-style architecture as colorful as a candy store. The city is divided into two sides: Punda, the original settlement, and Otrobanda, literally the "other side." Both sport picturesque harborfront buildings, and are connected by the largest bridge in the Caribbean, a free ferry, and the Queen Emma Pontoon Bridge for pedestrians, locally known as the "Swinging Old Lady" because of the way it moves out of the way for harbor traffic.

Beyond Willemstad, Curaçao becomes a three tiered countryside dotted with tall cacti trimmed with coastlines of the windswept and tranquil varieties. The Atlantic shoreline of the island is rugged and wild, with pounding surf, shady sea caves, and evidence of past volcanic action. Swimming is prohibited in the dangerous waters, but families will find plenty of calm waters along the placid Caribbean side of the island.

ARE WE THERE YET?
By Air

Curaçao International Airport lies just minutes from Willemstad and the nearby resort hotels. American Airlines serves with the island from Miami, ALM from Atlanta twice weekly. Air Aruba from Newark daily, Tampa four times a week, and Baltimore three times weekly. Guyana Airways flies from NY-JFK twice weekly.

Entry Requirements

US and Canadian citizens need to offer proof of citizenship in the form of a passport or a birth certificate and a photo ID. Travelers also need to show a continuing or return ticket.

WHICH ONE IS MY ROOM?

SONESTA BEACH RESORT AND CASINO CURAÇAO, *Piscadera Bay, Tel. 011/599-9-736-8800, Fax 011/599-9-462-7502. Toll-free reservations Tel. 800/766-3782. Winter rates $230-$335, Summer rates $160-$220. Credit cards accepted.*

See "Best Places to Stay with Kids" chapter for resort review.

PRINCESS BEACH RESORT AND CASINO, *Martin Luther King Boulevard, Tel. 011/599-9-736-7888, Fax 011/599-9-461-4131. Toll-free reservations Tel. 800/327-3286. Winter rates $210-$285, Summer rates $140-$205. Credit cards accepted.*

Located near the Seaquarium, this resort is nestled along a wide stretch of beach protected by a man-made breakwater. The three-story resort features rooms in Caribbean colors, as well as three restaurants, four bars, and a casino.

LION'S DIVE HOTEL AND MARINA, *Bapor Kibra, Tel. 011/599-9-461-8100, Fax 011/599-9-461-8200. Toll-free reservations Tel. 800/223-9815. Winter rates start at $150, Summer rates begin at $130. Credit cards accepted.*

Especially popular with divers, this hotel has everything scuba enthusiasts could want: a five-star dive center, dive courses, snorkel and boat dive trips, rentals, and a complete dive shop. Its 72 guest rooms are all air-conditioned, each with a balcony or a patio. The hotel also operates a shuttle to Willemstad and offers free admission to Seaquarium.

ACTIVITIES

This is an island without hasslers or pushy vendors, a place where your family can walk safely along the streets, dine at sidewalk cafes, and be greeted by friendly Curaçaoans.

Start with a visit to **Willemstad**, a historic city that bustles with activity but also takes a slower pace in its shopping district. Here you can take a guided tour aboard an open-air trolley or a self-guided walk for a look at Fort Amsterdam. And you can't miss the historic harborside shops, as colorful as Easter eggs.

Stroll through the streets and alleyways, then walk across the Wilhelmina Bridge to the **Floating Market**, one of Willemstad's most colorful sites. Here Venezuelans sell fresh fish and vegetables (a real commodity on an island without much agriculture). Stroll along the waterway booths and buy exotic tropical fruits or watch fishermen cleaning their catch for a buyer. Behind the stalls, colorful schooners make an excellent photo.

While you're in the city, make time for a visit to **Seaquarium**, *Bapor Kibra, Tel. 011/599-9-461-6666,* one of the Caribbean's finest marine exhibits and a definite winner with kids. Along with tanks of local fish, coral, and sponges, the aquarium also has several outdoor tanks with larger species—including sharks, sea turtles, and stingrays. Divers and would-be divers can take a dip here and feed the sharks through holes in an underwater Plexiglass wall. Complete instruction and equipment are provided. For those who want a drier look at these toothy denizens, just walk down into the Seaquarium Explorer, a semi-submarine parked by the shark tank.

After the Seaquarium have a dip at the Seaquarium Beach, a full-service beach with watersports, restaurant, bar, and plenty of action. There's a small admission charge. This is the beach where Curaçaoans and visitors come to see and be seen. Waters as calm as a lake make swimming inside the breakwaters easy and popular with families.

Curaçao has over three dozen additional **beaches** from which to choose, all located on the Caribbean side of the island. Some of the most popular are Knip Bay and Barbara Beach.

Curaçao may be a dry island, but you'll find plenty of other natural attractions. One is **Boca Tabla**, a sea cave carved by pounding Atlantic waves. Located on the road to Westpoint, the cave is a short walk off the road (wear sturdy shoes!). Kneeling in the darkness of the sea cave, you'll watch the surge of crystal blue waves as they come within feet of you, roaring into the cave and back out to sea. Above the cave, walk on the volcanic rock (stay on the pebble path) to the seaside cliffs for excellent photos. This stop is not recommended for families with young children but is a good stop for those with kids 10 and older who will stay by parents.

If you'd like to venture into a cavern, take a tour of **Hato Caves**, open daily except Monday. Guided tours take the two of you through the stalactite and stalagmite filled rooms, several which include pools or waterfalls.

Nature lovers should save time for a visit to **Christoffel National Park**, on the western end of the island. This wildlife preserve includes the island's highest point and 20 miles of trails that wind through local flora and fauna. Don't be surprised to see some native wildlife in the park; it is home to iguanas, donkeys, small deer, rabbits, and many bird species.

For a look at all these attractions, consider an **island tour**. Tours can be booked through hotel desks or call Taber Tours, *Tel. 376637*, for a rundown of their packages which include east and west end tours, Hato Cave tour, jeep safari, and sailing and sunset cruises.

WHAT CAN I BUY?

Curaçao's shopping opportunities keep many travelers busy, especially in downtown **Willemstad**. The prime shopping district is in **Punda**, just across the floating bridge. Cross the bridge and continue up Breede Straat, where you'll find most of the shops and boutiques aimed at vacationers, along with some charming sidewalk cafes.

The most obvious shop in Punda is the **J.L. Penha and Sons** department store, housed in a beautiful lemon-tinted colonial building constructed in 1708. You'll find just about everything in this department store, from perfumes to fine jewelry to collectibles.

Down **Breede Straat**, you'll find more appropriate shops for families. Stop by Sunny Caribbee for a look at many Caribbean collectibles, spices, and crafts. The Gomezplein plaza, just a couple of blocks up from the bridge, offers picturesque boutiques and a relaxed shopping atmosphere.

For lower priced purchases, take a turn off Breede Straat and enjoy a stroll down Heeren Straat or Keuken Straat. These streets are filled with electronics, inexpensive clothing, and housewares. It's a fun atmosphere where you'll have a chance to mix with residents.

These streets end at the water, where you'll find an entirely different shopping opportunity: the **Floating Market**. Schooners from Venezuela bring exotic fruits, vegetables, spices, and plants to this open-air market that's very popular with older residents. To reach the floating market, walk across the bridge at Columbus Straat. We highly recommend the market to enjoy a slice of island life and, for the photographers out there, to capture one of Curaçao's most colorful sights.

Americans are allowed to return to the US with $600 worth of purchases (per person) before paying duty.

PRACTICAL INFORMATION

Banks. Bank hours are 8am to 3pm. ATMs are available for use with Cirrus network cards.

Currency. The official currency is the Antillean guilder, exchanged at a rate of US $1=ANG 1.77.

Driving. Driving is on the right side of the road.

Electricity. The current is a little different from that found in the United States. Curaçao operates at 110-130 volts alternating current, 50 cycles.

Information. Call the Curaçao Tourist Board, *Tel. 800/ 270-3350 or 800/445-8266.* For additional information, contact the Curaçao Tourist Board office nearest you:

Miami office:
330 Biscayne Boulevard
Miami, FL 33132
Tel. 305/374-5811

New York office:
475 Park Avenue
Suite 2000
New York, NY 10017
Tel. 212/683-7660

Information on Island. Once you're on the island, stop by the Visitors Information Booth at the airport (just past customs) for brochures and maps. The tourism office is located at 19 Pietermaai in Willemstad; the local number is *461-6000.*

Web Site. Check out the official Web site at: *http:// www.interknowledge.com/curacao.*

ISLAND REPORT CARD

Transportation to island	B
Transportation around island	B+
Family Resorts	B
Family Restaurants	B-
Friendly atmosphere	A+
Activities for kids	B+
Weather	A+
New cultures for kids to experience	A+
Safety	A+

DOMINICAN REPUBLIC

"Can you see the mosquito?" asked the guide.

We peered at the amber, backlit in the museum display. The insect was frozen in the solidified sap. One day over 50 million years ago, that mosquito had made a fatal mistake: landing on sap from a now-extinct species of pine tree. His slender legs were caught in the sticky substance that over the years had formed a crystal coffin.

The mosquito, along with amber-encased termites, ants, fern, cockroaches, and even a tiny lizard, is found in the Amber Museum in Puerto Plata, Dominican Republic. This Caribbean nation is one of only a few sites on the globe where amber is found. The popularity of *Jurassic Park*, where fiction gave scientists the ability to use DNA found in the mosquito blood to spawn dinosaurs, brings visitors flocking to this museum on the north shore of the island.

Although its history, from the prehistoric amber to Christopher Columbus' first landing in the New World, is fascinating, it is the Dominican Republic's present day situation with which most travelers are familiar. The Dominican Republic shares the island of Hispaniola with Haiti, a tumultuous neighbor that frequently overshadows the popular vacation destination.

The second largest Caribbean island (only Cuba is larger), Hispaniola is a land of rugged mountains, palm-lined beaches, and two diverse cultures. Haitians speak French; Dominicans, Spanish. The leadership of Haiti has frequently been torn by assassinations and military takeovers while the citizens of the Dominican Republic enjoy the relative tranquillity of a stable, freely elected government. And while life has become a struggle for Haitians, Dominican Republic days are far more carefree, with plenty of time to dance to the throbbing sounds of merengue.

The Dominican Republic has long been heralded as one of the least expensive Caribbean destinations, some sources estimating it to be as much as 50 to 70 percent cheaper than its neighbors. Excepting such resorts as Casa De Campo where jet setters come to relax and where Michael Jackson and Lisa Marie Presley once wed, the island boasts inexpensive prices and bargain resorts.

Many resorts are found on the Dominican Republic's north side, a region nicknamed the Amber Coast. The Dominican Republic boasts the fastest growing tourism business in the Caribbean, with over two million visitors a year. We found that over 60% of the vacationers are European.

Most visitors arrive at Puerto Plata's La Union International Airport and journey to the resort area about twenty minutes away. A drive past fields of tall sugar cane with a backdrop of lush mountains takes many vacationers to Playa Dorada, a horseshoe-shaped complex containing 14 resorts, a casino, several discotheques, a two-story shopping mall, numerous restaurants, and a Robert Trent Jones-designed 18-hole golf course. Only guests and hotel vehicles are permitted within the Playa Dorada complex.

Playa Dorada is located on the Atlantic side of the island. Although the sea here is choppier that its Caribbean counterpart on the south shore, a gentle breeze makes it popular with windsurfers, boogie boarders, and families that enjoy playing in the surf. Other guests are just content to lie on the beaches lined with majestic palms.

Although Playa Dorada is almost a city within itself, travelers shouldn't miss Puerto Plata. Founded by Nicholas de Ovando in 1504 at the request of Christopher Columbus, this city is rich with history.

Dating back to the 16th century, the Fortaleza San Felipe still stands guard over the city and the harbor. Built by the Spaniards to protect the city from pirates, in this century it was used as a prison. The doors within the fort are only four feet tall, slowing down would-be attackers (and keeping tourists alert). The fort includes a small museum with a collection of period weapons and cannon balls.

Another fort stands at the top of Pico Isabel de Torres, one of the highest points in the Dominican Republic. The dome-shaped fortress is topped with a statue of Christ similar to one that overlooks Rio de Janeiro.

Santo Domingo is located on the island's southern shore. Here history buffs will find a wealth of Spanish Renaissance architecture to explore. The city was the first permanent European settlement in the New World and has been honored for its cultural landmarks by a United Nations proclamation.

Near Santo Domingo is located the nation's most lavish resort: Casa de Campo, as well as a host of other first-rate vacation destinations.

ARE WE THERE YET?
By Air

Puerto Plata is served by American and Continental Airlines. Santo Domingo is served by American and Dominicana Airlines. Casa de Campo boasts its own air service from American Airlines, the only resort that can make that claim.

Entry Requirements

US and Canadian citizens should bring proof of citizenship, either a passport or an official birth certificate with photo ID.

Getting Around the Island

With 12,000 miles of roads, getting around the Dominican Republic can be achieved many different ways. You can rent a car from a major agency at the airports and in the larger cities. You'll need your driver's license and a major credit card. You'll also need good reflexes to deal with the frequent displays of driving *machismo* you will encounter. One fortunate thing: driving is (more or less) on the right side. Taxis are a safer bet, but are fairly expensive and are unmetered; you'll need to negotiate a price before you embark. A variety of buses are also available from luxury lines to those with few creature comforts. The most basic transportation in the DR are the *guaguas,* unregulated taxi/buses which are usually crowded with locals. If you speak Spanish, riding the *guaguas* can be a good way to get the lowdown on what's happening.

WHICH ONE IS MY ROOM?

CASA DE CAMPO, *La Romana, Tel. 809/523-3333, Fax 809/523-8548. Toll-free US phone number Tel. 800/223-6620. Winter rates from $235, Summer from $125. Credit cards accepted.*

The Dominican Republic's most lavish resort is also one of the most activity-oriented in the Caribbean. You name it, you can do it at the plush resort sprawled over 7000 acres. Located in La Romana, American Airlines offers direct flights into Casa de Campo's own airport. The hotel operates kids' programs for ages three to five, and six to 12 years.

CLUB MED PUNTA CANA, *Provincia La Altagracia, Tel. 809/686-5500, Fax 809/687-2896. Toll-free US phone number Tel. 800/CLUB-MED. Winter from $120 per person. Credit cards accepted.*

See "Best Places to Stay with Kids" resort review.

JACK TAR VILLAGE, *Puerto Plata, Tel. 809/320-3800, Fax 809/320-4161. Toll-free US phone number Tel. 800/858-2258. From $165 in winter, from $110 in summer. Credit cards accepted.*

This resort is easy on the pocketbook and still offers families plenty of activity. The rooms here are separated from the beach by the golf course, but some days you can still hear the waves rolling in on this Atlantic side which is too rough for snorkeling but nice for a romp in the surf.

MELIA BAVARO, *Playas de Bavaro, Higuey, Tel. 809/221-2311, Fax 809/286-5427. Toll-free US phone number 800/33-MELIA. Credit cards accepted.*

Located in Punta Cana on the eastern end of the island, this 57-acre resort offers rooms in two-story bungalows and a two-story hotel for a total of nearly 600 rooms.

Children's activities are conducted daily, free for hotel guests. Kids under two years stay free with parents; children over two years are charged only 50% of the normal rate.

CLUB DOMINICUS BEACH, *Bayahibe, La Romana, 809/562-6001, Toll-free US reservations Tel. 800/898-9968. Winter rates from $120 double occupancy. Credit cards accepted.*

One of the Viva Resorts (others are found in Mexico and the Bahamas), this 500-room resort is located on a mile-long beach. The all-inclusive resort includes all meals (served buffet style), drinks, daily activities, sports, non-motorized watersports, and enrollment in the Kids' Fun Club.

Children under seven years of age stay free when sharing a room with a paying adult. Children age seven through 16 receive a 50% discount when sharing a room with two paying adults (maximum of two children per room).

WHAT ARE WE DOING NEXT?

The Jurassic Park buffs in your family have come to the right place. Amber-encased specimens were borrowed from the collection of Puerto Plata's **Amber Museum** to make the movie and today you can have a look at amber-encased mosquitoes, termites, ants, fern, cockroaches, and even a tiny lizard. This Caribbean nation is one of only a few sites on the globe where amber is found.

Housed in a two story Victorian structure, the museum features amber mined in the Septentrional mountains along the north coast.

The museum was founded by Didi and Aldo Costa, the Italian consulate in the Dominican Republic. Their collection of amber is the most extensive in the world.

When removed from the geologic layers on the mountainside, amber looks like an unspectacular stone. Cutting and polishing, however, reveals its true nature — not a stone at all but a translucent fossilized sap. Amber ranges in color from pale yellow to dark brown, depending on the surrounding soil. A rare blue tinted amber is colored by volcanic gas. The most treasured pieces of amber are those that have "inclusions" — leaves, insects or even small reptiles trapped in these crystal coffins.

The Amber Museum has numerous displays of amber and provides guided tours in several languages, including English. After a tour of the museum, most visitors head to the shop downstairs (even larger than the museum). Here shoppers find one of the north coast's largest selections of amber jewelry.

Dating back to the 16th century, the **Fortaleza San Felipe** still stands guard over the city and the harbor. Built by the Spaniards to protect the city from pirates, in this century it was used as a prison. The doors within the fort are only four feet tall, slowing down would-be attackers (and keeping tourists alert). The fort includes a small museum with a collection of period weapons and cannon balls.

Another fort stands at the top of **Pico Isabel de Torres**, one of the highest points in the Dominican Republic. The dome-shaped fortress is topped with a statue of Christ similar to one that overlooks Rio de Janeiro.

In Santo Domingo, historic attractions fill the **Colonial Zone**. Tour sites such as the Catedral Santa Maria la Menor, the first cathedral in the Americas and, according to some historians, the final resting site of Christopher Columbus.

At Casa de Campo, **Altos de Chavon** is well worth a visit. This family recreation of a 16th century art colony, complete with Spanish wrought ironwork and hushed courtyards, speaks of colonial style in a way no museum ever could.

WHAT CAN I BUY?

The most unique purchase in the Dominican Republic is **amber**, available at gift shops along the north coast. Amber prices vary from US $3 for small earrings to US $200 for a mosquito encased in amber to several hundred dollars for large, chunky necklaces or amber set in gold. The color of the amber affects the price as well. Generally the pale blonde amber is the least expensive.

Amber resembles plastic, so avoid buying from street vendors and check your item before purchasing. Amber possesses a slight electromagnetic charge, so genuine amber, when rubbed on a piece of cloth, should attract particles. Better stores, such as the Amber Museum Shop, also have an ultraviolet light for testing. Genuine pieces will glow under the light. Also, amber will float in salt water while plastic will sink.

For teenagers, popular souvenirs are **merengue cassette tapes**, and **larimar**, a blue stone similar to turquoise.

NOTE: Do not exchange more dollars than you will spend while in the Dominican Republic. Upon departure, you may only convert 30% of your pesos back to dollars with proper receipts.

PRACTICAL INFORMATION

Currency. The Dominican peso (RD) is the official currency. The exchange rate fluctuates but at press time was about RD $14=$1 US.

Electricity. 110 volt/60 cycles is used.

Information. For brochures on Dominican Republic attractions, call the Tourist Information Center, *Tel. 800/752-*

1151 in the US or 800/563-1611 in Canada, on weekdays from
8:00 to 5:00, eastern standard time. For additional information, write the office nearest you:

Chicago office:
561 West Diversey Parkway
Suite 214
Chicago, IL 60614
Tel. 773/529-1336

Miami office:
2355 Salzedo Street
Suite 307
Coral Gables, FL 33134
Tel. 305/444-4592

New York office:
1501 Broadway
Suite 410
New York, NY 10036
Tel. 212/575-4966

Montreal office:
2980 Rue Crescent
Montreal, Quebec
H3G 2B8
Tel. 514/499-1918

Toronto office:
35 Church Street
Unit 50 Market Square
Toronto, Ontario
M5E 1T3
Tel. 416/361-2126

Language. Spanish is the official language of the Dominican Republic. In tourist areas, English is spoken but away from the hotels you will need at least a minimal knowledge of Spanish.

Time. Atlantic Standard Time, one hour ahead of Eastern, is used throughout the year. Daylight savings time is not observed.

Web site. Get more Dominicana information at: *http://www.dr1/travel.html.*

ISLAND REPORT CARD

Transportation to island	B
Transportation around island	B-
Family Resorts	B
Family Restaurants	B-
Friendly atmosphere	B
Activities for kids	B
Weather	A
New cultures for kids to experience	A
Safety	B

JAMAICA

Spanning over 4,000 square miles, the Caribbean's third largest island has a little bit of everything: rivers, mountains, plains, forests, caves, and, of course, a beautiful coastline. Jamaica is an island that appeals to travelers who enjoy its pulsating reggae music, rich history, and bountiful attractions that highlight its lush, tropical beauty. Perhaps more than any other Caribbean island except St. Lucia, Jamaica is incredibly lush and fertile. Fruits, orchids, bromeliads, hardwoods, and ferns all thrive in this rich soil and bountiful environment. Sugar remains a major product.

Jamaica also offers several distinct destinations that lie a few hours' drive apart on roads that twist and wind beside a jagged coast and, on the eastern end, stands the Blue Mountains, with peaks that top 7,500 feet above sea level.

The capital city of Kingston lies on the south shore, a metropolitan area that's visited primarily for business rather than pleasure. Most vacationers head to the resort communities of the north shore. Quiet Port Antonio, once a hideaway for Hollywood stars, lies to the east. Heading west, the garden city of Ocho Rios is a popular favorite with couples. Montego Bay or Mo Bay is the first taste most visitors have of the island as it's home of the north shore airport. To the far west is Negril. Once a hippie haven, today it's the preferred vacation spot for many aging yuppies who have returned with their families to enjoy its laid-back atmosphere and unbeatable sunset views.

We have to admit that Jamaica is not for everyone. Many travelers, including some fellow travel writers, prefer to skip this island because of the problems that inevitably reveal themselves even to the casual traveler. Drugs are a problem on this island, and you will probably be approached by *ganja*-selling entrepreneurs. Although the resorts patrol their grounds and beaches above the high water line, when you step outside the boundaries of the resort be prepared. "I have something special for you" is a frequently used line that you can ward off with a friendly but firm "No, thank you."

But, in general, we've found that Jamaica has some of the friendliest inhabitants in the Caribbean. Service, even in all-inclusive resorts where tips are not even a question, is excellent. Taxi drivers are proud to tell you about the island, and we've even had drivers jump out of the car and pick herbs and plants along the route in describing their uses in the Jamaican household. We have visited this island more than any other in the Caribbean and it continues to hold a special place in the hearts of our family.

MEET THE JAMAICANS

There's no better way to really learn about Jamaica than to meet its residents in person. Two excellent programs allow visitors to join up with residents with shared interests.

Meet the People is a free program operated by the Jamaica Tourist Board that utilizes the services of over 500 volunteers on the island in different walks of life. Through the years, the program has matched stamp collectors, birders, private pilots, and travelers of many interests with islanders. The program is simple: just give the Jamaica Tourist Board office a call, *Tel. 800/233-4582 or 0888/995-9999 on island.*

Countrystyle, *Tel. 876/962-3725 or 876/962-3377 or 800/ JAMAICA, Fax 876/962-1461,* is another unique service. Owner Diana McIntyre Pike can arrange island experiences tailored just to the visitor's interest. Whether you'd like to visit a school, meet a family with kids the same age as yours, or plan a vacation that includes some home stays in small communities across the island, give Countryside a call.

ARE WE THERE YET?

By Air

Service into Montego Bay's Donald Sangster International Airport is available on American Airlines, Continental, Air Canada, USAirways, Air Jamaica, and Northwest Airlines. Service is available from New York, Newark, Baltimore/Washington, Philadelphia, Atlanta, Miami, Orlando, Los Angeles, Tampa, and Toronto.

By Ship

Most cruise ships arrive in Ocho Rios or Montego Bay. Both city's terminals are within easy distance of the craft markets and shopping centers.

Entry Requirements

American and Canadian citizens should ring along your passport or proof of citizenship: a certified birth certificate or naturalization certificate and a photo ID.

Getting Around the Island

Taxis are the easiest mode of travel and can be obtained at any resort. Look for red PPV license plates; these indicate legitimate taxis. Agree on the price with the driver before you depart.

Rental cars are pricey, and are available from most major rental companies. The speed limit is 30 mph in town and 50 mph on the highways, but be warned: Jamaica has some wild drivers! We've often seen two cars passing an auto at the same time, creating a three lane, one way road out of a two lane, two way highway. On top of that, you'll be driving on the left side of the road and dealing with roundabouts at every intersection.

JAMAICAN CHILDREN'S CHARITY
To benefit chronically ill Jamaican children, the Rebecca Pike Foundation for Sick Children was established in 1992. The foundation supports families who need financial help for critically ill babies and sick children who need specialized care and also assists in improving the maternity and pediatric care facilities at Hargreaves Memorial Hospital in Mandeville.

For more information, write the Rebecca Pike Foundation, PO Box 60, Mandeville, Jamaica, W.I. , *Tel. 876/ 962-3265, Fax 876/962-1461.*

WHICH ONE IS MY ROOM?
Montego Bay
ROUND HILL HOTEL AND VILLAS, *8 miles west of Montego Bay, Tel. 876/956-7050, Fax 876/956-7505. Toll-free reservations Tel. 800/237-3237. Winter from $330, Summer rates from $220 per room. Credit cards accepted.*

Located eight miles west of Montego Bay, this elegant resort is "old" Jamaica, a reminder of the time when guests came with their steamer trunks, brought the latest European fashions, and stayed for weeks. Today, this is where the rich and famous come to vacation; Ralph Lauren, Paul McCartney, and the Kennedys have been spotted on the guest register at this exclusive resort.

But, for all its luxury, this is also a family-friendly property. Complimentary nanny service is available for up to five hours daily; children under 12 are offered a 50% discount on any meal plan or the all-inclusive package. A special children's menu caters to young tastes.

Kids activities include a free tennis clinic available weekly, a donkey ride at the Monday night beach party, beach fun, glass bottom boat rides, and a weekly sailing trip. Young equestrians can take a pony ride at nearby stables.

HOLIDAY INN SUNSPREE, *east of Montego Bay, 876/ 953-2485, Fax 876/953-2840. Toll-free reservations Tel. 800/ HOLIDAY. Winter rates start at $150 per person; room-only rates begin at $80. Credit cards accepted.*

Over a decade ago, we spent our honeymoon at this resort located on the outskirts of Mo Bay. At that time, it was a standard Holiday Inn, albeit one with a private white sand beach, live entertainment every night, and restaurants which introduced us to Caribbean cooking.

But today this hotel has become even better. Following a major recent renovation, the 516-room Holiday Inn SunSpree Resort is now all-inclusive, offering guests a package that includes all their meals, drinks, non-motorized watersports, tennis, golf, daily activities, theme parties, shopping excursions, and a Great House tour. The Kids Spree Vacation Club accommodates infants through teens.

The Kidspree Centre recently instituted a new program called "Kid E Care" with private nanny. Daytime nannies service the guest room and also take care of the children. The cost is US $30 per child (US $5 per additional child) for a daytime nanny from 9am to 5pm; a 48 hour advance notice is needed. Evening nanny services run US $25 for one child; advance notice of 24 hours is needed. Evening nanny services run from 6pm to 1am.

During the Christmas holiday, the resort stages a Mini Miss Holiday Inn Pageant for young girls age 7 to 12. Prizes are offered and hotel management, guests, and local retailers serve as judges.

VERNEY'S TROPICAL RESORT, *3 Leader Avenue, Tel. 876/952-2875, Fax 876/979-2944. Toll-free US reservations Tel. 800/JAMAICA. Winter rates from $65 double room, summer rates from $45. Credit cards accepted.*

You won't find a friendlier inn in Montego Bay than Verney's. Tucked up above Montego Bay, this 27-room hotel makes you feel like you're returning home, thanks to owners Kathleen and Earnest Sterling. Rooms are basic and the property is not located on the beach, but the property is clean, friendly, and safe. All rooms include a private bath, air-conditioning, telephone, and TV. The hotel also has a pretty freshwater pool that overlooks the city and beyond it the sea, and free transportation to Doctor's Cave Beach in Montego Bay.

Verney's also includes a restaurant featuring traditional Jamaican dishes (so traditional, in fact, that many hotel concierges recommend the restaurant for travelers looking for a taste of the "real" Jamaica). Feel free to special order any dish for picky eaters, however.

Babysitting is available and special large rooms near the restaurant are very popular with families.

Negril

NEGRIL CABINS, *Norman Manley Boulevard, Tel. 876/957-4350, Fax 876/957-4381. Toll-free US phone number 800/382-3444. Winter from $154, summer from $136. Credit cards accepted.*

Negril is bordered to the east by the Great Morass, a swampland rich with peat, a substance that was considered as a possible energy source in the 1970s when scientists studied the feasibility of mining this resource. Environmental concerns about the possibility of damaging Negril's famous Seven Mile Beach put a stop to the mining plans.

During the study of the Morass, these researchers lived in cabins in Negril. Today, Negril Cabins utilizes those original structures plus several new buildings and operates as a resort for those who want to combine the luxuries of a hotel with the natural experience of camping. Visitors enjoy Swiss Family Robinson-style accommodations in cabins perched on stilts. Lush grounds are filled with indigenous Jamaican flora and fauna and dotted with colorful hummingbirds. Negril Cabins offer tours to the Royal Palms Reserve, located directly behind the property.

NEGRIL GARDENS, *Norman Manley Boulevard, Tel. 876/957-4408, Fax 876/957-4374. Toll-free reservations Tel. 800/752-6824. Credit cards accepted.*

This 65-room hotel is especially popular with European visitors, so much so, in fact, that the daily news fax is also offered in Italian.

We enjoyed a stay in one of the beachside rooms (less expensive accommodations are available across the road). Like other guests, we sunned on the hotel's stretch of Seven Mile Beach, watching the continuous procession of traffic. Hair braiders, a cappella singer, craftsmen, and more worked their way along the beachfront (although they are only permitted within a few feet of the water's edge).

XTABI, *Lighthouse Road, Tel. 876/957-4336, Fax 876/957-0121. Toll-free US reservations Tel. 800/757-4336. Credit cards accepted.*

Located on Negril's cliffs, this 16-room resort is an inexpensive way to enjoy Jamaica's western end. Each accommodation is an octagonal rondoval, most with uninterrupted views of the sunset. Take the ladder down to the sea to snorkel or sunbathe on the flat rocks that spill into emerald-colored water or to explore the sea caves carved along the cliff's edge. This resort is a real bargain, and its exotic atmosphere will make you feel like you've stepped off the beaten path. Because of its location on the rugged cliffs, this property is not recommended for families with young children but would be a good option for those with kids 12 and older.

Ocho Rios

RENAISSANCE JAMAICA GRANDE, *Tel. 876/974-2201, Fax 876/974-5378. Toll-free US phone number 800/HO-TELS-1. Winter rates from $340, summer from $320 ,double occupancy. Credit cards accepted.*

This beautiful beachfront resort has plenty of around the clock fun for even the most active of families. Step out to the sand beach or enjoy a romp in the Fantasy Pool, which is a clever replica of Dunn's River Falls complete with caves and bridges. Watersports include everything from snorkeling to waterskiing and out of the water the fun continues with tennis, aerobic classes, and more.

Kids 12 and under enjoy the "Club Mongoose" program here. Three programs team young guests with others their own age: two to four, five to eight, and nine to 12 years. This supervised program includes plenty of fun: picnics, beach parties, dance classes, cricket classes, and even an ecology awareness program. Some other interesting activities link guests with local residents. A pen-pal program teams up children with local kids to give them a chance to learn more about Jamaican culture and to keep the excitement of the Jamaica vacation going long after they return home. Also, once a week, the Club Mongoose program visits a local kindergarten. The program runs from 10am to 9pm daily and is free for all-inclusive guests, $15 per day for others. Admission in the program includes the "Club Mongoose" T-shirt. Baby-sitting is available from 9pm and can be arranged with the concierge.

Children eat, stay, and play free in deluxe or junior suite accommodations when sharing a room with parents on the all-inclusive plan. The all-inclusive plan covers buffet breakfast, lunch and dinner at a choice of restaurants to the dinner buffet theme party, late night snack, beverages, all non-motorized watersports, one glass-bottom boat excursion per guest, tennis, fitness center, daily program of activities, hotel taxes, tips, and airport transfers.

FRANKLYN D. RESORT (FDR), *St. Ann, Tel. 876/973-3067-70, Fax 876/973-3071; 888/FDR-KIDS or Toll-free reservations Tel. 800/654-1FDR. $1,700-$2,205 per person for 7 days. Credit cards accepted.*

See "Best Places to Stay with Kids" chapter for resort review.

FAMILY TRAVEL SURVEY

FDR recently conducted a family travel survey. What did they find?

• Children are traveling on planes much younger than ever before—one out of every two respondents say their children flew for the first time at age three or younger.

• Driving vacations have significantly decreased as compared to destinations reached by plane.

• Beach resort destination vacations have dramatically rose.

• Respondents rated food as the best lifesaver to keep kids entertained, rating significantly higher ahead of stuffed animals, friends, or games.

BOSCOBEL BEACH, *Oracabessa, Tel. 876/975-7330, Fax 876/975-7370. Toll-free reservations Tel. 800/859-SUPER. Winter rates $409-$663 for three nights, per person; Summer rates from $319-$503 for three nights, per person. Credit cards accepted.*

See "Best Places to Stay with Kids" chapter for resort review.

WHAT ARE WE DOING NEXT?

THE CONCIERGE RECOMMENDS...

David Ellis, Concierge at Renaissance Jamaica Grande, recommends the following for busy family travelers:

The kiddie center provides a wide variety of activities for children including pony rides, swimming, and disco. These activities may be participated in by other members of the family. Certain family style activities such as Pirates' Party, reggae Jamboree, and beach Olympics are organized for full family participation at our hotel.

Touring the Prospect Plantation is a recommended off-property event. For history enthusiasts, the Coyaba Museum is recommended.

Families staying at our hotel can do most things together, including dining, or separate as adults may feel the need to do.

Montego Bay

Several great houses, which once oversaw huge sugar plantations, are today notable visitor attractions. **Rose Hall**, *Tel. 876/953-2323*, is one of the best-known and is an easy afternoon visit for Montego Bay guests. This was once the home of the notorious Annie Palmer, better known as the White Witch. According to legend, Annie murdered several of her husbands and her slave lovers. Readers who would like to know more about the tales of Rose Hall can read the novel *The White Witch of Rose Hall*. The guided tour is excellent for older children but the recounting of the murders (including the burying of a live baby up to his neck near an ant hill) is too grisly for those under 10.

Jamaica may be the land of sun and fun but it's a birders' paradise as well. Bird lovers find one of the Caribbean's most unique sites at the **Rocklands Feeding Station**, *Tel. 876/952-2009*, in the village of Anchovy. This is the home of Lisa Salmon, 93, Jamaica's best-known ornithologist. Her home is a veritable bird sanctuary surrounded by clouds of grassquits, saffron finches, and, most especially, hummingbirds.

Salmon moved to the verdant hillside in April 1952 and found the site, located a short drive from the beaches of Montego Bay, filled with feathered friends. Through the years, Salmon worked as a bird advocate, achieving a limit on Jamaica's bird hunting season. In 1959 she opened the bird sanctuary and since that time travelers from around the world have hand-fed the regular guests of this bird diner. Tiny finches flutter around outstretched palms filled with birdseed while fast-as-lightning hummingbirds drink from a hand-held bottle of sugar water.

Visitors are invited between 3:30 and 5pm daily.

Next to Half Moon, **Rocky Point Stables**, *Tel. 876/953-2286*, offers horseback rides and lessons as well as pony rides.

Negril

Restless kids looking for a little traditional theme park fun find Jamaica's closest offering in Negril at **Anancy Park**, *Norman Manley Boulevard*. "Anancy was built as an attraction for the local community, as well as hotel guests," explains founder Dr. Garfield Munroe. "We are delighted to combine a fun environment with a learning experience. Visitors really get a chance to experience the history of Jamaica and have a good time doing it."

The park welcomes families with an 18-hole miniature golf course, go-kart racetrack, carousel, and power wheels for the youngest visitors. Families can also take a WaterSkeeter pontoon paddleboat in the small lake and youngsters can borrow a fishing pole right on the premises to try their luck on the well-stocked pond.

In spite of its emphasis on fun, the park also offers a look at the nature and culture of the area with a nature trail with markers explaining more about local plants and a cultural center that features varying programs. "We at Anancy feel that an existence of a nature park encourages a greater environmental awareness of and appreciation for the surrounding natural resources, by both visitors and locals," emphasizes Munroe.

Negril visitors don't have to venture all the way to Ocho Rios to enjoy waterfalls. Western Jamaica has a much quieter alternative in **Y.S. Falls**, *Tel. 876/997-6055*. These spectacular waterfalls cascade in steps through tropical forest. As spectacular (and far less crowded) as Dunn's River Falls, Y.S. is a Jamaican attraction that has remained untouched by hassling vendors and long lines. At the top, swimmers enjoy clear waters under a canopy of fern.

Nearby in the community of Black River, enjoy the **Black River Safari Cruise**, a popular day trip for Negril vacationers looking for a little respite from sun and sand. This hour and a half long tour takes travelers up the Black River, at 44 miles the longest river in Jamaica. The waters here are home to snook and tarpon, some reaching as large as 200 pounds. You may see spear fishermen with a snorkel, mask and speargun, swimming in the dark water stained by peat deposits. The fisherman's canoes are hand-hewn and burned out using a generations-old technique. Among their catch are tiny brine shrimp, sold by women in the St. Elizabeth parish along the roadside. Highly salted and spiced, these are a popular snack with locals and visitors.

The biggest attraction on the Black River are the **crocodiles**. Once hunted, these crocodiles are now protected but still remain wary. These reptiles can live as long as 100 years, so long that some have become known by local residents. One 15-foot-long specimen named Lester is seen nightly.

For a look at the countryside around Negril the way it used to be, consider at day at **Belvedere Estate**, *Tel. 876/ 952-6001 or 957-4170*, one of the first sugar cane plantations on the island. Located an hour from town, this estate is set up as a living museum with costumed guides to show you the ruins of the 1800's great house, the sugar factory, and the boiler where the juice of the cane is made into brown sugar. In the craft village, watch a weaver make coconut palms into baskets, talk to an herbalist about Jamaica's bountiful herbs, visit a canoe maker, and have a taste of island bread at the bakery. A traditional Jamaican lunch is included with the tour.

Ocho Rio

In Ocho Rio, the most popular attraction (one that just about every cruise ship passenger and resort guest enjoys—sometimes what seems like must be all at one time) is **Dunn's River Falls**. This spectacular waterfall is actually a series of falls that cascade from the mountains to the sea. Here you don't just view the falls, but you climb up the cascading water. Led by a sure-footed Jamaican guide (who wears everyone's cameras slung around his neck), groups work their way up the falls hand-in-hand like a human daisy chain. Be prepared to get wet and have fun, but don't expect a quiet, private getaway. This is Jamaica for the masses, and, no matter what day of the week, the masses do come. At the end of the climb, you'll be deposited into a hectic market for another opportunity to buy crafts, carvings, and the ubiquitous T-shirt.

West of Ocho Rio in the town of Oracabessa, 007 fans can visit the **James Bond Beach**. Located near Ian Fleming's home, Goldeneye, the beach has plenty of options for a day of activity: waverunners, helicopter tours, and horseback rides as well as beach bar and grill.

If you're serious about horseback riding, check out the **Chukka Cove Equestrian Centre**, *Tel. 876/972-2506 or 974-2239*, between Runaway Bay and Ocho Rios. Well known for its world-class polo matches, the center also offers guided horseback trips along the beach and in the mountains.

mlemlememlemlemlemlmemlmlmlmemlemlemlmlmemlmemlmemlmlmemlmlmemlmlmemlemlme priced) Half Moon Shopping Village, and our favorite, the Holiday Village Shopping Centre near Holiday Inn SunSpree. Look for Bob Marley T-shirts, rasta tams, woodcarvings, straw baskets, and more.

In Negril, the Hi-Lo Shopping Center offers a good selection of souvenir, liquor, music, and sportwear stores. The Hi-Lo grocery itself is an excellent shopping stop; pop in to purchase spices, hot sauces, and Blue Mountain coffee at prices far lower than you'll see in the hotel gift shops.

Ocho Rios is home to the Taj Mahal Shopping Centre, a complex of fine duty-free shops and other stores that sell souvenir items, liquor, and Blue Mountain coffee.

MAGIC TOYS

One of the most delightful products in Jamaica for both kids and adults alike are the creations of Magic Toys, a company based outside Mandeville. All hand-painted in vibrant tropical tones, Magic Toys are seen in the resorts throughout the Caribbean as decoration in public areas in the form of wall hangings, countertops, and more. Smaller pieces, from jigsaw puzzles to mirrors and picture frames, make perfect souvenirs. The creations each feature a tropical design such as parrotfish, bird of paradise, and Jamaica's own doctor bird. For the best prices and the largest selection, visit the studio outside Mandeville, *Tel. 876/990-6030*, or check in resort gift shops throughout the island.

In every resort area, be prepared for numerous offers by higglers, Jamaica's word for peddlers. Also be prepared for offers of "something special." *Ganja* or marijuana is widespread, but purchase or use of the drug is strictly illegal. Talk with your teens before a trip to Jamaica. Teenagers—especially boys—will be approached by salesmen in the larger resort areas.

A very legal agricultural product is **Jamaican Blue Mountain coffee**, considered one of the finest coffees in the world. Gift shops at the resorts and the airport sell the coffee in small burlap gift bags for about $1 US per ounce (less than half the price found in American coffee shops). You can find the coffee even cheaper at local markets.

PRACTICAL INFORMATION

Banking. Know before you go that ATM cards from US and Canadian banks are not accepted by Jamaican machines. You can obtain a cash advance on major credit cards at the banks, but this is a slow process (it took us close to two hours to obtain money in Negril recently). Banks are open 9am to 2pm Monday through Thursday, 9am to 4pm Friday.

Currency. The Jamaican dollar is the official tender; its exchange rate fluctuates frequently but at press time was about $1US=35J. US dollars are accepted throughout the island.

Driving. Driving is British style, on the left.

Electricity. The island uses 110volts/50 cycles, although 220 is used in some of the hotels. Adapters are not required for North American appliances.

Information. For questions or brochures, call the Jamaica Tourist Board, *Tel. 800/233-4582 or 305/665-0557.*

Information on Island. JTB operates a help line while on island, *Tel. 0888/995-9999 or 0888/995-4400.* You will also find several tourist offices across the island: Black River (Hendricks Building, *2 High Street, Tel. 876/965-2074),* *Kingston (2 St. Lucia Avenue, Tel. 876/929-9200),* Montego Bay *(Cornwall Beach, Tel. 876/952-4425),* Negril *(Coral Seas Plaza, Tel. 876/957-4243),* Ocho Rios *(Ocean Village Shopping Centre, Tel. 876/974-2582),* and Port Antonio *(City Centre Plaza, Tel. 876/993-3051).*

Language. English is the official language, although you'll frequently hear the Jamaican patois on the street, a combination of several languages.

Time. Jamaica is on Eastern Standard Time and does not observe Daylight Savings Time.

Web site. Get more Jamaica information at: *http://www.jamaicatravel.com/travel.html.*

ISLAND REPORT CARD

Transportation to island	A+
Transportation around island	B
Family Resorts	A+
Family Restaurants	A
Friendly atmosphere	A
Activities for kids	B+
Weather	A
New cultures for kids to experience	A
Safety	B

PUERTO RICO

Puerto Rico is an easy destination for families. It's a short airplane ride, just 2-1/2 hours from Miami and under four hours from New York. As a commonwealth of the US, travel here is easy and hassle free. No money to be exchanged. No immigration lines to endure.

And yet Puerto Rico has a culture as vast and exotic as those found anywhere in the Caribbean. The island can give young travelers a chance to try out their Spanish phrases. Or it can provide an opportunity to sample some Old World dishes spiced with a New World flavor. And best of all, this island offers a full menu of attractions to please every member of the family with fun that ranges from shopping to snorkeling, from historic forts to heady rainforests.

Your visit to Puerto Rico will likely begin in the capital city of San Juan. Pulsating with a big city atmosphere, San Juan is one of the most modern cities in the Caribbean and a hub for American Airlines. It's so large that it's divided into several districts. Tourists typically visit Condado, Isla Verde, and Old San Juan, the historical heart of the city. Here you'll find buildings so old and quaint they look more like part of a movie set than part of a modern downtown district.

But beyond the boundaries of San Juan, the sounds change to the slap of waves on the honey-colored shore or the peek of the tiny coqui (co-kee), a frog that's a national symbol of Puerto Rico. (It's said that the coqui can survive only on the island, so to be as Puerto Rican as a coqui is a declaration of national pride.) Here over 200 miles of coastline welcomes families with a hearty "Buenos dias."

ARE WE THERE YET?

By Air

Puerto Rico boasts excellent air service via the Luis Muñoz Marin International Airport in San Juan. The airport serves as the American Airlines hub for Caribbean flights. Service to San Juan is also available from the other major carriers. Carnival, Towers Air, Kiwi, Continental, USAirways, United, Delta, Northwest, United, and TWA each have flights to San Juan.

Daily nonstop service to San Juan is available from Atlanta, Baltimore, Boston, Charlotte, Chicago, Dallas, Detroit, Hartford, Miami, Nashville, Newark, New York, Orlando, Philadelphia, Raleigh-Durham, Tampa, and Washington D.C.

Entry Requirements

As a US commonwealth, passports or other documents are not required of American citizens. Luggage is inspected upon departure for agricultural reasons.

Getting Around the Island

You'll find that you have many of the same options in Puerto Rico as you do at home. Rental cars from the major agencies are available from AAA, Avis, Budget, Discount, Hertz, National, Thrifty, and other companies, especially in the San Juan area. Driving is on the right and signage is bilingual. However, realize that San Juan is a major metropolitan area and just as difficult to maneuver as any other city its size. The Old San Juan area is especially congested, with old, narrow streets.

Taxis are a popular choice, especially within San Juan. A new Taxi Turisticos program sets specified rates within certain zones. These taxis are white and bear the words Taxi Turisticos and a drawing of El Morro. These taxis are an excellent choice for first-time visitors. The drivers have received special training to serve the tourist zones. A drive from the airport to the Isla Verde area costs $8; a trip from the airport to Old San Juan runs $16.

> **MONEY**
> The US dollar is legal tender in Puerto Rico, but with a Spanish flair. Quarters are called pesetas, nickels are villones (pronounced ve-jo-nes), and pennies are centavos.

WHICH ONE IS MY ROOM?

WYNDHAM PALMAS DEL MAR RESORT AND VILLAS, *Humacao, Tel. 787/852-6000, Fax 787/852-2230. Toll-free reservations Tel. 800/WYNDHAM Winter rates from $249 for double occupancy, summer from $179. Credit cards accepted.*

See "Best Places to Stay with Kids" for resort review.

HYATT CERROMAR, *Dorado, Tel. 787/796-1234, Fax 787/796-4647. Toll-free reservations Tel. 800/233-1234. Winter from $405, summer from $205. Credit cards accepted.*

See "Best Places to Stay with Kids" chapter for resort review.

WESTIN RIO MAR BEACH RESORT AND CASINO, *Rio Grande, Tel. 787/888-6000, Fax 787/888-6637. Toll-free US reservations Tel. 800/WESTIN-1. Rates from $350-$550. Credit cards accepted.*

One of Puerto Rico's newest and most lavish hotels, the Westin is a 600-room resort located on the northeast coast. You name it, you'll find it here: two championship golf courses, a casino, 13 tennis courts, two oceanfront swimming pools, watersports, 11 restaurants, and more.

Club Iguana is named for the first residents of the Westin Rio Mar's two golf courses. This supervised children's program is housed in a three-room camp center with a TV room (which converts to a sleeping room for late night campers), an arts and crafts room, and a playroom. Fun includes arts and crafts, sailing clinics, tennis clinics, beginner through advanced golf lessons, horseback riding, volleyball, and beach activities.

The camp is available as a full- or half-day session. The full-day program runs from 9am to 3pm and costs $35 per child per day, including lunch, snacks, and a T-shirt. The half-day program runs in three-hour blocks, from either 9am to noon or noon to 3pm, and costs $20 per child, including snacks.

The Westin offers a Family Plan package that includes round-trip airport transfers, room, free dining for children under 12 from the kids' menu, buffet breakfast daily for two adults, a family picnic on the beach, souvenir disposable camera, one dinner for two, one hour Waverunner rental, one free day at the kids' club, and more. Summer rates for the three- to seven-night package, per room, double occupancy, range from $1,215 to $3,080, depending on the number of nights and choice of accommodation. Winter rates for the program run $1,665 to $4,515.

HYATT DORADO BEACH, *Dorado, Tel. 787/796-1234, Fax 787/796-2022. Toll-free reservations Tel. 800/233-1234. Winter rates from $495, summer from $170. Credit cards accepted.*

For families looking for the comfort of a resort that offers classic elegance and simplicity, Hyatt Dorado Beach fits the bill. With its low rise buildings overlooking a wide stretch of palm-lined beach, Hyatt Dorado Beach exudes a 50s feel in the finest tradition of Laurance Rockefeller's former Rockresorts.

Hyatt Dorado Beach is the sister property to Hyatt Cerromar, a high-rise resort that caters both to conference groups and families. While Cerromar has recently undergone an extensive renovation and many changes and additions, Dorado's strength lies in its sameness.

The simple guest rooms are decorated in West Indian style, with furniture inspired by Caribbean antiques including an armoire/TV center, daybed that folds out to a double sleeper, and, in second floor rooms, carved four poster beds with white linens. Standard amenities include AC, cable TV, minibar, in-room safe, direct dial telephone, electronic locks, and a marble bath and dressing area with sit-down vanity. Rooms open out to a balcony or a patio with views of the ocean, golf course, or, in the older three-story section, the swimming pool. Seventeen casita rooms feature split-level elegance that includes a private lawn and marble shower beneath a clear skylight.

Two swimming pools, including one with tournament lanes, are available, and guests enjoy reciprocal privileges at the Hyatt Cerromar, where they can enjoy use of the River Pool.

Nature walks on the property, featuring 600 species of tropical plants, are available. The resort features two 18-hole golf courses designed by Robert Trent Jones Sr. Guests also have privileges at the two courses at Hyatt Cerromar. Seven tennis courts, some lit for night play, are available. A tour desk arranges excursions into Old San Juan, El Yunque Rain Forest, Rio Camuy caves, shopping in the nearby town of Dorado, and other tours. At night, activity centers around the casino. Families enjoy Camp Hyatt children's program at Hyatt Cerromar.

EL SAN JUAN HOTEL AND CASINO, *San Juan, Tel. 787/791-1000, Fax 787/253-0178. Toll-free reservations Tel. 800/231-3320. Winter rates from $350, Summer from $250. Credit cards accepted.*

Located just minutes from the airport, this hotel could symbolize the elegance of San Juan. A lobby paneled in rich woods greets visitors, and just steps away the most elegant casino in the Caribbean offers games of chance managed by croupiers in black tie. At the same time family travelers will feel at home here as well. The pool area is beautifully land-scaped with tropical gardens, the perfect place to relax after a morning of touring or shopping in San Juan.

The Kids Club offers supervised activities for children age five to 12. Participants receive a T-shirt, membership card, and three "Sand Dollars" to use in the game room or at the poolside restaurant. The daily fee for program participation is $28 and includes lunch.

EL CONQUISTADOR, *1000 El Conquistador, Tel. 787/ 863-1000, Fax 787/860-3280. Toll-free reservations Tel. 800/ 468-5228. Winter rates $350-$495, Summer from $200. Credit cards accepted.*

Perched atop a 300-foot cliff, this is one of the grandest resorts in the region. With 918 guest rooms, it's not the place for those looking for privacy and to get away from the crowds, but you'll find just about everything else at this $250 million resort. Choose from an 18-hole championship golf course, a private marina with rental boats and charters for deep-sea fishing, scuba facilities, six swimming pools, seven tennis courts, a nightclub, casino, fitness center, salon, and luxurious shops. Not to mention a 100-acre private island, Palomina, where guests can be whisked on complimentary ferries. On secluded Palomina, families can enjoy snorkeling, nature trails, and siestas in hammocks stretched between tall palms.

The kids' program, Camp Coqui, is designed for kids age three to nine and nine to 13. This program is one of the most unique in the Caribbean. The kids' program is located on Palomino Island, just offshore and accessible by water taxi. With its own nurse located on the island and always in touch with the mainland by radio, the kids' program includes activities such as watersports, nature hikes, and island crafts. Special overnight programs are also available and give kids the chance to feel like Robinson Crusoe. The fee for the full-day program is $38 per child and includes lunch; a half-day program is $25 and does not include lunch.

WHAT ARE WE DOING NEXT?

Old San Juan is dotted with museums and historic sites. The best known is **Fuerte San Felipe del Morro** or **El Morro,** *Old San Juan, Tel. 787/729-6960.* This fort, one of the most photographed sites in the Caribbean, it contains a museum and is administered by the National Park Service. On its grounds, the Cuartel de Ballaja, once Spanish troop quarters, now houses the Museum of the Americas.

The park is open daily from 9am to 5pm; there is no admission charge. Start with a video on the site then take a self-guided tour. You'll find a map at the entrances, and exhibits throughout the park are posted in both English and Spanish. Even if you're not a history buff, this site is a family place where you can look out on the sea and enjoy a gentle tradewind. Bring along your camera for this scenic stop.

Nearby, **Casa Blanca**, *1 Sebastian Street, Old San Juan, Tel. 787/724-4102*, contains exhibits on 16th and 17th century life and on its most famous residents: Ponce de Leon and his family. (Actually Ponce de Leon died before the home was completed.) Built in the 1520s, the home was the city's first fortress and is now open for tours Wednesday through Sunday.

Puerto Rico is also rich in natural attractions, including what is called one of the finest cave systems in the world. The **Rio Camuy Cave Park**, *Route 102, Tel. 787/892-5845*, located 2-1/2 hours west of San Juan, was formed by large underground rivers. Today the park includes a new visitors center with reception area and cafeteria and a theater with AV presentation. Visitors reach cave level by trolley then follow walkways on a 45-minute guided tour.

Another natural attraction is **El Yunque National Forest**, *Highway 3 east between San Juan and Fajardo to Route 191 near Luquillo, Tel. 787/887-2875 or 787/766-5335*, the only tropical rainforest in the US National Forest Service. Forty-five minutes east of San Juan, the rainforest boasts 240 species of trees and flowers, including 20 varieties of orchids and 50 varieties of ferns. Walking trails carve through the dense forest, and guided tours are available.

Kids also enjoy the **Children's Museum or Museo del Niño**, *150 Cristo, San Juan*. Young visitors enter the museum through the legs of a large wooden figure then enjoy hands-on displays and activities from a village of playhouses to a "Visit the Dentist" exhibit where children can play dentist. The museum is open Tuesday through Thursday, 9:30am to 3:30pm, and weekends 11am to 4pm.

Families who will be exploring much of Puerto Rico should take part in the **Le Lo Lai VIP (Value in Puerto Rico) Program**, *Tel. 787/723-3135 or 722-1513*. Program participants pay $10 for a week's worth of activities that includes musical, folkloric, cultural, and natural attractions as well as discounts on sightseeing tours at Old San Juan, El Yunque, Rio Camuy Cave Park, and more.

Sports and Recreation

If your interests run more toward eco-tourism, you're in luck in Puerto Rico as well. One of our favorite excursions is a snorkel trip out to **Monkey Island**. More fun than a barrel of monkeys, this island of curious primates is located off the southeast coast of Puerto Rico. It's a sanctuary for hundreds of monkeys, and access to the island is prohibited. Visitors cannot actually step on land, but you can snorkel around the fringes of the island while excited primates hoot and holler at the intrusion. We found the snorkeling here excellent as well, full of colorful fans and bright corals. Coral Head Divers at Palmas Del Mar, *Tel. 787/850-7208*, offer scuba and snorkel trips to Monkey Island.

Baseball buffs are in the right place. Watch major league stars during the Winter League, from November through

January. The games take place nearly nightly in San Juan's Hiram Bithorn Stadium and tickets are just $6 and under.

WHAT CAN I BUY?

Shopping is a major activity for Puerto Rico visitors. Duty-free shopping is found at the Luis Muñoz Marin International Airport and at factory outlet shops in Old San Juan.

If you're looking for jewelry or factory outlets, check out the shops on Calle Christo and Calle Fortaleza in Old San Juan.

If you're looking for an island product, popular purchases are *cuatros* (small handmade guitars), *mundillo* (bobbin lace), and *santos* (hand carved religious figures).

PRACTICAL INFORMATION

Currency. The US dollar is the official currency.

Doctors. In an emergency, call 911. The doctors in Puerto Rico meet the same standards as those on the mainland of the United States.

Driving. Driving is on the right side. Most road signs are in both English and Spanish.

Electricity. The island uses 110 volts, 60 cycles.

Language. Both Spanish and English are the official language of Puerto Rico. You'll find plenty of English spoken in the resort areas and in San Juan but in the smaller communities most conversation is in Spanish.

Information. Contact the Puerto Rico Tourism Company, *Tel. 800/223-6350 in US, 800/667-0394 in Canada*. For additional information, contact the office nearest you:

Los Angeles office:
3575 West Cahuenga Boulevard
Suite 405
Los Angeles, CA 90068
Tel. 213/874-5991 or 800/874-1230

Miami office:
901 Ponce de Leon Boulevard
Suite 604
Coral Gables, FL 33134
Tel. 305/445-9112 or 800/815-7391

New York office:
575 Fifth Avenue, 23rd Floor
New York, NY 10017
Tel. 212/599-6262 or 800/223-6530

Toronto office:
41-43 Colbourne Street
Suite 301
Toronto, Ontario M5E 1E3
Tel. 416/368-2680 or 800/667-0394

Island Information. The Luis Muñoz Marin International Airport has an excellent tourist information booth near the baggage claim area.

Time. Puerto Rico is located in the Atlantic Time Zone, one hour ahead of Eastern. The island does not observe Daylight Savings Time.

ISLAND REPORT CARD

Transportation to island	A+
Transportation around island	A-
Family Resorts	A
Family Restaurants	A-
Friendly atmosphere	A
Activities for kids	B+
Weather	A
New cultures for kids to experience	A
Safety	B+

ST. KITTS & NEVIS

They're often referred to as "the way the Caribbean used to be." Life is quiet and unspoiled on this two island nation where most guests stay in small, locally owned plantation inns that recall the heritage of the Caribbean with period antiques, wide porches to pick up gentle trade winds, and an atmosphere that appeals to travelers who are independent and ready to strike out on their own.

Rugged and tropical, both islands are excellent destinations for hikers, birders, and nature lovers. St. Kitts is the larger of the two, spanning 68 square miles. The island covers 23 miles in length and at its widest point five miles across. For its size, St. Kitts offers varying terrains that range from semi-arid to rain forest, from flat to nearly impassable. Most of the population lives on St. Kitts with a large percentage in the capital city of Basseterre (pronounced bos-tear). Modern life and ancient history live hand-in-hand as the island is sprinkled with historic sites that date back both to pre-history and to the days of colonization.

Development has, thankfully, been slow on St. Kitts. Although the island has one all-inclusive property, most hotels are locally owned and managed and provide a genuine Caribbean experience. They're found sprinkled throughout the island, both at seaside destinations and high in the hills overlooking fields that were formerly part of plantations.

The most noticeable feature of St. Kitts is Mount Liamuiga (pronounced Lee-a-mweega), usually fringed with a ring of clouds. This dormant volcano, elevation 3,792 feet, is home of the island's tropical rain forest and an excellent destination for eco-travelers. Guided tours take visitors to the far reaches of the forest for a look at this ecosystem.

One area presently being eyed for development is the Southeast Peninsula, a site that, until a few years ago, could only be reached by boat. Since the days when the British and the French fought for domination of the small island of

St. Kitts, the Southeast Peninsula remained impenetrable. Although it was blessed with white sand beaches and palm-fringed coves, this rugged area was inhabited only by a few die-hard residents who traveled by boat and by troupes of green vervet monkeys and shy white-tailed deer. Today the Dr. Kennedy Simmonds Highway, a $14 million road, links this final frontier with the rest of the Caribbean island.

Just two miles away from St. Kitts lies the tiny island of Nevis (pronounced NEE-vis), covering a total of 36 square miles. Columbus first named this island because of the ever-present cloud that circled Mount Nevis, giving it almost a snow-capped look. Today the cloud still lingers over the mountain peak. Home to only 9,000 residents, this country cousin has a charming atmosphere all its own, plus a good share of plantation houses where guests can enjoy a look back at Caribbean history.

Recently the citizens of Nevis voted for independence from St. Kitts so the coming months and years may bring some changes in the political structure to this tiny isle.

Monkeys

Ownership of the Caribbean islands frequently flipped between countries during the early days of European settlement. When the former government left, it was not uncommon for the new country to be left with reminders of the earlier residents in the form of architecture, forts, and city names.

But when the French were deported from the islands of St. Kitts, they left more than Gallic names at cities such as Basseterre. They also left behind their monkeys.

The French had imported a few vervet or green monkeys from Africa as pets during their century of rulership. When the British took over the island, they deported their enemies. However, they refused to allow the monkeys on the ships, and the primates were turned loose on the mountainous island. The tropical climate, miles of untamed rainforest, and plentiful vegetation agreed with the furry creatures, so much in fact, that today the monkey population is estimated to be two and a half times larger than the human population in this twin island federation.

The monkeys do not have a prehensile tail, so they're often seen on the ground, scampering across a lawn in search of a fallen mango. Social like other monkeys, the green monkeys often travel in groups of 30 or 40. Early mornings and late evenings are the best times for spotting the most common resident of St. Kitts and Nevis.

ARE WE THERE YET?

By Air

Most visitors first arrive at St. Kitts' Robert Llewelyn Bradshaw International Airport (formerly Golden Rock Airport) with daily jet service from the USAmerican Airlines providing daily service from the Caribbean hub in San Juan.

From St. Kitts, air service to Nevis' small Newcastle Airport is served by commuter flights from St. Kitts. Air St. Kitts Nevis, *Tel. 869/465-8571 on St. Kitts, on Nevis Tel. 869/469-9241*, and Nevis Express, *Tel. 869/469-9756*, whisks visitors from island to island in less than 10 minutes.

By Ship

St. Kitts' new $16.25 million cruise ship terminal is located in Basseterre. Visitors arrive just off Pelican Mall, a new establishment with 26 shops that feature tropical clothing, locally made goods, and tourist items. Kittitian architecture makes this mall different from the typical mall you might see back home.

Nevis is presently constructing a new cruise port in Charlestown.

By Ferry

To reach Nevis, most travelers travel by ferry rather than air. Ferry service is available several times daily between the two islands aboard *The Caribe Queen*; the journey takes about 45 minutes and costs $20 EC (about US $8) round trip. Departure is from Basseterre, St. Kitts and arrival is in Charlestown, Nevis. An excellent family option is a catamaran cruise between two islands.

WHICH ONE IS MY ROOM?

HORIZON VILLAS RESORT, *Tel. 869/465-0584, Fax 869/465-0785. Toll-free reservations Tel. 800/830-9069. Rates start at $160. Credit cards accepted.*

This condominium resort is an excellent destination for families. You'll feel like you have made your home on this beautiful island during a stay in these lovely villas. Perched up on a hillside with a path down to a crescent-shaped beach, the villas are comfortable, cozy, and maintained by a friendly staff. Guest facilities include a pool and a lovely little strip of beach.

BIRD ROCK BEACH HOTEL, *Tel. 869/465-8914, Fax 869/465-1675. Toll-free reservations Tel. 800/621-1270 or 223-9815. Rates start at $140 during winter months, $75 during summer and fall. Credit cards accepted.*

Scuba divers especially enjoy Bird Rock, a property just five minutes from the airport or from Basseterre. The hotel is home of St. Kitts Scuba and divers can head right off the dock on the dive boat. The hotel is simple and clean and rooms include cable TV, air conditioning, telephone, and balcony or patio. Facilities include restaurant, dockside BBQ grill, pool, bars, tennis, fitness center, scuba.

JACK TAR VILLAGE ST. KITTS BEACH RESORT AND CASINO, *Tel. 869/465-8651, Fax 869/465-1031. Toll-free reservations Tel. 800/999-9182. Rates for the all-inclusive resort start at $115 per day per person. Credit cards accepted.*

Renovated after Hurricane Luis, this all-inclusive resort is recommended for families looking for activity. The resort offers plenty of organized fun and evening entertainment as well as a golf course. The fun comes in an all-inclusive package, so all activities, along with food and drink, are included in the price. Although it is not located directly on the beach, it's just a short walk to the sand and surf.

The Kids Klub offers supervised activities for children 3 to 12 with activities that range from sandcastle building to scavenger hunts. All participants receive souvenirs such as hats, sunglasses, beach pails, and shovels.

The cool, tile floor rooms include air conditioning, cable TV, and telephone. As a clue to the resort's fun level, the pools are deemed the "quiet pool" and the "rowdy pool" where you might witness bingo or pool volleyball. Other guest facilities include golf, tennis, bicycling, fishing in the resort lagoon, nightly entertainment, casino action, two restaurants and several bars, gift shop, and duty free shop.

Children under 6 (under 12 during the summer season) stay and eat free when they share a room with parents, making this an especially popular property for anyone keeping an eye on the budget.

FORT THOMAS HOTEL, *Basseterre, Tel. 869/465-2695, Fax 869/465-7518. Toll-free reservations Tel. 800/851-7818. Winter rates from $100, Summer rates from $100. Credit cards accepted.*

This hotel has one of our favorite swimming pools, a giant in the style of 1950s hotel pools. Located in walking distance of downtown Basseterre, the Fort Thomas Hotel has recently refurbished guest rooms, as well as one of the island's largest swimming pools. Facilities include a restaurant and bar, that impressive Olympic size swimming pool, lawn and table tennis courts, and beach shuttle.

OCEAN TERRACE INN, *Basseterre, Tel. 869/465-2754, Fax 869/465-1057. Toll-free reservations Tel. 800/524-0512. Rates from $93 winter, $76 summer. Credit cards accepted.*

We love this small hotel just steps from downtown Basseterre. Just a short walk from Fisherman's Wharf restaurant (a property under the same ownership), Ocean Terrace Inn or OTI is a favorite with returnees to St. Kitts and with business travelers. The hotel has views of Basseterre Bay and Nevis; many of the recently renovated guest rooms overlook a pool with swim up bar and a hot tub. Beautiful landscaping and walks made of stone divided with low growing grass connect the hotel with two bars. Families can take a complimentary shuttle to Turtle Bay on the island's southeast peninsula for a day of watersports and beach fun then enjoy an evening at the hotel that might include a solo guitarist nightly in the Harbour View Restaurant or a show by the Coronets Steel Orchestra on Friday nights.

FOUR SEASONS NEVIS, *Pinney's Beach, Tel. 869/469-1111, Fax 869/469-1112. Toll-free reservations Tel. 800/332-3442 US, 800/332-3442, Canada. Rooms start at $500 per night during the winter season. Credit cards accepted.*

This resort is the most luxurious accommodation on Nevis and indeed one of the top resorts in the Caribbean. Boasting a championship golf course, 10 tennis courts, two outdoor Jacuzzis, 24-hour room service, and more, this resort is for those looking for a little pampering. Children enjoy the Kids for All Seasons complimentary program with supervised activities.

When word went out that the Four Seasons was coming to Nevis, doomsayers predicted the end of the quaint atmosphere for which Nevis is known. However, during the hotel's construction, Hurricane Hugo hit the island and the Four

Seasons' bosses stopped building and put crews to work cleaning up the island. Today, the tiny island inns coexist peacefully with this corporate giant.

The Four Seasons Nevis sprawls across grounds dotted with coconut palms and other carefully tended fauna. Guests can enjoy a round of golf, scuba, windsurf, or just sun around the pool, cooled by Evian sprayed on guests by mindful pool attendants.

NISBET PLANTATION BEACH CLUB, *Tel. 869/469-9325, Fax 869/469-9864. Toll-free reservations Tel. 800/742-6008. Rooms begin at $335 during winter season. Children under 12 stay for $60 nightly; under 5 for $20 nightly. Children under 2 are free. Seven night minimum stay is required for arrivals during peak Christmas holiday week. Credit cards accepted.*

This plantation was the former home of Admiral Nelson's bride, Fanny Nisbet. The plantation today is a 38-room inn boasting one of Nevis's most striking vistas: a quarter-mile palm-lined walk from the greathouse to one of Nevis's finest beaches. Guests stay in lemon-tinted bungalows scattered throughout the property. Today the greathouse of this former coconut plantation is home to an elegant restaurant and bar. Other facilities include beach, pool, and tennis courts.

MONTPELIER PLANTATION INN, *Tel. 869/469-3462, Fax 869/469-2932. Toll-free reservations Tel. 800/223-9832. Rooms start at $225 for singles, $280 for doubles during peak season; additional guests are $70. Children under 12 stay for $50 per night, under 5 years of age for $25 per night, and under 2 years of age for $10. Children's rates apply only when the child shares the room with two adults. Credit cards accepted.*

Travelers may have heard of this classic plantation inn because of one of its most famous guests: Princess Diana. When Diana and her children visited Nevis, they opted for this hotel's quiet seclusion. Both royalty and honeymooners are offered peace and quiet in this very British hotel located on the slopes of Mount Nevis.

Princess Diana focused the eyes of the world on Montpelier, but it was hardly the property's first brush with royalty. On March 11, 1787 Admiral Horatio Nelson married Fanny Nisbet in front of a royal audience right on these grounds.

Today the plantation includes a 16-room inn that exudes a dignified British air appreciated by travelers who come to the Caribbean for peace and quiet. The inn provides shuttle service to the beaches and evenings here are spent at the open-air restaurant that features classical cuisine with many local ingredients. The rooms are decorated in a tropical style and include telephone, ceiling fan, hair dryer, tea and coffee maker and patio; electricity is 220 volts with a 110 volt shaver adapter. Facilities include swimming pool, tennis court, restaurant and bar.

The inn also has a private stretch of beach along Pinney's Beach with lounging facilities. Complimentary transportation to the beach is available daily. Montpelier closes annually from late August through early October.

MOUNT NEVIS HOTEL AND BEACH CLUB, *Tel. 869/ 469-9373, Fax 869/469-9375. Toll-free reservations Tel. 800/ 75-NEVIS. Rates from $190 in winter, $130 in summer. Credit cards accepted.*

Those looking for a simpler accommodation will find some of the island's best views at this cozy hotel. This family-operated property sits perched high atop Round Hill estate with a view of the Caribbean and of nearby St. Kitts. The view is best enjoyed from the open air restaurant, a facility that's well-known for its innovative cuisine. Rooms here offer a telephone, air conditioning, cable TV, and video players. Facilities include a pool, with a good view of the sea, that helps travelers cool off on hot days, and the hotel also has a beach facility. The Mount Nevis Beach Club has a restaurant and beach Pavilion.

HURRICANE COVE BUNGALOWS, *Oualie Beach, Tel. 869/469-9462, Fax 869/469-9462. Winter rates start at $145 for a one-bedroom unit to $395 for a three bedroom, three bath unit with a private pool; summer rates fall to $100 and $275 respectively. Credit cards accepted.*

Independent travelers looking for the self-sufficiency of a housekeeping unit—as well as some of the most splendid views on the island—will love these stylish bungalows. Each of the 10 hill-hugging cottages was constructed in Scandinavia, broken down and reassembled on a slope overlooking St. Kitts in the distance. Today they're all open-air and furnished with Caribbean artwork. One-, two-, and three-bedroom bungalows with kitchens are available, and guests can walk down to the beach.

OUALIE BEACH HOTEL, *Tel. 869/469-9735, Fax 869/469-9176. Toll-free reservations Tel. 800/682-5431. Rates start at $135 in the winter months, $100 in the summer. Credit cards accepted.*

Families will find one clear choice on Nevis: Oualie Beach Hotel. Home of Nevis's only dive shop and windsurfing operator, this hotel also offers a fine stretch of sand, 22 charming Caribbean bungalows with screened seaside porches and a comfortable atmosphere. Oualie (pronounced Wally) is the old Carib Indian name for Nevis and translates as land of beautiful water. Cribs are available as well as a kids' menu.

Rooms here are spacious and perfect for quick dashes to the beach. Four units include full kitchens. All rooms include a minibar, hair dryer, electronic safe, direct dial telephone, cable TV; air conditioning is offered in the deluxe and studio units. Facilities include SCUBA, deep sea fishing, windsurfing and sailing. They are available for guests and non-guests alike.

WHAT ARE WE DOING NEXT?
St. Kitts

A day's worth of sightseeing is found on St. Kitts, more if you're especially interested in historic sites. Budget a day for an overall look at the sights, which range from historic homes and museums to natural formations and Indian petroglyphs.

Don't miss the **petroglyphs**, *located near Romney Manor,* carved many years ago by the Carib Indians. While you're stopped here, check out the handicrafts sold next door by a neighbor who creates turtles and bird feeders from coconut shells. (Kids love the coconut shell turtles—their heads bob up and down on a spring.)

Just beyond the petroglyphs lies **Caribelle Batik**, *Romney Manor, Tel. 869/465-6253,* a stop worth making even if you don't want to shop. Here you can watch batik in progress and buy the finished product in the form of shirts, wraps, and wall hangings. (Even if you don't want to buy, it's worth a trip to Romney Manor just to visit the ruins of the stately greathouse and the grounds shaded by trees that date back hundreds of years.) The closest thing that St. Kitts has to a botanical garden, these grounds are home to many tropical plant species. You can't miss the huge Saman tree, said to be the largest tree in the Caribbean. On the drive to Caribelle Batik, look for the historic aqueducts along the side of the road, a reminder of the island's early water system.

Continue around the island and don't miss a visit to **Brimstone Hill Fortress National Park**, *Tel. 869/465-2609/6211,* one of the top historical attractions in the Caribbean. From over 800 feet above sea level, you'll enjoy one of the best views found on any of the islands. On a clear day, you can view Nevis, Montserrat, Saba, St. Martin, and St. Barts.

Brimstone Hill is nicknamed "The Gibraltar of the West Indies," and is one of the most amazing attractions in the Caribbean, a mandatory stop for anyone interested in military history. The structure took over a century to construct of volcanic stone and is named for the faint sulfur smell sometimes encountered here. At this site, the French and the British fought for control of the island, a battle first won by the French and the next year won back by the British.

Wear good walking shoes and bring along drinking water for your look at Brimstone Hill. (At the parking level, you'll find a small concession that sells water, soft drinks, and snacks.) Your first stop should probably be the brief film that gives an overview of the site and its rich history at the Visitors Orientation Centre.

From the parking level, walk up the cobbled path to the citadel. Here a view of up to 70 miles makes neighboring islands seem just a stone's (or a cannonball's) throw away. From this lofty peak, it's easy to imagine the British forces keeping an eye on the seas over two centuries ago.

The citadel has two levels. Museums featuring Amerindian artifacts, British and French memorabilia, and St. Kitts items are located in the stone rooms. The fort is open daily from 9:30 to 5:30. Admission is $5.

SAFETY TIP

At Brimstone Hill, visitors can climb upstairs for additional views. Families with young children, however, **be careful**. There are no railings on the second level and, between glare, wind, and a floor that is black with hundreds of years of weathering, it can be tough to see just where the second level opens into the first floor courtyard. Keep young children by the hand here.

Nevis

Nevis has two spectacular beaches custom made for families. **Pinney's Beach** is one of the island's best, the waters here are protected by reefs and popular with snorkelers, swimmers, and sunbathers. **Oualie Beach** is the most active beach on Nevis, with watersport operations.

The main community in Nevis is the city of **Charlestown**. On Tuesday, Thursday, and Saturday mornings, the place to be in Charlestown is the **Market Place**. Here kids can experience a real slice of Caribbean life at a market that bustles with locals shopping for Caribbean fruits, vegetables, and seafood.

In Charlestown, save some time for a stop at the **Museum of Nevis History**, *Tel. 869/469-5786*. This small museum includes exhibits on indigenous people, Nevis's first residents approximately 4,000 years ago. Other displays include the island's political history, slavery, home crafts, churches, and more. The museum is housed in the home that was the birthplace of Alexander Hamilton, first Secretary of the US Treasury. Exhibits recall the life of this famous Nevis resident. The museum is open Monday through Saturday. If you visit one of Nevis's museums, admission to the second (see Horatio Nelson Museum, below) is half price. Admission is US $2 (children under 12, $1).

Another excellent stop is the **Nelson Museum**, *next to Governor's House, Belle Vue, Tel. 869/469-0408*. The name Horatio Nelson is heard throughout the Caribbean as a naval hero. Today his life is remembered at the Nelson Museum, the largest collection of Nelson memorabilia in the Western hemisphere. Paintings, china, figurines, and remembrances of the naval leader are found here along with displays on Nevisian history. The finest museum in St. Kitts and Nevis, it is well worth a visit. The museum is run by the Nevis Historical and Conservation Society; hours are Monday to Friday 9am to 4pm and Saturday 10am to 1pm. Admission is $2 for adults, $1 for children.

Ready for a little ghost story? Time to make a stop at the **Eden Brown Estate**. These ruins, formerly an estate of a wealthy planter, were the site of a true tragedy. The legend goes that on the eve of his wedding a bridegroom planter and his best man got into a duel and both men were killed. The bride-to-be went mad and is said to haunt the ruins today. The site is grown over and is little more than a few stone walls, but for those with an active imagination it's an interesting stop.

Sports & Recreation

Once the last Kittitian frontier, the **Southeast Peninsula** is now accessible by a modern highway. Some of St. Kitts most beautiful sights and beaches are located along this area, which is also home to many vervet monkeys. (Look for them in the early mornings and late evenings.) **Turtle Beach** is the most popular beach on the peninsula (actually the only one where you might have a little company). On the drive, you'll pass a salt pond with a distinct pink hue, the result of many tiny kroll shrimp. Birders will enjoy this region for its unspoiled opportunities to spot some of the island's species.

With its towering volcano, lush rainforests, and beautiful beaches, St. Kitts offers a full menu of **hikes**. You'll find plenty of soothing walks along powdery beaches for families but also lots of rugged walks and hikes for those with older children and teens.

Guided tours of the rainforest are a popular option, most combining a guided ride with a hike. A far more strenuous hike is to the crater rim of Mt. Liamuiga, an all day excursion only for those ready for a challenge.

Rainforest and volcano tours are available from several operators. **Greg's Safaris**, *PO Box 65, Basseterre, St. Kitts, West*

Indies, 869/465-4121 or 465-5209, Fax 869/465-1057, offers a half day guided Rainforest Safari through mountain trails into the Oceanic Rainforest. Visitors have a chance to look for birdlife, cross springs, identify exotic wildflowers, and enjoy the mist shrouded forest.

Greg's Safari's also offers a full day Volcano Safari. This strenuous trip includes a rugged hike up the volcano to view the mile-wide crater rim, and a chance to see the cloud forest and steaming sulphur vents in the volcanic region. The hike is a tough one, so come prepared with very good walking shoes.

Kriss Tours, *Tel. 869/465-4042*, offers half and full-day tours of the rainforest and, a full-day tour, of the volcanic rim. **Tropical Tours**, *Tel. 869/465-4167*, offers a St. Kitts island tour, half-day rainforest tour and cave explorer tour, and volcano crater tour.

These two islands also offer plenty of diving fun. The most common dive sites are found on the western side of the island in the calmer Caribbean waters. Here visibility runs as much as 100 feet.

Horseback buffs, both trained and prospective, can take their pick of facilities. **Ira Dore's Stable** at Garner's Estate (sign up at your hotel activity desk) offers a combination trail and beach ride on Saturdays and Sundays. Located in the Newcastle area of the island, a horseman will teach you English style riding if needed. Rides last about 1 1/2 hours and cost $40 per person.

The Nevis Equestrian Centre, *Cole Hill, Tel. 869/469-2638*, offers guided tours of the Saddle Hill area, the historic plantations, Nelson's Lookout, historic Gingerland, and other scenic points. Many of the trails offer good views of neighboring islands. Rides last about 1 1/2 hours and cost $45 per person.

The Hermitage, *Tel. 869/469-3477*, has an equestrian center and offers 1 1/2 hour trail ride through historic

Gingerland. Escorted trail rides are English style and taken at the pace of the least skilled rider. Headgear is provided. For riders over 250 pounds, two Belgian horses are available. Riding lessons are also available at The Hermitage. And for those who'd rather let someone else take the reins, plantation carriage rides are offered. The relaxing two or three mile ride travels through historic Gingerland on hilly backroads where vacationers can witness traditional West Indian life. The carriages are authentic Creole adaptations of mid 19th century Victorian styles and are constructed of West Indian mahogany.

WHAT CAN I BUY?

The best shopping stop is St. Kitts' **Caribelle Batik** at Romney Manor. Here you can watch **batik** in progress and hear an explanation of the step-by-step process involved. You can buy the finished product in the form of shirts, wraps, and wall hangings. Prices are reasonable and the batik makes a colorful souvenir of your island visit. We purchased a batik of a string band that brings back good memories of our island stays. (Even if you don't want to buy, it's worth a trip to Romney Manor just to visit the stately greathouse and the grounds shaded by trees that date back hundreds of years. The grounds here are some of the most beautiful in the Leeward Islands.)

In Basseterre, duty-free devotees will find plenty of selection at **Pelican Mall** on the waterfront. This two-story mall, designed with Kittitian architecture and tropical colors, features duty-free shops selling everything from china to liquor to Cuban cigars. Twenty-six shops make this a popular stop, especially for cruise ship passengers who come in from the new cruise ship berth adjacent.

Stamp collectors will be familiar with Nevis because of its often-sought stamps. Stop by the Philatelic Bureau in Charlestown for the best selection. While you're in

Charlestown, stop by the **Handicraft Cooperative**. Located near the Bureau of Tourism, this little shop is a must for arts and crafts shoppers and anyone looking to bring back a Nevisian souvenir. Look for wood carvings, small artwork, and even Nevisian honey here. It's a terrific place for kids to shop with just a few dollars and to pick up a special souvenir that's Nevisian-made.

One of the best stops is **Nevis Pottery** in Newcastle, where artisans craft the local clay soil into various vessels. The pots are finished over a fire of coconut shells behind the shop. The shop is open Monday through Friday and is located near the Newcastle Airport.

PRACTICAL INFORMATION

Currency. The Eastern Caribbean (EC) dollar is legal tender. It is exchanged at a rate fixed to the US dollar: $1 US=2.68 EC.

Driving. Driving is British style on both islands, on the LEFT side of the road.

Information. For brochures and maps of the islands, contact the St. Kitts and Nevis Tourism Office, *Tel. 800/582-6208,* or write *East 75th Street, New York, NY 10021. Fax your information request to 212/734-6511 or e-mail skbnev@ix.netcom.com.*

In Canada, contact the tourism office at *365 Bay Street, Suite 806, Toronto, Ontario M5H2V1. Call for information at 416/368-6707 or Fax 416/368-3934.*

Information on Island. While on St. Kitts, stop by the Basseterre office on the first floor of Pelican Mall for assistance, brochures, and maps. In Nevis, the tourism office is located in Charlestown.

Web site. An excellent source of St. Kitts and Nevis information is the Web page for the islands, accessible at: *http://www.interknowledge.com/stkitts-nevis.*

ISLAND REPORT CARD

Transportation to island	B
Transportation around island	B+
Family Resorts	B
Family Restaurants	B
Friendly atmosphere	A+
Activities for kids	B
Weather	A
New cultures for kids to experience	A
Safety	A+

ST. LUCIA

Jagged peaks clothed in velvety tropical plants, honey-colored beaches shaded by towering palms, and everywhere, colorful blooms and greenery: this is a true garden of Eden.

This is St. Lucia, one of the most beautiful islands in the Caribbean. Orange, lime, lemon, mango (over 100 varieties, we learned), breadfruit, plum, and coffee trees cover the landscape. Pineapples sprout alongside the highway. Spices like vanilla, nutmeg, and cinnamon grow in thick profusion.

But most evident are the bananas. Not just banana trees, but banana plantations. Miles of bananas that stretch to the horizon.

Along with its reputation as a drive-through grocery market, St. Lucia is also abloom with color from a million blossoms: tall flame flowers, orchids, hibiscus, shrimp plants, and more.

Most famous are the Pitons, located in the southwest region of the island. Gros Piton, the shorter but fatter of the two, and Petit Piton are among the Caribbean's most recognizable landmarks.

ARE WE THERE YET?
By Air

Unlike most Caribbean islands, St. Lucia is served by two international airports, so pay close attention here. More than one couple has booked flights into one airport only to discover that their hotel was across the island, over an hour's (expensive) taxi ride away.

The main airport is Hewanorra, located on the southern end of the island. It's the larger of the two airports, with jet service from American Airlines, Air Canada, BWIA, and several European carriers. Hotels near the Pitons are only a short taxi ride from the Hewanorra terminal.

On the northern end of the island lies Vigie International Airport, located in the cities of Castries. This is closest to the bulk of the island's hotel properties, but it is served primarily by smaller carriers such as American Eagle, LIAT, and BWIA with daily service from New York and Miami.

By Ship

Cruise passengers arrive either in Castries or Soufriere. The Castries port is in easy walking distance of duty-free shopping and the Castries market.

Getting Around the Island

For years, St. Lucia was renown for its poor roads, winding potholed terrors that made travel slow and uncomfortable. In 1995, however, the island completed a major road refurbishment project, and we're glad to say that we found travel from one end of the island to the other both speedy and easy.

Taxis are the most common means of transportation for vacationers, but be advised that a journey from the north end of the island to the Piton region is an expensive one: about US $50 one way. Rental cars are available from the airports and the major hotels; look for Avis, Budget, or National Car Rental. You'll need to obtain a local license from the immigration desk at either airport, police station, or from the larger rental dealers. You will also need to present your local driver's license.

Taxis can also be rented by the hour for a private tour. Work out the price with the driver before you leave, but estimate about US $20 per hour.

Tour companies also offer a wide array of guided full- and half-day tours of the island. Visit the rain forest in a open-air jeep (book early for this one since space is limited), take a bus tour to the volcano, the botanical gardens, and the waterfalls, or enjoy a combination tour with a drive down the coast and a catamaran ride back. Sunlink Tours offers a good selection of tours and we found the guides very knowledgeable about everything from island vegetation to history.

Entry Requirements
US citizens need either a passport or birth certificate and a return or onward ticket.

WHICH ONE IS MY ROOM?

ANSE CHASTANET, Soufriere, Tel. 758/459-7000, Fax 758/459-7700. Toll-free reservations Tel. 800/223-1108. Winter from $385 (including breakfast and dinner), summer from $166 with no meals. Credit cards accepted.

For vacationers looking to put as little as possible between the Caribbean and themselves, St. Lucia's Anse Chastanet offers a place where the barriers between guests and the great outdoors are frequently as minimal as three exterior walls.

The vision of architect Nick Troubetzkoy, this hillside resort rises from a quiet bay and palm-lined beach to offer views of St. Lucia's spectacular twin Piton mountains. The architect-owner designed this singular resort to scale the hillside with guest accommodations that offer unique features that offer visitors open-air showers, trees that sprout right up through guest rooms, and open walls where views are uninterrupted by windows or screens.

The resort atmosphere is pure St. Lucian. Anse Chastanet's owners work to preserve the island's natural and cultural resources. "Our allegiance is to the island," points out Troubetzkoy. The resort utilizes island-made furnishings, cloths, foods, and artwork both to offer the guests a genuine island experience and to nurture the culture and economy of St. Lucia. Although it has long been considered one of the most romantic resorts in the Caribbean, Anse Chastanet also is a family experience for families with children five years and older. (Open walls and steep walkways make it inappropriate for families with infants and toddlers.)

Marine biology classes are held two times a week for children age 5 to 11. Children 12 and older can participate in a Learn to SCUBA course to lead to certification. Another choice for children 12 and over and adults is the "Dive 'n' Discover" course to introduce non-certified divers to the reef.

The simple guest rooms are decorated in West Indian style, with furniture that is produced on St. Lucia, usually from the Soufriere region. Beds, chairs, and couches are covered in a simple madras, the national cloth of St. Lucia, and covers are changed every three months to provide a different look for frequent return guests. Rooms are all oversized, ranging from 900 to 1,600 square feet.

Amenities include hair dryers, refrigerators, coffee makers, and ceiling fans. Although they're not always necessary, for guests' convenience mosquito nets are provided, along with electric mosquito coils. Telephones are not available in rooms; an outdoor bank of phones for guest use is located near the main office. Guests check for messages on a chalkboard posted nearby.

CLUB ST. LUCIA, *Castries, Tel. 758/450-0551, Fax 758/450-0281. Toll-free US and Canadian reservations Tel. 800/777-1250. Winter rates from $284 for family room, summer from $256 for family room. Credit cards accepted.*

Located on 50 acres in the northern tip of St. Lucia, this all-inclusive resort is a favorite with families. Over 370 guest rooms include standard, ocean view, and family rooms, with an air-conditioned bedroom with king size bed, a separate living room with ceiling fan and convertible couch that can sleep two children, and a patio area.

Family activities range from use of two swimming pools (one with a shallow child area), two beaches, two tennis courts (plus complimentary membership at the St. Lucia Racquet

Club on hotel grounds), free tennis clinics, sunfish sailing, snorkeling, water-skiing, canoeing, and windsurfing as well as beach cricket, golf clinics, bicycling, volleyball, and classes in everything from local dancing to coconut carving.

The all-inclusive program includes all meals, beverages, taxes, service charges, evening entertainment, daily sports and recreational activities, watersports, tennis, and the daily supervised children's program.

Children age four to 12 are welcome at the kids' club, which operates from 9:30am to 12:30pm and 2pm to 5pm. Activities include field trips, videos, face painting, T-shirt designing, cooking classes, and games. Special activities are also organized for teenagers.

WHAT ARE WE DOING NEXT?

St. Lucia has one of the most unique children's programs in the Caribbean. "Safari Summer", designed by the National Trust, is designed for family vacationers to learn more about St. Lucia's heritage and to have fun.

Three age groups are included in the activities and all are supervised by counselors, many of them local teachers. Pigeon Island Summer Club is aimed at children aged 5-8; Kids' Safari Summer is for children aged 9-12, and Teen Tours is for vacationers from ages 13 to 18. Activities range from hikes and nature walks to photography, crafts, folk dances, and drumming. Teen participants can also enjoy field trips to the mangroves, wildlife sanctuaries, and coastal trails.

The cost of the program is $15 per day or $60 per week or $120 for the full two week program. For dates of upcoming Safari programs, call the St. Lucia Tourist Board, *Tel. 800/456-3984 or 212/867-2950.*

On the northern reach of the island lies **Pigeon Island**, a 35-minute drive from Castries. No longer a true island but connected to the main island by causeway, Pigeon Island has a long history as everything from a pirate hideout to a

232 CARIBBEAN WITH KIDS

military fort. The ruins of the fort can still be seen at Pigeon Island National Park, a popular day trip for north shore vacationers and the site of many of St. Lucia's festivals.

Most guests stay on the northeast section of the island near **Castries**, the island's largest city with a population of 60,000. This capital city was destroyed by fire several times, but some colonial period wooden structures still remain. You'll see several of them as you head south on Government House Road. This twisting, climbing slice of road is slow going but offers you a great view. Save time for a stop across from the Governor's House for a panoramic look at the city. From atop Morne Fortune, hill of good luck (not such good luck for the French soldiers who resided here in the 18th century; they were plagued with yellow fever), you'll have a postcard view over Castries Harbour, Vigie Peninsula and Pigeon Island.

Continuing south, the road soon drops into a veritable forest: the first of several **banana plantations**. Driving past this display of the island's number one crop, you'll see blue plastic bags hanging from many trees. These cover the bananas themselves to shield the crop from insects and bruising by the banana leaves. The banana plant yields only one crop during its lifetime, a process that takes nine months to bear fruit.

Marigot Harbour, located just off the main road, is the next stop. This magical harbor, often considered to be the most beautiful in the Caribbean, is dotted with yachts from around the globe. If you don't have your own, don't worry. The Moorings, a company headquartered in the British Virgin Islands, can rent you a yacht with or without a crew to enjoy a sailing vacation of your own. Landlubbers will enjoy the scenic harbor as well, and may recognize it from the movie *Dr. Doolittle*.

South of Marigot, the road passes through many small communities and fishing villages. Make time for a walk around **Anse La Raye** (Beach of the Ray), a traditional St. Lucian fishing village. Enjoy a walk along the waterfront to view the hand-crafted fishing canoes painted in bright primary colors and the various fishing nets and traps used in these waters. In town, stroll past traditional Caribbean homes with lawns outlined in conch shells, past the large Roman Catholic church, and make a stop in the authentic Creole bakery for a treat.

The **Soufriere** region is the heartland of the island's many attractions. There's no denying that the most scenic part of the island is this south-central region. Starting with the rain forest and continuing down to the Pitons, this spectacular region is the breadbasket of the island. Every tropical fruit and vegetable thrives in this rich region, which is sparsely populated.

For many families, the most fascinating area is the **rain forest**. You'll need a guide to enter the restricted rain forest region, so sign up for a guided tour with one of the island's tour operators. Hiking tours are available with guides from the Forestry Department. You'll walk through the dense foliage, swim in a tropical waterfall, and learn more about the plants that make up this fragile ecosystem. And, if you're lucky, you may have the opportunity to see the rare St. Lucian parrot .

This area is also home to a unique **Sulphur Spring volcano**, often called the "drive-through volcano." Actually, visitors cannot drive or walk through the volcano anymore (a few years ago a Rasta guide fell through a weak part of the crust—and fortunately received only severe burns). Groups walk only to the edge of the volcano which last erupted two centuries ago. With the smell of sulphur heavy in the air, you'll see jets of bubbling water black with ash and bubbling with gases released from deep in the earth's core. (Leave your silver jewelry back at the hotel for this trip. The gases can cause silver to tarnish.)

Sports & Recreation

Another major attraction of St. Lucia is its **scuba diving**. Anse Chastanet is considered to be the top dive spot on the island and one of the best in the Caribbean. The reason? Extraordinary fish life, coral formations, and sponge growth right off shore. Divers and snorkelers can enjoy spectacular underwater exploration just yards from the beach.

St. Lucia's **beaches** run from golden brown to a salt-and-pepper mixture of sand and volcanic elements. Some of the most popular beaches are Anse Chastanet, Anse Cochon, and Reduit Beach. Sunbathers take note: topless and nude sunbathing is prohibited throughout St. Lucia.

For fun away from the water, Trim's National Riding, *Tel. 758/450-8273*, offers **horse and carriage rides**. All levels of riders are accommodated on guided rides along the Caribbean or Atlantic beaches.

WHAT CAN I BUY?

Castries, the island's largest town, is also its top shopping area. Here you'll have a choice between malls and markets for everything from fine jewels to handmade crafts that capture the island spirit.

Pointe Seraphine is the island's duty-free port. Here you'll find well-known chains such as Little Switzerland, Colombian Emeralds and Benetton. (Remember to bring your passport and return airline tickets to take advantage of the duty-free shopping. Items can be taken with you at point of purchase.) Pointe Seraphine is open weekdays, and on Saturdays, until 1pm only. Like most shops in St. Lucia, the mall is closed on Sundays.

Outside of Castries, make a stop at **Caribelle Batik** for handmade batik shirts, wraps, and scarves. In Choiseul, stop by the **Choiseul Arts and Crafts Center**. This town is known as the crafts center of the island, and here you'll find straw, wood, and clay handcrafts, all manufactured locally.

For teen shoppers, another local item that's a good reminder of your vacation is perfume. **Caribbean Perfumes**, located in Castries, captures the scents of the islands with perfumes for both men and women. Caribbean Perfumes are sold at shops across the island, including most resort gift stores.

PRACTICAL INFORMATION

Currency. The Eastern Caribbean (EC) dollar is the official currency. The exchange rate is fixed to the US dollar at US $1 equals EC $2.65.

Electricity. The current on the island is 220 volts, 50 cycles. Some hotels offer 110 volts, 60 cycles. Also, socket styles vary, although most are the three-pin style with square plugs (UK).

Hospitals. Four hospitals are available on the island. Most hotels have a doctor on call that will make "house" calls.

Information. Contact the St. Lucia Tourist Board, *Tel. 800/456-3984.* For additional information, write the St. Lucia Tourist Board, *820 Second Avenue, 9th Floor, New York, NY 10017.* In Canada, write to *130 Spadina Avenue, Suite 703, Toronto, Ontario M3V 2L4, Tel. 416/703-0141, Fax 416/703-0181.*

Information on island. Contact the Tourist Board at Pointe Seraphin in Castries, *Tel. 758/452-5968.*

Web site. Check out the official site of the St. Lucia Tourist Board for up-to-date information on the island: *http://www.interknowledge.com/st-lucia.*

ST. MARTIN/SINT MAARTEN

This island calls itself "a little European and a lot Caribbean." It's a fitting description of a most unusual political situation: two nations sharing a single, small piece of land. The smallest mass on the globe shared by two nations, it's a peaceful neighboring of French and Dutch that offers vacationers twice the cultural experience. Travelers can enjoy fine French food, topless French beaches, Dutch architecture, and Dutch casinos that ring with baccarat and roulette all in an atmosphere that's definitely West Indian.

Although the border is almost superficial, there are distinctions between the two countries. Mention "St. Martin" and many visitors will immediately think of fine dining and charming sidewalk cafes. French is heard in the markets and there's no mistaking that this is *la partie francaise.*

The Dutch influence is felt far less strongly in Sint Maarten than the Gallic influence in St. Martin. Although the official language taught in the schools, Dutch is rarely heard on the street. And although it falls under the government of the Netherlands Antilles and the Kingdom of the Netherlands, the US dollar reigns here. The atmosphere is strictly West Indian with an eye toward American commerce. US dollars are accepted freely and shopping on the Dutch side is more American-style than in St. Martin, which features more European-style shops.

ARE WE THERE YET?

By Air

Air service is available at two airports on the island: Princess Juliana International Airport on Dutch St. Maarten and L'Esperance Airport in Grand Case on the French side. The French airport is served only by a few commuter flights from St. Barts and Guadeloupe and private planes. Most travelers arrive in Dutch Sint Maarten.

Travel time to the island from is 2 1/2 hours from Miami, 3 1/2 from New York, 4 1/2 from Dallas, 5 from Montreal, and 8 hours from Paris.

Princess Juliana is a major airport and a Caribbean hub for inter-island travel. Service is available from American Airlines, Continental, USAirways, Northwest Airlines, and others from Europe.

By Boat

In Philipsburg, Sint Maarten, the new $2.5 million Captain Hodge Wharf, can accommodate up to 600 passengers an hour (triple the size of the former tender pier). It's the first step in a $60 million master improvement plan for the area.

The new wharf includes a Tourist Information Center and is now the disembarkation point for over 650,000 cruise ship passengers annually. The site is named for Captain Arsene Hodge who, beginning in 1938, operated the first government ship delivering mail, passengers, and goods between St. Maarten and Saba, Statia, and St. Kitts.

The new wharf regularly welcomes cruise passengers from Carnival, Costa, Norway, Cunard, Club Med, Celebrity, and other lines.

In Marigot, the cruise pier is located at the market and is used to tender cruise passengers to this area. It sports a new look, thanks to renovations that occurred during the filming of the movie *Speed 2: Cruise Control.*

Entry Requirements

US citizens need a current passport, an expired one less than five years old or other proof of citizenship (a birth certificate with raised seal or a notarized copy along with driver's license) and a return or onward ticket. Immigration is in the airport only; there is no border check between the French and Dutch sides. Canadian citizens need to present a valid passport as well as a return or onward ticket.

WHICH ONE IS MY ROOM?

French St. Martin

LA SAMANNA, *Tel. 011/590-87-6400, Fax 011/590-87-8786. Toll-free reservations Tel. 800/854-2252. Rates run $575-$900 in winter months, $325-$575 in summer, including breakfast. Credit cards accepted.*

This 80-room resort is often cited as one of the Caribbean's most luxurious. A member of Rosewood Hotels and Resorts, whose other properties include Little Dix and Caneel Bay, this resort features rooms with cool white interiors, bamboo and mahogany furniture, and a genteel atmosphere. La Samanna was closed by damage from Hurricane Luis, but has reopened with a fresh face and restored grounds.

ESMERALDA RESORT, *Orient Beach. Toll-free reservations Tel. 800/622-7836. Rates start at $180-$210 in low season. Credit cards accepted.*

From the action packed waters off Orient Beach, the green roofs of Esmeralda Resort are easy to spot. Fifteen villas, accommodating 54 guest rooms, are sprinkled across the low rise hills that rise up from Baie Orientale. Each villa includes its own swimming pool; accommodations offer air-conditioning, satellite TV, telephones, fully equipped kitchenettes, and private terraces. A poolside restaurant, L'Astrolabe, offers continental cuisine.

LE MERIDIEN AND L'HABITATION LE DOMAINE, *Anse Marcel, Tel. 001/590-87-6700. Toll-free reservations Tel. 800/543-4300. Rates run $300-$500 at L'Habitation or $380-$600 at Le Domaine in the winter months; $190-$350 and $220-$380 in the summer months respectively. Credit cards accepted.*

These two adjoining resorts, L'Habitation and Le Domain, are located on the island's northeast coast, tucked into Marcel Cove. Surrounded by a 150-acre nature preserve, the resort is landscaped with bougainvillea, hibiscus, and oleander. Guest rooms, with bright Caribbean colors, include 251 rooms at L'Habitation with garden or marina views and 145 rooms and suites at the newer wing, Le Domaine. Facilities include swimming pools, private white sand beach, shuttle service to casinos, Philipsburg, and Marigot. Watersports activities are deep sea fishing, marina activities, motorboat, sail, power, and glass bottom boating, sailing and catamaran boating, scuba diving, water skiing, canoeing, jet skiing, kayaking, and more. Horseback riding, racquetball, squash, fitness center, and tennis also available.

Villas

Several villas rental companies offer families the option of staying in a fully furnished villa, complete with cooking facilities and plenty of room. Contact these villa rental companies for information: **Carimo**, *Tel. 011/590-87-57-58, Fax 011/590-87-71-88*, **Immobilier St. Martin Caraibes**, *Tel. 011/590-87-55-21*, **West Indies Immobilier**, *Tel. 011/590-87-56-48*, **International Immobilier**, *Tel. 011/590-87-79-00*, **Sprimtour**, *Tel. 011/590-87-58-65*, and **Interprom**, *Tel. 011/590-87-32-46*.

Dutch Sint Maarten

MAHO BEACH HOTEL AND CASINO, *Simpson Bay, Tel. 011/599-5-52115, Fax 011/599-5-53180. Toll-free reservations Tel. 800/223-0757. Winter rates from $225, summer from $155. Credit cards accepted.*

This 600-room hotel is located within walking distance of plenty of action for those who are looking for nightlife. A high-rise built around a sprawling freshwater pool, this resort is the heart of the nightlife because it is the home of the island's largest casino and just across the street from one of its most popular nightspots: Cheri's Cafe. However, we found many members of the resort staff less than personable and encountered difficulties several times during our stay.

DIVI LITTLE BAY, *Philipsburg, Tel. 011/599-5-22333, Fax 011/599-5-23911. Toll-free reservations Tel. 800/367-3484. Rates start at $150-$225 in low season. Credit cards accepted.*

Perched on a peninsula between Great Bay and Little Bay, this newly reopened property offers spectacular views. The 159-room resort offers typical hotel rooms as well as studios and one-bedroom units. Facilities include a restaurant, pool, and water activities center.

GREAT BAY BEACH HOTEL, *Philipsburg, Tel. 011/599-5-22446, Fax 011/599-5-23008. Toll-free reservations Tel. 800/223-0757. Winter rates start at $180 per person for double occupancy; summer rates start at $135 per person with double occupancy. Credit cards accepted.*

Located ten minutes from downtown Philipsburg, this 285-room hotel offers visitors 24-hour fun. Daytime activities include watersports (wave runners, sailboats, windsurfing, snorkeling, paddleboats), tennis, beach, and two swimming pools. Rates are all-inclusive and include transfers, three meals daily, drinks by the glass, sunset cruise, sightseeing tour, windsurfing, snorkeling, and sailing, scuba clinic, and more.

PELICAN RESORT AND CASINO, *Pelican Key, Tel. 011/599-5-42503, Fax 011/599-5-42133. Winter rates from $114, Summer from $95. Credit cards accepted.*

This all-suites property is located on the beach and is a good choice for families. Rooms include fully equipped kitchens; families can select from hillside, poolside, or beachfront accommodations. Five swimming pools (not to mention the beach) keep waterlovers happy. A children's pool is available, along with a children's playground and baby-sitting.

Adults find plenty of activity as well including tennis, watersports, spa, and a shopping arcade.

Villa Rental Companies

These rental companies handle a variety of island properties:

Caribbean Concepts	Tel. 800/423-4433
Caribbean Resorts and Villas	Tel. 800/955-8180
Condo and Villa Authority	Tel. 800/831-5512
Coral Shore Villas	Tel. 800/942-6725
Island Properties	Tel. 800/738-9444
Leslie's Vacation Villas	Tel. 800/888-0897
Unusual Villas and Island Rental	Tel. 804/288-2823
Vacation Home Rentals	Tel. 800/633-3284

WHAT IS THERE TO DO?

There's no denying that St. Martin's beautiful **beaches**, nearly 40 in all, are one of this island's top assets. Whether you're looking for pulsating action or blissful privacy, you'll find it somewhere on the island. On the French side, topless sunbathing is standard and nudity is permitted on the nude beach at Orient Bay, so prepare your children first if you plan a visit to this bustling beach.

One of the top destinations for families is **Butterfly Farm**, Tel. 011/590-873121. This "ferme des Papillons" is a unique attraction and well worth the drive for anyone interested in butterflies. You'll enter the butterfly's world and stroll among plants in which they make their home. The colorful insects are free-flying, gracefully floating and flitting from plant to plant as they eat. Eighty species of butterflies are found at this farm including many longwings and flames. These tropical species reproduce all year so you can see the butterflies in different life stages. The most famous butterfly in the world, the morpho, is seen floating like blue crepe paper from plant to plant. Its blue tint was once used to make watermarks for US bills. Bring along your camera for this tour.

The farm is open from 9 to 4:30; guided tours are $10. Once you have bought a ticket, you're welcome to come back any time during your visit.

Sports & Recreation

Horseback riders will find plenty of action on both sides of St. Martin. Bayside Riding Club, *Tel. 011/590-873664, Fax 011/590-873376*, offers beach rides, riding lessons, pony rides, and even horse leasing. Beach rides follow the surf and, if you're on the island at the right time, full moon rides can be a unique experience. Bayside Riding Club is located next to Orient Bay on the road to Le Galion Beach.

Caid and Isa, *Tel. 011/590-87-32-79*, at Anse Marcel (near Le Meridien) offers two rides daily at 9am and 3pm except on Sunday. Six paso finos are stabled and available for hire at $40 for a 2 1/2 hour excursion that goes over the hills of Anse Marcel to the beach of Petites Cayes, also known as Anse de la Pomme d'Adam or Adam's Apple Cove.

St. Maarten offers **scuba diving** for first timers and advanced divers. Visibility ranges from 75 to 125 feet in these waters which are home to a wide array of marine life. Waters are warm year around, averaging 70 degrees.

Good visibility makes **snorkeling** popular around St. Maarten's beaches. The top snorkel spot is Little Bay Beach, with good reefs and calm waters except during a southeast wind.

Snorkel trips are also available from several operators. Sand Dollar, *Tel. 011/5995-42640*, offers three hour snorkel excursions to Creole Rock. Departing at 10am and 2pm from Pelican Marina Tuesday through Saturdays, the trips includes sightseeing through Simpson Bay Lagoon, Marigot harbor, Friar's Bay, Happy Bay, and Grand Case, and use of snorkel equipment, view boards, and drinks.

For many travelers, a good day's adventure is **sailing** around the island, a little snorkeling, and a deck picnic or perhaps an elegant sunset sail to watch the lights come out in Dutch Sint Maarten.

Costs vary by activity and operator. Catamaran cruises run about $45 a person for a half day sail and range from $50-$70 for a full day cruise. Power boat excursions run about $95 for a full day. Sailboat cruises average about $65-$70 for a day sail. Lagoon cruises cost about $28 per person and dinner cruises run about $60.

Day Excursions

Explore neighboring St. Barts with a quick trip aboard the Voyager 2, *Tel. 011/590-87-20-28, Fax 011/590-87-20-78*, which departs from Marigot to Gustavia, St. Barts at 9am and 5:45pm daily (reservations required for Sunday departure). The hour and a half trip aboard the high-speed boat is comfortable, air conditioned, and includes a stocked bar. Round trip is $50 plus a $9 tax. A package including lunch and an island tour is available for $80 plus a $9 tax and, considering the dining prices on St. Barts, is a real bargain. Car rental is available for day trippers as well for $40.

From Grand Case, St. Barth Commuter offers day trips to nearby St. Barts. Flights depart on Wednesdays from Grand Case a 9am and return at 4:30 p.m. Round trip air fare, including taxes, is US $80. A minimum of six participants, maximum of nine is required. Bookings are accepted only until the preceding Monday at 3pm. Additional flights are available to Anguilla, Antigua, Barbuda, Guadeloupe, Nevis, St. Kitts, and Statia. For information, contact St. Barth Commuter, Customer Service, Aeroport de Grand Case, *Tel. and Fax 011/590-87-75-70*.

Sint Maarten's proximity to other islands give vacationers the opportunity to visit St. Barts and Saba (take a day trip to Anguilla from Marigot in French St. Martin). The Edge Ferry Service offers two excursions. Travel to Saba, the tiny island that's really a volcanic peak, on Wednesday,

Friday and Sunday. Departure is at 9am from Pelican Marina at Simpson Bay, return is at 5pm The trip takes one hour and costs $60 round trip. Or, for a Gallic experience, travel to nearby St. Barts (or St. Barts), a 45-minute excursion aboard the ferry. The 9 to 5 trip runs Tuesday, Thursday, and Saturday; cost is $50 roundtrip plus a $7 port charge. For information or reservations on either trip, *call Tel. 011/ 5995-42640/42503 extension 1553 or Fax 011/5995-42476.*

WHAT CAN I BUY?

French St. Martin

On the French side, the best shopping is in the capital city of Marigot. A crafts market near the cruise terminal offers jewelry, T-shirt, souvenir items, carvings, and paintings (we were especially taken with the Haitian artwork available here). We've bought lots of inexpensive children's gifts in this market: wooden turtles that open to hold jewelry or small treasures for $10, painted wooden animals from Haiti for $3, and for teens inexpensive silver jewelry starting at about $10 and pareos for about $10.

Marigot also is home to boutique shops open 9am to 12:30pm and 3 to 7pm.

Dutch Sint Maarten

In Philipsburg, shops line Frontstreet, the narrow boulevard nearest the waterfront. In these duty-free stores, electronic goods, leather, jewelry, and liquor (especially guavaberry liqueur) are especially good buys. (For the best prices, shop on days when the cruise ships are not in port.) No duties are charged in or out of port (one of the few such ports in the world), so savings run about 25-50% on consumer goods at this popular duty-free stop. Shop carefully, though, and know prices on specific goods before you leave home. Some items are not such bargains.

Most shops are found on Philipsburg's Frontstreet. Typically, shops open at 8 or 9am and remain open until noon, then reopen from 2 to 6 daily. When cruises ships are in port, most shops remain open through the lunch hours.

PRACTICAL INFORMATION

Currency. The official currency for the French side is the French franc; the Dutch side uses the Netherlands Antilles guilder. However, you'll rarely see either currency. US dollars are used almost exclusively on both sides of the island.

Information. For information on Sint Maarten, call Tel. 800/ST MAARTEN for information on the Dutch side of the island including transportation, accommodations, and activities or write:

St. Maarten Tourist Office
675 Third Avenue, Suite 1806
New York, NY 10017
Tel. 212/953-2084
Fax 212/953-2145

For information on the French side, call "France On Call," *Tel. 900/990-0040.* This is a toll call and provides information on all lands which are part of France. You can write the French Government Tourist Office nearest you:

New York office:
444 Madison Avenue
New York, NY 10022

California office:
9454 Wilshire Boulevard, Suite 715
Beverky Hills, CA 90212

Chicago office:
676 N. Michigan Avenue, Suite 3360
Chicago, IL 60611

Montreal office:
1981 Avenue McGill College, 490
Montreal, Quebec, Canada H3A 2W9

Toronto office:
30 St. Patrick Street, Suite 700
Toronto, Ontario, Canada M5T 3A3

Information on Island. While on island, you'll find an information center at the cruise terminal in Philipsburg:

St. Maarten Tourist Bureau
Walter Nisbeth Road, 23
Philipsburg, St. Maarten
Netherlands Antilles
Tel. 011/5995-22337
Fax 011/5995-22734

On the French side, stop by the St. Martin Tourist Office near the waterfront in Marigot; the office is open Monday through Friday 8:30 to 1, 2:30-5:30 and Saturday from 8 to noon.

Web sites. Check out the Dutch Sint Maarten web site at this address: *http://www.st-maarten.com*. The French Martin site is located at *http://www.interknowledge.com/st.martin*.

ISLAND REPORT CARD

Transportation to island	A
Transportation around island	A-
Family Resorts	B
Family Restaurants	B
Friendly atmosphere	B
Activities for kids	B+
Weather	A
New cultures for kids to experience	A+
Safety	B

TRINIDAD & TOBAGO

Trinidad and Tobago may share membership in the same independent republic. They may share the Trinidad-Tobago currency, the TT dollar. And they may both enjoy the same idyllic climate, located south of the hurricane zone and rarely disturbed by the storms that can ravage other Caribbean islands in the summer and fall months.

But that's where the similarities between these two islands stop. Like city and country cousins, Trinidad and Tobago each have their own unique personalities and their own distinct attributes.

Trinidad is by far the largest, both in terms of population and size. This anvil-shaped island bustles with activity in Port of Spain, the capital city that's also a capital in the world of Caribbean commerce. Here you'll hear accents from residents who have relocated from around the world to work in this modern metropolis. The Indian influence is stronger here than anywhere else in the Caribbean, and is seen in the faces of islanders, the architecture, food, and religion of the island, where nearly one quarter of all residents are Hindu.

Both islands are especially popular with nature lovers and are veritable gardens of Eden for families to enjoy.

ARE WE THERE YET?
By Air

Trinidad's Piarco International Airport is served by American Airlines and BWIA. The airport is located about a half hour drive from Port of Spain, a taxi ride of about $20 US.

You can reach Tobago's Crown Point International Airport, near the town of Scarborough, on American Eagle from San Juan or via a 20-minute flight on Air Caribbean, *Tel. 868/623-2500.* Air Caribbean passengers should reconfirm their flight arrangements the day before flying; these inter-island hops are very popular especially on holidays and week-ends and many passengers are wait-listed for seats.

By Ferry

Ferry service connects Trinidad and Tobago. The journey, a six-hour trip, is usually taken only by those bringing autos to Tobago.

Entry Requirements

You must show a valid passport to gain admittance to Trinidad or Tobago.

Getting Around the Island

Taxis are a common means of transportation on both islands. Driving in Port of Spain is a little like participating in a stock car race, so most vacationers opt for a cab. Inexpensive options are the maxi taxis, vans which cover different areas of the island (locations are designated by the color of the stripe on the side of the vans). Maxi taxis stop anywhere along their routes.

In Tobago, taxis also frequent Scarborough's streets, but visitors on the north end of the island may find rental cars a better option. Thrifty Car Rental and several local companies offer rentals from Crown Point airport.

WHICH ONE IS MY ROOM?

Trinidad

TRINIDAD HILTON, *Port of Spain, Tel. 868/624-3211 ext. 6040, Fax 868/624-4485. Toll-free US phone number Tel. 800/HILTONS. Winter rates $235-$255, Summer rates $225-$255. Credit cards accepted.*

Conrad Hilton's personal project still exudes an air of comfort and elegance amid a bustling city. This hotel is known as the "upside-down Hilton" because the lobby and ground level make up the top floor and the guest rooms are located downhill.

Visitors are met by walkways of smooth teak, grown on the island and used in furniture and railings throughout the hotel. Rooms are similar to those found in other traditional business-oriented hotels, but all include a private balcony overlooking Queen's Park Savannah. Carnival is held directly across the street from the hotel, so during that time come prepared to party—like it or not.

THE NORMANDIE HOTEL, *Port of Spain, Tel. 868/624-1181-4, Fax 868/624-1181. Winter and summer rates from $86. Credit cards accepted.*

The Normandie Hotel is small (53 rooms) and is an intimate place in which to enjoy the downtown region in a setting much like a country inn. This property may be small in size, but, it has a large number of amenities to offer its guests: an excellent shopping arcade and cultural events scheduled every month. Rooms here are simple, and for the most room consider a split level loft, perfect for families. A freshwater pool is available.

Tobago

COCO REEF RESORT, *Coconut Bay, Tel. 868/639-8571, Fax 868/639-8574. Toll-free reservations Tel. 800/221-1294. $198-$220 for rooms ($350-$1500 for suites) in high season. Credit cards accepted.*

From an entrance highlighted by a Classic Rolls Royce Silver Cloud parked beneath a columned porte-cochere to a breezy, open-air public area filled with wicker furniture, the mood here is one of elegance combined with a relaxed Caribbean atmosphere. The hotel requests no jeans, T-shirts, or shorts in public areas after 7pm

Europeans make up the bulk of Coco Reef's clientele, led by Germany and England, each with 35% of the guest list. Americans, mostly from the Northeastern states, compose 18% of the Coco Reef's visitors. Coco Reef's guests include honeymooners, couples, and families with children.

Supervised activities are available for children, and families can have the services of a nanny during their stay.

One hundred ocean view rooms make up the bulk of the property, each with Saltillo-tiled patios or balconies. Other categories include superior rooms with no ocean view, six suites, five villas, a presidential suite, and the sunset villa, with a private lawn and decks overlooking the sea.

All rooms include air conditioning, satellite TV, a mini-refrigerator, direct dial telephone, hair dryer, and twice daily maid service. Wicker furniture and walls decorated with hand stenciling emphasizing the pineapple, the theme of the hotel and the symbol for hospitality, complete a cozy look for the rooms.

Coco Reef is located between two top Tobago beaches, but the hotel itself is situated on a small man-made beach. Protected by a breakwater, the calm waters are excellent for young swimmers. Snorkeling, windsurfing, and Sunfish sailing are offered nearby. Pool lovers will also find a freshwater pool or, for more active recreation, two Har-Tru tennis courts are lit for day or night play; lessons are available from the resort pro. Guests also have complimentary access to a fitness center, part of a complete spa facility.

LE GRAND COURLAN, *Black Rock, Tel. 868/639-9667, Fax 868/639-9292. Toll-free US phone number Tel. 800/INSIGNIA. Early winter rates from $410. Credit cards accepted.*

Tobago's most elegant resort features a new spa with a teak floor for aerobics, massage rooms, juice bar, hot and cold Jacuzzis. Based upon the Eastern philosophy that right angles create stress, the spa walls are curved.

GRAFTON BEACH RESORT, *Black Rock, Tel. 868/639-0191, Fax 868/639-0030. Toll-free US phone number Tel. 800/223-6510. Winter rates from $225-$400, summer from $162-$300. Credit cards accepted.*

Grafton Beach Resort exudes fun. At the 114-room property all rooms include TV, minibar, and air conditioning. Families enjoy a freshwater pool as well as watersports and squash on property. Activities also include deep sea fishing, horseback riding, sailing, and kayaking.

PLANTATION VILLAS, *Black Rock, Tel. 868/639-9377, Fax 868/639-0455. Toll-free US phone number Tel. 800-74-CHARMS. Winter rates $495 (for four people). Credit cards accepted.*

For villa lovers, these two-story homes are a dream come true. They lie just steps from the sea and from both Le Grand Courlon and Grafton Beach Resorts. The villas, with a full kitchen, living and dining room, and three bedrooms, are filled with locally crafted furniture. Perfect for families, each home tempts residents with wide porches across the back of the homes, overlooking a tropical garden. A freshwater pool is available for guests' use and is adjoined by a bar.

Housekeeping services are provided daily, and cooking and baby-sitting are also available.

REX TURTLE BEACH, *Courland Bay, Tel. 868/639-2851, Fax 868/639-1495. Toll-free US phone number 800/255-5859. Winter rates from $140 per person all-inclusive, summer rates from $110 per person. Credit cards accepted.*

The Rex hotel chain is well known among UK travelers, but its offering should also be a favorite with North American vacationers. Like its name suggests, this hotel is located right on a beach favored by turtles as a nesting site. The atmosphere here is casual and fun, enjoyed by an international array of visitors who come to soak up Tobago's sun. The hotel offers 125 rooms, each with oceanview.

BLUE WATERS INN, *Speyside, Tel. 868/660-4341, Fax 868/660-5195. Toll-free US phone number 800/74-CHARMS.*

Winter rates from $130, summer rates from $85. Credit cards accepted.

This beachfront hotel is casual and fun. Situated on the edge of Batteaux Bay, this resort is perfect for families who plan to spend time enjoying nature, either on the resort's 46 acres of tropical foliage or in the clear waters best known as the home of giant manta rays. Activity is the name of the game here, and it comes in forms such as scuba diving, snorkeling, windsurfing, glass-bottom boat tours of the reef, deep sea fishing, tennis, and more.

> ### CARNIVAL
>
> When it comes to festivals, no island can beat Trinidad at Carnival. This is more than a festival; it's a way of life. Held the Monday and Tuesday prior to Ash Wednesday, this pre-Lenten blowout is preceded by weeks of parties, balls, competitions, and calypso shows. J'ouvert, Carnival Monday, starts at 2am as Trinidadians take to the streets in costume. Partiers practice Carnival dances: chipping (a slow shuffle down the street), jumping up, and wining. Soca music pulsates from giant trucks while steel pans deliver traditional calypso sounds.
>
> Should you visit Trinidad during Carnival? Only if you're looking for pulsating action around the clock. Otherwise, stick to other weeks for a visit to this island. Tobago is quiet during Carnival but it's traditional for merrymakers to recuperate with a Tobago vacation following Carnival festivities, so crowds are larger than usual during that time as well.

WHAT ARE WE DOING NEXT?

Nature tours definitely rank as a top attraction on Trinidad. The **Asa Wright Nature Centre**, *Tel. 868/667-4655*, is the island's top spot for naturalists and birders, who can enjoy guided walks on nature trails or go off on their own in search of multi-color hummingbirds and many of the island's other tropical species. Near Port of Spain, the **Caroni Swamp**, *Tel. 868/637-9664 Fax 868/625-6980*, is a sanctuary that's home to the scarlet ibis, and in the sunset hours the sky turns truly scarlet as these birds come in to roost in the mangroves. Boat tours are available for a closer look at these beautiful birds.

Although Trinidad is not known for its beaches, **Maracas Bay**, located on the north shore, is a popular spot with both tourists and residents. About an hour from Port of Spain, the drive to this area is a treat in itself, winding through the Northern Range with views of forests where species such as howler and capuchin monkeys, ocelot, Amazon parrots, and wild pigs can be found. Make a stop at the Hot Bamboo Hut for a taste of spicy mango slices in pepper and a beautiful view of the coastline. Nearby, Maracas Bay offers a full day of fun, with complete changing facilities, chair rentals, watersports, and local food such as "shark and bake," a fast food snack made with fresh shark encased in a pancake sandwich.

In Port of Spain, the **Queen's Park Savannah** is a top stop. This central park, encircled by what's termed the world's longest roundabout, is home to cricket fields, botanical gardens, and tall trucks selling green coconuts. Enjoy a walk around the Savannah, which is lined with grand historic homes, and stop for a drink of coconut water.

Nature attractions are also a big draw on Tobago. Of special interest are the **leatherback turtles** who come to nest on the leeward side of the island between March and August. Come out after sunset between 7pm and 5am for the best chance of viewing these large marine turtles when they come ashore to lay between 80 and 125 eggs in the sand. The tiny offspring make their run for the sea about two months later.

Sports & Recreation

Cruising Tobago's calm waters is a fun a way to look at the island's beautiful coast. The Loafer, *Tel. 868/639-7312,* a 50-foot catamaran, departs from Buccoo Reef, the most popular beach on the island for all day cruises as well as sunset sails and full moon dinners. The all-day trip includes a swim at the **Nylon Pool**, a calm, shallow area in the sea formed by a sandbar close to the surface where guests of all swimming levels enjoy a swim.

Divers often head straight to Speyside, located on the northern tip of the island. Here they might have the opportunity to swim with giant manta rays; dolphins, turtles, whale sharks and porpoises are sometimes spotted. This area is especially rich, with a profusion of coral growth and marine life, because of Venezuela's Orinoco River. The river's nutrients flow through the Guyana current that brushes Tobago and provides the island with some of the Caribbean's best diving.

WHAT CAN I BUY?

The best purchase on Trinidad and Tobago for children are **steel pans**. Child-size drums are available for under $10 and are marked with the notes; some also come with simple song books. The magical sound of the pan will bring back the vacation memories for months to come and is just about indestructible.

You can find steel pans for sale at the Piarco International Airport in Trinidad. Here duty-free shops tempt those departing with local liquor, electronics, watches, jewelry, and more. There's also a good selection of locally made items ranging from hot sauces to copper jewelry to tiny steel pans.

Port of Spain is also home to several sprawling **malls**. The newest and most complete is the Grand Bazaar, an open-air extravaganza with fine shops much like you'd find at home offering clothing, jewelry, Indian clothing, the ubiquitous T-shirt, and spices in a large supermarket.

Non-shoppers will love Tobago: it's tough to spend money on this island. The most colorful shopping is found in

Scarborough's **open-air market**, where tropical fruits and vegetables explode in an artist's palate of colors. Sample a few items (watch out for the fiery Scotch Bonnet peppers!) and buy a bottle of homemade hot sauce and packaged curry, some of the island's top buys.

For more traditional shopping, check out the shops at Coco Reef. Here you'll find jewelry, clothing, and small souvenir items.

PRACTICAL INFORMATION

Currency. The official currency is the Trinidad-Tobago dollar. The exchange rate fluctuates but at press time the rate was $1US equals about 5.80TT.

Driving. Driving is on the LEFT on both islands.

Information. Call the Trinidad and Tobago Tourist Office, *Tel. 888/595-4TNT.*

Information on Island. In Trinidad, contact the Tourism and Industrial Development Company of Trinidad and Tobago, *10-14 Phillips Street, Port of Spain, Tel. 868/623-1932.*

On Tobago, stop by the tourism offices at IDC Mall in Scarborough, *Tel. 868/639-4333.*

Web site. Check out the official web site at: *http://www.tidco.co.tt.*

ISLAND REPORT CARD

Transportation to island	B
Transportation around island	B+
Family Resorts	B
Family Restaurants	B-
Friendly atmosphere	A
Activities for kids	B+
Weather	A+
New cultures for kids to experience	A+
Safety	B

TURKS & CAICOS

We really don't want to write about the Turks and Caicos.

No, it's not a case of, as our mothers always told us, "If you can't say something nice, don't say anything at all." And it's certainly not that we didn't fall in love with the miles of endless beaches or the almost palpable sense of tranquillity in these islands just off the tip of the Bahamas.

It's just that we feel we've discovered a slice of paradise. And we just don't want the rest of the world to know about it. But, as our mothers also always warned, "Share and share alike." Others searching for their own piece of paradise may find that this archipelago of nearly 40 islands, most uninhabited, will fit the bill.

The Turks and Caicos (pronounced Cay-cos) are located 1-1/2 hours from Miami, tucked halfway between the tip of Florida and Puerto Rico. This British crown colony, ruled by a governor appointed by the Queen, is better known to the world of banking than among travelers. With its tax-free status, use of the English language and the US dollar as official currency, and with the stability of the British government backing the islands, the Turks and Caicos have been a popular off-shore banking center for American corporations for many years.

We found that the same attributes that make these islands so attractive to businesses also make them appealing to travelers. A trip to the islands is quick thanks to daily jet service from Miami. Once there, travel around the islands, although on the left side of the road, is easy, and we didn't need to take time to learn a foreign currency or exchange rate. And the political stability of this government has brought a sense of security to the Turks and Caicos, resulting in an incredibly low rate of crime. Beaches are safe and uncrowded, and tourists can enjoy late night walks from property to property on the beaches of the main island, Providenciales.

Just how uncrowded these islands are is very obvious when arriving in Providenciales, better known as simply Provo. Although this island boasts the largest portion of the Turks and Caicos population of 15,000, it is still open and unsettled. This sickle-shaped island is dotted with scrubby growth, short palms and climbing sea grapes. Chalky limestone roads wind across the flat island, connecting settlements like Blue Hills and The Bight.

But the traveler to Provo will soon realize that its desert terrain is just a backdrop to the beaches and clear waters that are the main attractions. On some parts of the island the beaches stretch for miles, dotted only with the footprints of iguanas or shorebirds. You won't find beach vendors or hagglers on these shores, just a few tourists and locals enjoying snorkeling or a swim in the gentle surf. High rises are forbidden, with resorts built no taller than three stories.

For most visitors, the real attraction of Provo is the luxury of being able to do nothing at all. Days are spent on the beach or in water so clear that it is often cited as one of the top scuba destinations in the world. Visibility averages 80 to 100 feet or better, and the water temperature ranges from 82-84 degrees in the summer and 75-76 in the winter months. Beneath the calm waves swim colorful marine animals as exotic as hawksbill turtles, nurse sharks, and octopus. With a one mile vertical coral wall located offshore, Provo is a diver's paradise.

To protect the ecology of the islands, the Turks and Caicos have established an extensive national park and nature reserve system. Over 31 national parks dot the islands: Provo's Princess Alexandra National Park, with 13 miles of protected beaches; the NW Point Marine, with spectacular wall diving; and Chalk Sound, with small boat sailing on the west end of the island, just to name a few. National park rules make it illegal to hunt or fish, remove any animal or coral, moor vessels over 60 feet except on fixed buoys or drive boats within 100 yards of the shoreline.

One of the most protected treasures around the islands is JoJo the dolphin. This wild dolphin has been sighted for 12 years along the north coast of Provo, the only case ever documented of prolonged interaction between an individual wild dolphin and humans. Often spotted swimming along the north shore or near boats, JoJo is protected and the government has declared him a national treasure.

Although it is a rarity to spot JoJo, vacationers are certain to spot wildlife on daytrips to nearby Water Cay. Located northeast of Provo, this small island is the home of numerous iguanas that greet boat passengers and happily pose for photos just yards away. Snorkeling cruises take visitors from Provo to this island most every afternoon.

But snorkeling, scuba diving, golfing, and even iguana watching take a back seat to Providenciales' real draw: pure relaxation.

Although the chain is composed of nearly 40 limestone islands, only eight are considered destinations. Providenciales or Provo is home to about 6,000 residents and to most of the tourist industry. The capital of the Turks and Caicos is the island of Grand Turk, a short hop from Provo. This seven-mile square island has some historic buildings and the national museum, a must-see for history buffs.

Other inhabited islands include North Caicos, the most verdant island in the chain; South Caicos, a fishing center; Middle Caicos, home of several sea caves; and Salt Cay, a tiny island of only 300 residents that was once the world's largest producer of salt.

ARE WE THERE YET?
By Air
Visitors to the Turks and Caicos arrive on Providenciales. Service from Miami is available from American Airlines daily and Turks and Caicos Airways six days a week.

To island hop, book a seat aboard an inter-island charter flights with Turks and Caicos Airways, Tel. 649/946-4255, Fax 941-5781.

By Ferry
Government-operated ferry service between Grand Turk and Salt Cay is available Monday, Wednesday, and Friday for $5 per person.

Entry Requirements
US visitors are required to have proof of citizenship such as an official birth certificate or voter registration card and photo identification, or a passport. Visitors must also show a return ticket.

Getting Around the Island
Rental cars are available, but they can be tough to obtain and expensive — about $45 a day for a full-size. Once you have a rental car, you'll find that gasoline prices are equally expensive: about $2.50 a gallon. Taxi service is easier. (Check out the neckties hanging from every taxi driver's rear view mirror. They're required attire for drivers picking up a fare at the airport.)

WHICH ONE IS MY ROOM?
BEACHES TURKS AND CAICOS, *Providenciales, Tel. 649/946-8000, Fax 649/946-8001. Toll-free reservations Tel. 800/BEACHES. Summer rates from $865 for three nights, per adult. Credit cards accepted.*

Part of the Sandals family of resorts, this all-inclusive is a favorite with families. Located on the 12-mile beach at Grace Bay, this 224-room resort is open to singles, couples and families.

Dining includes a variety of restaurants. Reflections is the main dining room and features buffet servings of breakfast, lunch and dinner. Sapodilla's and Schooners serve adults only while families are welcome in the Arizona Bar and Grill for Tex-Mex cuisine or the Teppanyaki restaurant Kimonos, which has family seating from 6 to 7 nightly.

Watersports include snorkeling and scuba diving (a resort course is offered for all guests 12 years and older), aqua trikes, windsurfing, kayaking, sailing, hobie cats, and view boards for a peek at what lies beneath the sea's waves. Two swimming pools cool down guests once they leave the beach, and a special Toddler's Pool and Activity area keeps young visitors happy.

Children are also kept entertained at the supervised areas. A nursery is available for infants and toddlers while the Cuda Kids Club keeps older children happy at the children's pool, kids gazebo, playground, table tennis, pool table facilities, and at classes in everything from sandcastle building to reggae. Video game buffs will love the Sega Center with state-of-the-art video games (all complimentary). Teens also have special activities including disco nights, movie nights, sports tournaments, and more.

OCEAN CLUB, *Providenciales. Tel. 649/946-5880, Fax 649/946-5845. Toll-free reservations Tel. 800/457-8787. Winter rates begin at $190 for studio suite; in off season $150- $405. Credit cards accepted.*

Starting as a simple time share, the property has grown to full resort status with a small shopping arcade, convenience store, watersports concession, restaurant, beach grill, two bars, and more. The all-suite Grace Bay property still functions as a time share, but now takes its place alongside other full service resorts on this 12 mile stretch of beach.

Expansive rooms greet even those guests who chose the smaller accommodations at Ocean Club. With white tile floors, wicker furnishings, sliding glass doors opening to screened patios and balconies, and numerous windows, suites here are sunny and styled in a casual beachfront decor. Every room includes air conditioning, fully equipped kitchens or kitchenettes, cable TV, direct dial phones with voice messaging, in-suite washer and dryer, and daily maid service. Family-friendly features such as rollaway beds, baby cribs, and high chairs are available. Two children under 12 stay with parents free in the same suite.

The resort's white sand beach is one of its top assets, located just steps from the suites. Water lovers can also choose from two freshwater pools, including a freeform pool that's a favorite with young vacationers. Art Pickering's Provo Turtle Divers, located at the resort, offers dive excursions and watersports including snorkel trips, bonefishing and deep sea fishing, parasailing, scuba certification, and more.

Guest facilities include a fitness center with stationary bikes, universal station, stair climbers, and free weights.There is also massages and aromatherapy at the fitness center or in-room with Ocean Club's licensed massage therapist. Tennis is available day and night on a lighted court.

A dining shuttle operates nightly for drop-offs at island restaurants; a shopping shuttle runs three days a week, primarily to the island supermarket so guests can stock their kitchens. The front desk staff arranges for rental cars, scooters, bicycles, and baby-sitters as well as island tours and day sails aboard private sailing charters such as the *Beluga*, a 37-foot catamaran.

TURQUOISE REEF RESORT AND CASINO, *Providenciales, Tel. 649/946-5555 Fax 649/946-5522. Toll-free US phone number 800/992-2015. Winter rates from $190.Credit cards accepted.*

The only casino in the country is found at this beachside hotel. Easy to spot with its turquoise roofs, the full service hotel has comfortable rooms, an excellent beach, and a relaxed atmosphere. Families will find plenty of outdoor ac-

264 CARIBBEAN WITH KIDS

tivity including watersports, a dive shop, tennis, and a freshwater pool at the beachfront property.

LE DECK, *Grace Bay, Providenciales, Tel. 649/946-5547, Fax 649/946-5770. Toll-free US phone number 800/528-1905. Winter rates $160-$182, Summer rates $125-$145. Credit cards accepted.*

Le Deck has comfortable rooms sporting a recent refurbishment, an excellent restaurant, and a central location. Nothing fancy, but you can't beat the Grace Bay location. The beachfront property includes a freshwater swimming pool.

EREBUS INN, *Turtle Cove, Providenciales, Tel. 649/946-4240, Fax 649/946-4704. Toll-free US phone number 800/645-1179. Winter rates $140-$165, summer rates $105-$130. Credit cards accepted.*

Overlooking Turtle Cove Marina, this modest inn is a charming spot for those on a budget—plus it offers a great view. Amenities include a gym and a freshwater pool as well as an excellent restaurant on property.

TURTLE COVE INN, *Turtle Cove, Providenciales, Tel. 649/946-4203, Fax 649/946-4141. Toll-free US phone number 800/887-0477. Winter rates from $95, Summer from $55. Credit cards accepted.*

When divers come up for air, many head to this resort where they find an on-site dive center and packages including two tank morning dives. Located directly off the marina, rooms here are simple but include telephone, cable TV, and a private balcony. A freshwater pool is available for guests along with a casual restaurant and bar.

WHAT ARE WE GOING TO DO NEXT?

> ### ASK THE CONCIERGE
> Mare Joinville at Beaches Turks and Caicos Resort and
> Spa says, "Come with an open mind and the sky is the limit."
> Some recommended activities include:
>   Tour to Little Water Cay (Iguana Island)
>   Silver Deep Island Tours
>   Private family picnic on private cays
>   Parasailing
>   Snorkeling at the White House
>   Sailing our pristine waters on a Hobie cat or sunfish
>   Cycling the island
>   Touring the world's only Conch Farm
>   Touring our historic North West Point
>   Deep Sea Fishing or Sports Fishing

With the number of tourists relatively low, you'll find
that the number of attractions are equally sparse. Don't expect the shopping of St. Thomas or the reggae clubs of Jamaica or the submarine rides of Grand Cayman at this destination. For most families, the real attraction is being able
to do nothing at all. Days are spent on the beach or in the
water that's so clear it's often cited as the world's top scuba
destination.

One unique attraction is the **Conch Farm**, *Providenciales,
Tel. 649/946-5849*, the only farm in the world that raises
Queen conch, the shellfish that's become a favorite meal
throughout much of the Caribbean. On a guided tour, you'll
see conch in various stages, from the larvae in the hatchery
to juveniles about 4mm in length, to adulthood. In Provo,
the product of this unique farm is served at the Anacaona
Restaurant and the Tiki Hut.

History buffs will find reason enough to take a day trip
to Grand Turk to visit the **Turks and Caicos National Museum**, *Grand Turk, Tel. 649/946-2160*. We think this is one

of the most fascinating museums in the entire Caribbean. The main exhibit features the Molasses Reef shipwreck, which occurred in the Turks and Caicos nearly 500 years ago. The Spanish caravel hit the reef and quickly sank in only 20 feet of water where it remained until the 1970s. Once excavated, it was recognized as the oldest European shipwreck in the New World.

The museum, located in a 150-year old house on the island's main street, features artifacts from the wreck with interactive displays, video presentations, and scientific exhibits.

The name of this wrecked ship was never learned because, like drug-running planes of today, this was a ship with an illegal booty. Kept off the official records of Spain, the ship was carrying slaves probably bound for the plantations of nearby Hispaniola.

Sports & Recreation

Scuba diving and **snorkeling** are the top attractions of these islands. Visibility ranges from 80 to 100 feet or better and water temperatures hover at about 82 degrees in the summer and 75 or so in the winter months. Beneath the calm waves swim colorful marine animals as exotic as hawksbill turtles, nurse sharks, and octopus. With a one mile vertical coral wall located offshore, Provo is a diver's paradise.

You'll find top **dive operators** here as well. In Provo, call Dive Provo, *Tel. 800/234-7768*, Turtle Inn Divers, *Tel. 800/359-DIVE*. In Grand Turk, check with Blue Water Divers *Tel. 649/946-2432*, Sea Eye Diving, *Tel. 649/946-1407*, and Aquanaut, *Tel. 649/946-2160*; in Salt Cay call Porpoise Divers *Tel. 649/946-6927*.

Save a day to cruise over to **Water Cay**, an island inhabited by friendly iguanas and tropical birds.

WHAT CAN I BUY?

There is a new shopping complex in Provo called Ports of Call, designed to resemble an old Caribbean seaside town. Look for restaurants, crafts and art in this new development near Grace Bay.

Conch (pronounced Konk) shells make a wonderful souvenir from these islands. Stop by the Conch Farm to purchase a beautiful shell.

PRACTICAL INFORMATION

Currency. The US dollar is the official currency of these islands.

Driving. Driving is on the LEFT.

Information. Call the Turks and Caicos Tourist Board, *Tel. 800/241-0824.*

Web site. Checked out *http://caribbean˜supersite.com/turks/* for additional information.

ISLAND REPORT CARD

Transportation to island	A
Transportation around island	B+
Family Resorts	B
Family Restaurants	B-
Friendly atmosphere	A
Activities for kids	B+
Weather	A
New cultures for kids to experience	B
Safety	A+

US VIRGIN ISLANDS

License plates proudly proclaim that this is "America's Paradise." It's the United States' own vacationland, a place to dance to a Caribbean beat, swim in some of the region's clearest waters, or do some "limin'," the Virgin Islanders' word for just kicking back and enjoying a taste of paradise.

The US Virgin Islands offer three distinct vacations for families. **St. Croix** boasts some of the best of the other US Virgin Islands: the bustle of St. Thomas and the eco-tourism of St. John. In St. Croix's cities of Christiansted and Frederiksted, duty-free shopping is on a smaller scale than St. Thomas' Charlotte Amalie, but you'll still find enough jewelry, leather goods, perfume, and china to keep even the most dedicated shopper happy. On the island's far reaches, eco-tourists can hike through a sultry rain forest or enjoy an unparalleled snorkeling trail where fish as bright as gumdrops swim among century-old coral.

On the south shore, Frederiksted is the quieter of the island's two cities, a sleepy port that springs to life when a cruise ship pulls into town. After Hurricane Marilyn wrecked havoc on St. Thomas, the popularity of this cruise destination soared and several new shops popped up on the city's waterfront streets.

Nature lovers, set your sights for tiny **St. John**. This is the eco-tourism capital of the Caribbean, an island where the two of you, from the luxury of a beautiful resort or a posh villa or the inexpensive accommodations of a tent or cabin, can hike, snorkel, and tour an island where two-thirds of the land is preserved as a national park.

The stewardship of the island's natural beauty began with Laurance Rockefeller. Developer of Caneel Bay Resort, the multi-millionaire donated much of the island to the National Park Service in the 1950s. Today, preservation of this island's resources lies in the hands of the park service and a developer named Stanley Selengut, a leader in the world of eco-tourism who operates several eco-friendly properties on the island. St. John leads the world in sustainable tourism resorts where guests make a minimal impact on nature.

St. Thomas is the most bustling of the Virgins. This is the destination for any shoppers in your family. St. Thomas' Charlotte Amalie (pronounced a-mal-yah) has a busy cosmopolitan atmosphere with a Caribbean charm all its own.

But beyond Charlotte Amalie's boundaries, the island enjoys a slower pace. Here, on overlooks high above the city's lights, families can share some of the Caribbean's most glorious sunsets. On the island's fringe of powdered sugar beaches, you can catch up on your limin' — just lazing the days away beneath towering palms.

ARE WE THERE YET?

By Air

American Airlines offers flights from JFK/New York, Miami, and Washington/Dulles via San Juan. Direct service from Baltimore/Washington is available aboard USAirways, and service from Atlanta is available on Delta. Direct flights from Miami are also available on Prestige Airways.

American Airlines (from Miami and New York's JFK) and Delta (from Atlanta with a stop in St. Thomas) have daily service to St. Croix. USAirways flies to St. Croix from Baltimore/Washington.

Take a day trip between St. Thomas and St. Croix with a quick hop between islands on the **seaplane**, which departs from downtown Christiansted and arrives in downtown Charlotte Amalie. Seaborne Seaplane, *Tel. 340/777-4491*, provides shuttle service between the two islands; rates are about $50 each way.

By Ferry

Ferry service from St. Croix to St. Thomas is available on the "FastCat" catamaran ferry operated by Gold Coast

Yachts, *Tel. 340/777-FAST.* The trip from downtown Christiansted to downtown Charlotte Amalie takes one hour.

St. John does not have an airport, so you'll arrive by boat. Most visitors arrive via ferry service from St. Thomas, *Tel. 340/776-6282* . From Red Hook, it's a 20-minute, $3 one way cruise; from Charlotte Amalie the journey costs $7 and takes 25 minutes. A private water taxi from Red Hook is a wonderful luxury; call Per Dohm's Water Taxi, *Tel. 340/775-6501.*

Getting Around the Islands

Taxis are easy to obtain. In Christiansted, stop by the taxi stand on King Street, in Frederiksted the taxi stand is at Fort Frederik. Licensed taxi services bear a license plate that begins with "TP." In St. Thomas, taxis are parked at the Vendors' Market.z`

Another option is bus service, an inexpensive way to get around the island and feel like a local. Clean and air-conditioned, the bus service costs about $1. For routes and more information, call *Tel. 340/773-7746.*

Rental cars are readily available; all you'll need is a valid U.S. driver's license. Remember, though, that driving is on the left side of the road.

Traveling among the USVI is as easy as moving from city to city. You can hop a ferry or seaplane (between St. Croix and St. Thomas), and there's no need to show documents on arrival.

Entry Requirements

You'll need proof of identity upon airport check-in, but incoming Americans do not need to pass through immigration. It's a good idea to bring along your passport, however, in case you decide to take a day trip to the nearby British Virgin Islands.

WHICH ONE IS MY ROOM?

St. Croix

WESTIN CARAMBOLA BEACH RESORT, *Estate Davis Bay, Tel. 340/778-3800, Fax 340/778-1682. Toll-free US phone number 800/228-3000. Winter rates $275-$370, Summer rates $185-$270. Credit cards accepted.*

Overlooking Davis Bay, the Westin Carambola Beach Resort is the most lavish resort on the island. We loved this hotel from the moment our transport began descending the steep hill on the island's western side and we caught sight of the hotel's trademark red roofs. Scattered throughout the lush grounds, the guest rooms are housed in two-story villas, each with louvered windows and private, screened porches.

No matter where you stay, you're only steps away from the beach along walkways that wind through grounds filled with hibiscus, bougainvillea, oleander, elephant's ear, philodendrons, banana trees, and towering palms.

CHENAY BAY BEACH RESORT, *Green Cay, Tel. 340/773-2918, Fax 340/773-2918. Toll-free reservations Tel. 800/548-4457. Cottage: $150-$235; Family Units: $225-$395. Credit cards accepted.*

Cheney Bay offers a Cruzan Kidz program for children 3-12. The complimentary program runs from 9am to 1pm weekdays and includes tennis lessons, snorkel trips, beach hikes, shell hunts, treasure hunts, and other activities.

The whole family can enjoy Chenay's activities as well. Complimentary snorkeling, tennis, kayaks, and floating mats are provided to guests. And, with its bay location, the calm waters are perfect for young swimmers.

Guests stay in one of 50 West Indian-style cottages, each with kitchenette, mini-bar, cable TV, and private deck with either a garden or ocean view. Family units are two connecting cottages and offer plenty of room for busy children.

THE BUCCANEER, *Shoys, Tel. 340/773-2100, Fax 340/778-8215. Toll-free US phone number 800/255-3881. Winter rates begin at $210, Summer rates start at $175. Credit cards accepted.*

No other hotel in St. Croix , and few in the Caribbean, boasts the impressive history of The Buccaneer, located east of Christiansted. Once owned by Charles Martel, one of the Knights of Malta, the estate had walls three feet thick and was tucked just behind a hill to hide it from view of pirates. Later, the stately manor was the residence of the young Alexander Hamilton.

Today, the original estate is supplemented with modern rooms to complete the 146-room resort but the rich historic atmosphere remains. Every week, guests and staff come together at the manager's cocktail party, hosted in a stone sugar mill that stands as a reminder of the island's early plantation past.

History at the Buccaneer doesn't just end with the facilities — it extends to the resort owners as well. Today the ninth generation of the Armstrong family to reside on St. Croix operates the expansive resort.

The Buccaneer is also well-known for its sports facilities, especially tennis and golf. Eight tennis courts are located halfway down the hill from the main house. Golfers can take their best swing at an 18-hole course with views of the sea. Packages with unlimited golf are available.

One of the top Christmas activities planned by a resort is found at The Buccaneer on St. Croix in the US Virgin Islands. The "Twelve Days of Christmas" kids camp keeps children in the holiday spirit of fun with supervised activities from 10am to 6pm . Children enjoy beach fun, tropical arts and crafts, and outdoor games.

And, of course, the spirit of Christmas rings true here as well. Santa arrives by, what else, a dingy pulled by eight tiny seahorses! For New Years, the celebrations include a tropical luau and fireworks.

HOTEL ON THE CAY, *Christiansted, Tel. 340/773-2035, Fax 340/773-7046. Toll-free US phone number 800/524-2035. Winter rates start at $189, Summer rates at $125. Credit cards accepted.*

Known to its fans as "Hot C," this charming property is located on a tiny cay with an unbeatable view of Christiansted. Protestant Cay rises from the turquoise waters of the harbor just a one minute ferry ride (free for guests) from downtown.

Along with 55 guest rooms (each with a kitchenette), Hotel on the Cay also offers the only beach in downtown Christiansted. It's enjoyed by guests from many nearby hotels who pay the toll of what must be, considering its length, the priciest ferry ride in the Caribbean: $3 per person for the round trip haul.

HIBISCUS BEACH HOTEL, *4131 LaGrande Princesse, Tel. 340/773-4042, Fax 340/773-4668. Toll-free US phone number 800/442-0121. Winter rates run $180-$190, Summer rates $130-$140 Credit cards accepted.*

The 37 guest rooms, each with an ocean view, here are pretty no frills but perfect for the traveling family on a budget. The hotel has a pretty stretch of beach, and this property is very convenient, just 15 minutes from the airport and about 10 minutes from Christiansted. The best feature, however, is its Friday night dance show, a wonderful introduction to the island's heritage for every member of the family. Every Friday, the hotel offers an unbeatable show that pulses with the fervor of island dancing and music. Authentic local steps are performed by the Caribbean Dance Company. The show is available with dinner or as show only. Reservations are required for this popular presentation.

TAMARIND REEF HOTEL, *501 Tamarind Reef, Christiansted, Tel. 340/773-4455, Fax 340/773-3989. Toll-free*

US phone number 800/619-0014. Winter rates start at $160. Credit cards accepted.

This is one of our favorite budget-priced accommodations in the Caribbean, thanks to sparkling clean rooms, an excellent snorkel trail, and the hotel's friendly on-site owners, Dick and Marcy Pelton. The 46-room property is located east of Christiansted just off the reef. All of the rooms include a refrigerator, coffee maker, air conditioning, phones, and many also include kitchenettes. The atmosphere here is laid-back and comfortable, perfect for families to enjoy the tranquil east end of St. Croix and the snorkel trail in the inlet just in front of the hotel.

Just a few steps from the hotel, the Green Cay Marina is home to boats that offer daily tours to Buck Island as well as deep-sea fishing excursions and scuba diving trips.

HOTEL CARAVELLE, *444 Queen Cross Street, Tel. 340/773-0687, Fax 340/778-7004. Toll-free US phone number 800/524-0410. Winter rates start at $142, Summer rates run $102-$112. Credit cards accepted.*

This modest European-style hotel is especially convenient for those who want to immerse themselves in the shopping of Christiansted. Located downtown right on the waterfront, this 43-room inn is within walking distance of just about everything in Christiansted, from art galleries to the historic fort to fine dining. It's an excellent choice for anyone on a budget, and you can splurge with the penthouse suite with a living room, full kitchen, large bedroom, and two baths for less than the cost of a standard room at many other island properties.

St. John
WESTIN ST. JOHN, *Tel. 340/693-8000, Fax 340/779-4500. Toll-free US phone number. 800/WESTIN-1. Winter from $425, Summer from $245. Credit cards accepted.*

At press time, the Westin (formerly the Hyatt) was just reopening following damage from Hurricane Marilyn and a purchase and redo by the Westin resort family. This resort has long been one of the Caribbean's nicest, a place where guests feel like they're being swept into paradise. Guests are transported to the resort like visiting royalty aboard a private yacht. You'll arrive on St. John at the hotel dock, and soon be off to your room, one of 280 guest accommodations on a hillside over Great Cruz Bay.

CANEEL BAY, *St. John, USVI, Tel. 340/776-6111, Fax 340/693-8280. Toll-free US phone number Tel. 800/928-8889. Winter rates run $350-$700, Summer rates $250-$425. Credit cards accepted.*

Caneel has the air of old-world Caribbean elegance that tells you, without a word, that this resort was a Laurance Rockefeller development. Tucked within the Virgin Islands National Park, Caneel boasts seven beaches and a natural beauty that is surpassed only by the resort's high quality service. Spread out across the lush property, 171 cottages combine "casual elegance" with "St. John camping" to come up with a property where you can feel like you are camping while enjoying plenty of pampering. Cooled by trade winds and a ceiling fan, each cottage has furnishings from the Philippines, screened walls that are open to a pristine view, and cool terrazzo floors as well as an ice chest for daily ice delivery.

Guests check in when they arrive at the airport in St. Thomas and board private ferry service to the resort. Upon arrival, kids are given a special gift and a personalized letter welcoming them to the resort. Complimentary punch is served to kids on the ferry ride over to their home away from home. After check in, children find milk and cookies waiting in their room with a selection of toys chosen for their age. (The ferry service is available several times daily so guests can hop to St. Thomas for a little shopping.) Private ferry service is also available three times a week to the resort's sister property, Little Dix Bay, on Virgin Gorda. (Bring along your passport or proof of citizenship to take this jaunt to the British Virgin Islands.)

Along with plenty of complimentary diversions (including the Peter Burwash International tennis program), introductory scuba diving clinic, windsurfing, Sunfish and kayaks, and movie presentations, other activities are available at additional charge: half- and full-day sails, beach barbecue, sunset cocktail cruise, guided snorkel trips, fishing charters, massages, and boat charters.

Children find plenty of fun at Caneel as well. Turtle Town, the children's center, offers plenty of fun and education. "In Turtle Town, our young visitors learn to appreciate the beauty of our island by going on treasure hunts and nature walks, making arts and crafts with local natural materials, listening to pirate tales, taking Caribbean dance lessons and much more," explains Joanna Werman, Caneel Bay's Children's Program Director.

Each day's fun in Turtle Town follows a special theme. On Marine Life Day, kids enjoy shore exploration, search for sea turtle nests, enjoy aquatic arts and crafts, watch a Sea Life slide show and more. Other themed days include An Island Home (with nature walks), A World of One/East To Be Me Day (featuring local culture), Mystery Day (with a scavenger hunt and costumed hunt for pirate treasure), Magic Day (complete with magic shows and lessons), and Family Fun Day (highlighted by events for the family such as a ride on the Atlantis Submarine or a look at the island's ancient petroglyphs).

Cost for the program is $50 per day per child and includes a full lunch. Caneel Companions, a baby-sitting service, is also available during the day and evening hours. The cost is $10 per hour with a three hour minimum.

However your family chooses to enjoy Caneel, there's one thing sure to please everyone: the resort's beaches. Here seven pristine stretches of sand are available, so guests can visit a different beach every day. Guests can hop aboard the resort shuttle for quick drop off at any of these beaches; don't forget to request a picnic lunch to take along!

CINNAMON BAY CAMPGROUNDS, *Cruz Bay, Tel. 340/776-6330 or 693-5654, Fax 340/776-6458. Toll-free reservations Tel. 800/539-9998. Winter rates for bare sites are $17 (bare sites) and $75-$105 for cottages, Summer rates are $20 for bare sites and $70-$75 for cottages. Credit cards accepted.*

Campers keep the bare sites, tents, and screened shelters of this popular campground full year around. Managed by Caneel Bay, this campground is located on the grounds of the national park and features accommodations near beautiful Cinnamon Bay Beach, St. John's longest stretch of sand.

Tents (which measure 10' x 14') are outfitted with four cots with bedding, a solid floor, an ice chest, water container, and cooking and eating utensils. Outdoors, a propane stove and lantern, charcoal grill, and picnic table are available.

Cottages (15 x 15 feet) are actually screened shelters with the same features as well as electricity. All accommodations share bathhouses with cool water showers.

The atmosphere is very relaxed, as campers enjoy the Caribbean at their campsite, on the beach, and on daily ranger-led tours of the national park. Don't be surprised to see a family of wild burros roaming the grounds.

The most family cottages are units 10A through D, a seashell's throw from the water. Tent site 21 is the closest to the water, and bare site 24 is best for beach buffs. We hear that you practically have to inherit a reservation to secure these most-popular sites, but give it a try anyway.

MAHO BAY CAMPS, *Cruz Bay, Tel. 340/776-6240, Fax 340/776-6226. Toll-free reservations Tel. 800/392-9004. Winter rates from $95, summer from $65. Credit cards accepted.*

From the minute you arrive at Maho, you'll know that this is no ordinary campground. From the help-yourself center where guests leave unused food, toiletries, books, and other items for other guests' use to the network of raised boardwalks that connect the tent cabins and protect hillside vegetation, this resort's focus is on environmental camping.

Every 16' x 16' unit has screened sides with roll down privacy shades, a sleeping area with mattress-covered beds and bedding, a futon sofa that pulls down into a sleeper, a cooking and dining area with cooler, propane stove, and fan, and an outdoor balcony. Barbecue grills and bathhouses are scattered throughout the property.

ECO-TOURISM IN ST. JOHN

Plush robes, imported shampoos, and well-stocked mini-bars have always been popular hotel amenities, but on one Caribbean island the demand calls for propane stoves, insulated coolers, and clotheslines.

St. John may be the smallest of the US Virgin Islands but it is a giant in the world of eco-tourism. Along with lavish hotels such as the Westin St. John and Caneel Bay, St. John also offers camping designed to allow vacationers to bring down the walls that separate hotel guests from nature.

Four campgrounds invite visitors who are ready to rough it in varying degrees. At Cinnamon Bay Campgrounds, located in the national park, campers select from bare sites, canvas tents, and screened shelters. At Maho Bay Camps, guests enjoy screened tent cottages, connected by a network of raised boardwalks. Nearby, Harmony Resort offers camping luxury with kitchens, balconies, and ceiling fans. A closer inspection reveals, however, that this is no ordinary resort. Running on solar energy, the cabins are built entirely of recycled materials. Sawdust and trash bags assume a new life as sturdy deck materials; recycled cardboard now serves as siding.

Now Stanley Selengut, founder of both Maho and Harmony, has gone a step further in offering an ecological choice for St. John guests. Concordia eco-tents feature high-tech reflective materials that keep the interior cool beneath the Caribbean sun, solar energy that powers appliances and heats showers, and compost toilets that minimize waste. And, in keeping with the Rockefeller connection with eco-tourism, Laurance's niece, Abby, heads the work on waste management at the resort.

"Eco-tourism should be on our shoulders because we're on some of the most beautiful land in the world," explains Selengut.

HARMONY, *Cruz Bay, Tel. 212/472-9453, Fax 212/861-6210. Toll-free reservations Tel. 800/392-9004. Winter rates from $180, summer from $95. Credit cards accepted.*

As its name suggests, this was designed to be a resort in tune with nature. Solar power, recycled materials, low flush toilets, and a complete awareness of the environment makes this an eco-sensitive resort, but with a higher number of creature comforts than are found at its sister property, Maho. These units include energy-efficient refrigerators, a computer to track energy use, comfortable furnishings (either two twin beds in the bedroom studio units or two queen beds in the living room studios), private baths, a deck with furniture, and kitchen.

ESTATE CONCORDIA, *Cruz Bay, Tel. 212/472-9453, Fax 212/861-6210 . Toll-free US reservations Tel. 800/392-9004. Winter rates for cottages from $135, summer from $95 (Eco-tents $95 in winter, $60 in summer). Credit cards accepted.*

Like Harmony, Estate Concordia also takes the eco-tourism-with-style approach. Located on the more remote south shore, these units and the neighboring eco-tents are more widely spaced across the landscape than the units at Harmony and Maho. These canvas tent cottages are specifically designed to be light on the land, to rely on high-tech advancements such as ultra light reflective materials, and to provide facilities such as compost toilets, while at the same time being ecologically friendly.

Villas

St. John boasts a number of exquisite private villas for the ultimate in privacy. For brochures of these homes, many with private pools, contact a villa broker such as Catered To...Ltd., *Tel. 800/424-6641*, Vacation Vistas, *Tel. 340/776-6462*, Windspree, *Tel. 340/693-5423*, McLaughlin Anderson Vacations, Ltd., *Tel. 800/537-6246 or 800/666-6246*, Caribbean Villas, *Tel. 800/338-0987*, Destination St. John, *Tel. 800/562-1901*, and Villa Portfolio, *Tel. 800/858-7989.*

St. Thomas

RITZ-CARLTON GRAND PALAZZO HOTEL, *6900 Great Bay, Tel. 340/775-3333, Fax 340/775-5635. Toll-free US phone number 800/241-3333. Winter rates run $385-$525, Summer rates run $265-$355. Credit cards accepted.*

Just as you would expect from a member of the Ritz-Carlton family, this resort is really grand. This is one of the most elegant hotels in the Caribbean, an ultra-luxurious resort designed to make its visitors feel like royalty. From the moment you enter the marble entry of this resort styled to replicate a Venetian palace, you'll know that this is a step above even the luxurious resorts for which the island is known. Maintaining a one-to-one guest to staff ratio, the resort is for those vacationers who are ready for privacy and pampering.

The hotel's hibiscus-colored roofs dot the shoreline of Great Bay. Here, amid stark white buildings punctuated with bougainvillea and other tropical splendors, await some of the island's most luxurious guest rooms. Marble baths, seersucker robes, and French doors leading out to private balconies greet guests. Away from their rooms, visitors continue to enjoy the finest in amenities, including sailing, snorkeling, and a private yacht. Nanny service is available for families.

Children under 18 stay free in parents' room.

MARRIOTT FRENCHMAN'S REEF BEACH RESORT, *#5 Estate Bakkeroke, Tel. 340/776-8500, Fax 340/776-3054. Toll-free reservations Tel. 800/524-2000. Winter rates from $325, Summer rates from $195. Credit cards accepted.*

This hotel-style property is popular with conventions and meetings but it also makes a fine place to bring along the family, whether you're on island for business or pure fun.

Marriott Frenchman's Reef sits high above the sea and boasts a fresh new face after a $45 million renovation. Families can enjoy plenty of activity together: tennis, golf, snorkeling, sailing, or even a water ferry ride into Charlotte Amalie for a day of duty-free shopping.

Kids 18 and under stay free when sharing a room with parents.

MARRIOTT MORNING STAR, *Estate Bakkeroke, Tel. 340/776-8500, Fax 340/776-3054. Toll-free reservations Tel. 800/232-2425. Winter rates from $325, Summer rates from $195. Credit cards accepted.*

Morning Star lies just down the road from Frenchman's Reef but is better designed for families with young children. Like Frenchman's Reef, the resort offers just about any activity you could select: sports, watersports (enjoyed right off the beach at this property), water taxi service into town, and more. However, here families can stroll right from their rooms to the beach, always a favorite with young children anxious to hit the water right away rather than wait for a shuttle.

SAPPHIRE BEACH RESORT AND MARINA, *Smith Bay Route 6, Tel. 340/775-6100, Fax 340/775-4024. Toll-free reservations Tel. 800/524-2090. Winter rates $295-$385, Summer rates $225-$275. Credit cards accepted.*

Sapphire Beach Resort and Marina is perched on one of the island's most beautiful stretches of sand and offers excellent snorkeling in calm, shallow waters just offshore. Located about half an hour from the airport, this resort includes beachfront and yacht harbor view suites and villas, each with fully equipped kitchens, television, and daily maid service.

If you're traveling with children, the complimentary KidsKlub, a day-long, complimentary program for children ages 4 to 12. Children enjoy swimming, sandcastle building, arts and crafts, story telling, sing-alongs, and more. A NiteKlub and Teen Scene program is also available to guests. This year, the KidsKlub will be better than ever. The resort is enhancing their facilities by adding a 10,000-square-foot swimming pool and a new 3,500-square-foot KidsKlub designed for younger children. A separate teen arcade is also being added, along with a new retail area for the whole family.

Presently, the KidsKlub runs from 8:30am to 5pm daily and includes activities such as swimming, sandcastle building, games, arts and crafts, water bingo, story telling, and more. From 6:30pm to 10pm, the NiteKlub is available for $15 and includes dinner, movies, and activities such as storytelling and crafts. In-room baby-sitting is also available.

Families also have free use of snorkel gear as well as windsurfers and sunfish sailboats. Other watersports are available for a fee: parasailing, deep sea fishing, sea kayaking, scuba diving, and half and full-day sails.

Sapphire Beach extends its welcoming spirit to families with a "Family Fun Vacation" package. Children 12 and under stay and eat for free (kids 18 and under stay for free) when accompanied by their parents. Each of the three on-site restaurants have children's menus. More kid pleasers: every room includes satellite TV with the Disney Channel.

BOLONGO BAY BEACH CLUB AND VILLAS, *four miles from Charlotte Amalie, Tel. 340/775-1800, Fax 340/775-3208. Toll-free reservations Tel. 800/524-4746. Winter rates from $225, Summer rates begin at $145. Credit cards accepted.*

A favorite with family travelers, Bolongo Bay offers 75 guest rooms in standards and superior (beachfront) rooms. All rooms include air-conditioning, ceiling fan, color cable television, private balcony, safe, and telephone. Some rooms include an efficiency kitchen.

284 CARIBBEAN WITH KIDS

Many guests opt for the "all-inclusive" plan with all meals, unlimited beverages, non-motorized watersports, tennis, basketball, beach volleyball, use of spa and fitness center, all-day sailing excursion to St. John, snorkel cruise, introductory scuba lesson, hotel taxes and gratuity in a one price package. If you think you'll be spending much of your time off property, a Continental plan is available with Continental breakfast, watersports, introductory scuba lesson, beach volleyball, tennis basketball, and use of fitness center (and, if you stay for seven nights, the all-day sailing cruise).

Active kids will enjoy Bolongo's many sports offerings: two lighted volleyball courts, two lighted half courts at the basketball club, two tennis courts, a five-star PADI training facility for teens interested in scuba, and an array of watersports that includes water cycles, kayaks, canoes, paddle boats, windsurfers, sunfish, sailboats, snorkel gear, and swim mats.

Children under 12 stay free in the same room with parents (when parents book Continental plan). Cribs are complimentary and baby-sitting services with a licensed day-care provider are available.

RENAISSANCE GRAND BEACH RESORT, *Tel. 340/ 775-1510, Fax 340/775-2185. Toll-free US phone number 800/ HOTELS-1. Winter from $335, summer from $155. Credit cards accepted.*

See "Best Places to Stay with Kids" chapter for resort review.

SECRET HARBOUR BEACH RESORT, *6280 Estate Nazareth, Tel. 340/775-6550, Fax 340/775-1501. Toll-free reservations Tel. 800/524-2250. Winter rates start at $265, Summer rates begin at $169. Credit cards accepted.*

Perched on a beautiful swath of sand, this resort offers beach-front studios or one and two bedroom suites, each with fully equipped kitchens, cable TV, air-conditioning, ceiling fans, and beachfront balconies or patios, all looking right out to sea and, in the evenings, to the setting sun.

WYNDHAM SUGAR BAY BEACH CLUB AND RE-SORT, *6500 Estate Smith Bay, Tel. 340/777-7100, Fax 340/ 777-7200. Toll-free US reservations number 800/WYNDHAM. Winter from $396, summer from $288. Credit cards accepted.*
See "Best Places to Stay with Children" chapter.

SAPPHIRE VILLAGE, *Smith Bay Route 6, Tel. 340/775-2600, Fax 340/775-5901. Toll-free reservations Tel. 800/874-7897. Studio $115 in summer, $150 in winter. 1-bedroom $140-$170. Credit cards accepted.*

Adjacent to the Sapphire Beach Resort, these condominiums offer full housekeeping units for busy families. Studio and one-bedroom suites all include a small kitchen, air-conditioning, TV, phone, in-room safe, private balcony, and maid service.

Guests can use the watersports facilities at the Doubletree, enjoying glass bottom boat rides, snorkeling, paddle boats, or even arranging a sail to the nearby British Virgin Islands.

The beach at Sapphire has long been cited as one of the top on St. Thomas and it's not a claim without justification. A white swath of sand meets the turquoise sea and the waters remain shallow for many yards. A shallow reef comes within feet of the beach, perfect for young snorkelers.

Cribs are available for $10 per night.

SECRET HARBOURVIEW VILLAS, *east end of St. Thomas, Tel. 340/775-2600, Fax 340/775-5901. Toll-free reservations Tel. 800/874-7897. Studio $140 in summer, $220 in winter. 1-bedroom $170-$270; 2-bedroom $250-$360. Credit cards accepted.*

Located eight miles from Charlotte Amalie and one mile from Red Hook, families have their choice of 25 condos at this quiet harbor. Sizes range from studios to two-bedroom suites and each includes a fully equipped kitchen, microwave, air-conditioning, TV, telephone, in-room safe, and maid service. All the condos overlook the beach from a private balcony.

The waters outside these units are perfect for young swimmers. Protected by the harbor, the sea here is usually calm and still, the perfect place for an afternoon swimming lesson.

Cribs are available for $10 per night.

CHARTERED YACHTS & VILLA VACATIONS

One of the most exciting ways to explore the Virgin Islands is aboard a chartered yacht. It may sound like the getaway reserved exclusively for the rich and famous, but many families find that these are as reasonable as a floating condominium. These luxurious vessels boast the niceties of a fine hotel room, including private bath, gourmet meals, and television and VCR, and come crewed with a captain and cook. Call Regency Yacht Vacations, *Tel. 800/524-7676*, for information on these unique excursions, where the itinerary is selected based on your needs. A few vessels are small enough for two person charters, but most accommodate between four and 12 persons. Prices are all-inclusive.

Another good option for families are villa homes. For brochures of these homes, many with private pools, contact a villa broker such as Catered To...Ltd., *Tel. 800/424-6641*, Vacation Vistas, *Tel. 340/776-6462*, Ocean Property Management, *Tel. 800/874-7897*, Windspree *Tel. 340/693-5423*, McLaughlin Anderson Vacations, Ltd., *Tel. 800/537-6246 or 800/666-6246*, Caribbean Villas, *Tel. 800/338-0987*, and Villa Portfolio, *Tel. 800/858-7989*.

WHAT ARE WE DOING NEXT?
St. Croix

ST. CROIX KIDS' FUN

Jane Watkins, public relations representative for St. Croix's Finest, recommends the following activities for families while on the largest of the US Virgin Islands:

1) Wahoo Willy's: One of very few restaurants on St. Croix that offer a kids' menu. It is a fun, open air restaurant on the harbor. Choose from frozen drinks, wood oven pizza, local dishes and more. Kids love to watch as the seaplane lands on the water and taxis in to the neighboring dock. Located in Hotel Caravelle, Christiansted.

2) Kayak around Green Cay: A Federally protected island (home to the endangered Ground Lizard) just off Tamarind Reef Hotel's beach. Guests of Tamarind Reef Hotel have free access to non-motorized watersports (snorkeling equipment, kayaks, windsurfers); non guests can rent the equipment. The trip to Green Cay is not far and kids 12 and older get there and back with relative ease. Younger kids should go on a two-person kayak with a parent or older sibling. Tamarind Reef Hotel is located east of the island. Tamarind Reef Hotel's snorkeling trail is awesome—a must do!

3) The Caribbean Dance Company performs every Friday night (during season) at 8:30pm at the Hibiscus Beach Hotel. Kids and parents love the show. The performances are of dances native to the Caribbean islands and dancers wear the traditional costumes that go with each dance. The final dance is the Rainbow, where the performers invite the guests to join them on the dance floor. (Kids love this!)

The best way to see what St. Croix has to offer you and your mate is to get an overview aboard a guided island tour. **St. Croix Safari Tours**, *Tel. 340/773-6700 or 773-9561 evenings*, offer excellent tours in open air safari vehicles with bench seats. Tours last about five and a half hours and include visits to both island cities, as well as all the major attractions.

The lavish lifestyle enjoyed by plantation owners during the 19th century is preserved at the **Whim Greathouse**. Here we toured an elegant home that combined English gentility with Caribbean practicality, filled with fine imported furniture as well as floor-to-ceiling shuttered windows and cool plank floors. If you're lucky, you'll be able to sample some freshly-made johnny cakes, baked in the plantation's detached cookhouse. (And don't miss the gift shop filled with Caribbean cookbooks, perfumes, and crafts.)

St. Croix's southern city, **Frederiksted**, lies just a few miles from the former plantation house. A stop for many cruise ships (a new dock was constructed here in 1994 to replace damage done by Hurricane Hugo), the town is a smaller version of Christiansted with a red, rather than yellow, fortress guarding the waterfront. Shopping includes duty-free boutiques featuring china and crystal to a vendor's market for inexpensive T-shirts and jewelry.

In Fredericksted, children enjoy a look at the **St. Croix Aquarium**, *Caravelle Arcade, Tel. 340/773-8995*. This small aquarium takes a look at the marine life that lives just offshore through tank exhibits as well as videos, microscope displays, and more.

St. Croix's best treasures, however, are not the man-made ones but the natural areas found at opposite ends of the island. From Frederiksted, take Rt. 76 or the Mahogany Road north for a trip to the **rainforest**. The small rainforest has thick vegetation where the sunlight is filtered through mahogany, yellow cedar, and Tibet trees. This forest is also home of **LEAP**, the Life and Environmental Arts Project, where skilled artisans craft everything from sculptures to spoons from the hardwoods found in the rain forest.

St. John

The biggest attraction of St. John is the national park. Start with a visit to the **Virgin Islands National Park Visitors Center**, located on the waterfront in Cruz Bay. Here you'll find information on hiking, camping, snorkeling, and guided programs.

After you have your bearings, head out to the park by taxi or rental jeep. Hike on one of the many marked trails, snorkel the **guided underwater trail** at Trunk Bay, stroll along the self-guided Cinnamon Bay Nature Trail, or visit ruins of Annaberg Sugar Plantation.

St. Thomas

One of the top family adventures on St. Thomas is a ride aboard the **Atlantis submarine**, *Havensight Mall, Tel. 340/ 776-5650.* The 30-passenger vessel gives travelers an unbeatable view of the coral reefs and marine life. The entire experience takes two hours including a narrated boat ride out to the dive site and a one-hour dive. The excursion costs $72 for adults and $27 for children age four to 14 years, $36 for teens 14 to 17.

Island tours are an excellent way to get an overview of St. Thomas. Most are conducted in open-air, safari-type buses and include pickup from your hotel and scenic stops at Drake's Seat and Mountain Top, a panoramic stop where you'll have a great view of the British Virgin Islands. Mountain Top claims to be the inventor of the banana daiquiri a complimentary drink is included in most tour prices. Check with your hotel for pick-up times.

Sports & Recreation
St. Croix

Horse lovers can enjoy St. Croix's rainforest on horseback. **Paul and Jill's Equestrian Stables**, *Tel. 340/772-2880 or 772-2627*, offers rides through this lush area.

Just off the coast of the far northeast side of the island lies St. Croix's other natural treasure: Buck Island. Several outfitters take snorkelers on half and full day trips to this island to swim along the **Buck Island Reef National Monument**. Here, in about 12 feet of water, snorkelers follow a marked trail for a self-guided tour of this undersea world. Several companies offer tours to this site, including Big Beard's Adventure Tours, *Tel. 340/773-4482*, Capt. Heinz's Teroro II, *Tel. 340/773-3161*, and Mile Mark Watersports Tel. *340/773-2628*, a very friendly group of operators who have a store in downtown Christiansted near the Old Scalehouse.

If the two of you are ready to head below the water's surface, there are plenty of **dive operators** to take you to coral formations and offshore wrecks in the St. Croix vicinity. In Christiansted, call Mile Mark Charters, *Tel. 340/773-2628*, VI Divers Ltd., *Tel. 340/773-6045*, or Cane Bay Dive Shop, *Tel. 800/338-3843 or 340/773-9913*; in Frederiksted, try Cruzan Divers, *Tel. 340/772-3701*.

BE THE FIRST AMERICANS TO SEE THE SUNRISE

Daylight creeps slowly over the sea, fading an ink-black sky littered with stars and staining the horizon mango red. But this is not just another sunrise.

This is Point Udall, the easternmost spot in the territorial United States. On this secluded coast, located on the island of St. Croix, the US first greets the sunrise. As dawn's rays bathe the Point in light, red Senapol cattle begin another day of grazing on nearby scrub-covered hills. Along a rocky shoreline, where even on the busiest days the sea-grape trees far outnumber the sunbathers, visitors find themselves virtually alone to enjoy daybreak an hour before it reaches the mainland.

Later in the day, St. Croix promises world-class snorkeling and diving at Buck Island Reef, duty-free shopping in quaint alley boutiques, and leisurely strolls to admire the fine Dutch architecture. But first, on a solitary stretch of beach, America's wake-up call is coming in.

Be advised, the road to Point Udall is rugged and requires a four-wheel-drive vehicle and that the last downhill stretch is best traveled on foot.

St. John

St. John is the only island in the Caribbean that offers snuba, a unique blend of scuba and snorkeling that allows would-be divers to descend to 20 feet below the surface. Snuba St. John, *Tel. 340/693-8063*, hooks guests up to a floating air tank so "C" cards are not required. The cost is $49 and includes equipment, a 1/2 hour orientation, and a one hour dive.

St. Thomas

Deep sea fishing is a favorite activity for many visitors, albeit a pricey one. Charters run about $400 for a boat (holding up to six passengers) for a half-day excursion.

Snorkeling is an excellent way to view the marine life in St. Thomas' waters. Coki Beach is a top spot for many snorkelers; another excellent reef is found at the Doubletree Sapphire Beach Resort, where marine life can be found in waters just two or three feet deep.

Day sails to the British Virgin Islands are very popular; bring along your passports or citizenship papers for every member of your family for this trip. Sails leave from many of the hotels in the morning and return before dinner and run about $60 per person. One excellent operator we recommend is the *Daydreamer*, a trimaran trip that comes with food, snorkel gear, float mats, snorkel vests, and shade to protect tender young skin. Trips include sails to Jost Van Dyke in the British Virgin Islands (bring passports for that one), sails to St. John including continental breakfast and lunch, half day sails, and sunset cruises. Call Captain Glen for reservations, *Tel. 340/775-2584.*

WHAT CAN I BUY?

St. Croix

In Frederiksted, at a small crafts market located just west of the cruise pier the two of you can shop for homemade hot sauces, T-shirts, and inexpensive jewelry, usually entertained by a live band. There's a fair amount of additional shopping down the street in pricey waterfront shops. For local art, stop by the Frederiksted Gallery, which offers paintings, sculpture, and pottery with an island touch.

Shopping in St. Croix means a trip to Christiansted or Frederiksted. Until recently, most shopping took place in Christiansted, the larger of the two communities, but as the cruise ship business has grown, Frederiksted is offering more duty-free shops aimed at those who have only a few hours to shop.

One of our favorite Christiansted shops is the American West India Company (Strand Street), which also has branches in Key West and on Sint Maarten. This shop offers items from throughout the Caribbean: amber jewelry from the

Dominican Republic, art from Haiti, sauces from Jamaica. Caribophiles should save time for a look around this interesting shop.

Larimar, the light blue semi-precious stone known as "the gemstone of the Caribbean," is also sold at many shops on St. Croix. The largest collection is at Larimar Mines in both Frederiksted (on the waterfront) and Christiansted (on the Boardwalk behind King's Alley).

A unique memento of your St. Croix visit is a mocko (rhymes with cocoa) jumbie, seen at Carnival and other special celebrations. The mocko jumbie sways high above the crowd on tall stilts covered with bright pants and wears elaborate headgear. A remembrance of an African tradition, the mocko jumbie is now a Virgin Islands cultural icon. You can buy brightly colored statues of the mocko jumbie at Silver and Tings (Pan Am Pavilion on Strand St.), Many Hands (Pan Am Pavilion), and Folk Art Traders, or gold and silver pendant interpretations at Sonya's.

St. John

St. John offers a very different shopping experience than nearby St. Thomas. Duty-free shopping is available, but by far the emphasis here is on hand-made items: clothing, pottery, jewelry, and artwork.

The most concentrated shopping is found at Mongoose Junction in Cruz Bay across from the National Park dock. Here, look for batik fabrics at the Fabric Mill, beautiful ceramics at the Donald Schneel Studio, where kids can buy "worry stones" made of sand and glass for just a few dollars.

St. Thomas

This is where serious duty-free shoppers come to seek out bargains from around the globe on jewelry, perfumes, leather goods, and gemstones.

The Waterfront Highway (Kyst Vejen), Main Street (Dronningens Gade) and Back Street (Vimmelskaft Gade) run parallel to the waterfront of Charlotte Amalie. These streets, and the alleys that connect Waterfront Highway and Main Street, are filled with non-stop shops. Start near the Vendor's Plaza (good for crafts purchases and inexpensive T-shirts), then begin your walk down crowded Main Street, where the sidewalks are always packed with shoppers and the street is continually lined with taxis and jitneys.

Our favorite shops are tucked in the alleys, refuges from the crowds where you can shop, dine or drink in a little peace. Here the walls are brick, recalling the area's history. In the 19th century, this was the Danish warehouse district.

PRACTICAL INFORMATION

Currency. The US dollar is the official currency.

Driving. Driving is on the left side of the road on each of the Virgin Islands.

Information. For brochures on St. Croix and the other United States Virgin Islands, *Tel. 800/USVI-INFO.*

Information on Island. Information booths are found in both the St. Croix and St. Thomas airports. On St. Croix, stop by the tourist office in Christiansted, located downtown in the Old Scalehouse.

Web Site. Check out *http://www.usvi-on-line.com* for additional information.

ISLAND REPORT CARD

Transportation to island	A+
Transportation around island	A-
Family Resorts	A
Family Restaurants	A-
Friendly atmosphere	A
Activities for kids	B+
Weather	A
New cultures for kids to experience	B+
Safety	B+

APPENDIX - CARIBBEAN TOURIST BOARDS

Anguilla Tourist Information Office
P.O. Box 1388
Old Factory Plaza
The Valley, Anguilla
Tel. 800/553-4939 or 264/497-2759

Antigua and Barbuda Tourist Office
610 Fifth Avenue
Suite 311
New York, NY 10020
Tel. 888/268-4227 or 212/541-4117

Aruba Tourism Authority
1000 Harbor Boulevard
Weehawken, NJ 07087
Tel. 800/TO-ARUBA or 201/330-0800

Bahamas Tourism Centre
150 East 52nd Street
28th Floor North
New York, NY 10022
Tel. 800/4-BAHAMAS or 212/758-2777

Barbados Tourism Authority
800 2nd Avenue
2nd Floor
New York, NY 10017
Tel. 800/221-9831 or 212/573-9850

British Virgin Islands Tourist Board
370 Lexington Avenue
Suite 313
New York, NY 10017
Tel. 800/835-8530 or 212/949-8254

Cayman Islands Department of Tourism
420 Lexington Avenue
Suite 2733
New York, NY 10170
Tel. 800/346-3313 or 212/682-5582

Curaçao Tourist Board
475 Park Avenue South
Suite 2000
New York, NY 10016
Tel. 800/3CURAÇAO or 212/683-7660

Jamaica Tourist Board
801 2nd Avenue, 20th Floor
New York, NY 10017
Tel. 800/233-4JTB

Puerto Rico Tourism Company
575 5th Avenue, 23rd Floor
New York, NY 10017
Tel. 800/223-6530 or 212/818-1866

St. Kitts and Nevis Tourism Office
414 East 75th Street
New York, NY 10021
Tel. 800/582-6208 or 212/535-1234

St. Lucia Tourist Board
820 Second Avenue
9th Floor
New York, NY 10017
Tel. 800/456-3984 or 212/867-2950

St. Martin French Government Tourist Office
610 5th Avenue
New York, NY 10020
Tel. 900/990-0040

St. Maarten Tourist Office
675 Third Avenue
Suite 1806
New York, NY 10017
Tel. 800/786 2278

Trinidad and Tobago
Sales, Marketing, and Reservations Tourism Services
7000 Boulevard East
Guttenberg, NJ 07093
Tel. 201/869-0060

Turks and Caicos Tourist Board
PO Box 128
Pond Street
Grand Turk
Turks and Caicos Islands
Tel. 800/241-0824 or 649/946-2733

US Virgin Islands Division of Tourism
1270 Avenue of the Americas
Room 2108
New York, NY 10020
Tel. 800/372-USVI or 212/332-2222

INDEX

THINGS CHANGE!

Phone numbers, prices, addresses, quality of food, etc, all change. If you come across any new information, we'd appreciate hearing from you. No item is too small! Drop us an e-mail note at: Jopenroad@aol.com, or write us at:

Caribbean With Kids
Open Road Publishing, P.O. Box 284
Cold Spring Harbor, NY 11724

TRAVEL NOTES

311